THE ONE-ACT PLAY TODAY

The One-Act Play
Today
A DISCUSSION OF

THE TECHNIQUE, SCOPE & HISTORY

OF THE CONTEMPORARY SHORT

DRAMA *Edited by William Kozlenko*

Essay Index Reprint Series

 BOOKS FOR LIBRARIES PRESS
FREEPORT, NEW YORK

First Published 1938
Reprinted 1970

STANDARD BOOK NUMBER:
8369-1473-2

LIBRARY OF CONGRESS CATALOG CARD NUMBER:
70-105022

PRINTED IN THE UNITED STATES OF AMERICA

CONTENTS

v

CONTENTS

CONTENTS

THE ONE-ACT PLAY TODAY

INTRODUCTION

FROM its antecedents as a convenient curtain raiser, the one-act play has grown to maturity as an adult form in the contemporary theatre. Once again—as once before, in the ebullient days of Strindberg, Lady Gregory, Yeats, Synge, the *Théâtre Libre*, O'Neill, and the Provincetown Theatre—the one-act play has become an impressive form with which creative dramatists seek to forge new ideas and to project exciting, vivified characters onto the stage. Moreover, experimentation in the drama has been effected recently not in the three-act play, which has long been used as a laboratory of experimentation, but in the short drama, especially the *social drama*. Look, for example, at Odets' *Waiting for Lefty*, a short multi-scene play of vigorous impact, utilizing for its swiftly contrived episodes a film technique of dissolves, black-outs, flash backs, and fade-ins, and at Irwin Shaw's *Bury the Dead*, a singularly trenchant play combining fantasy with realism.

This tendency on the part of our young venturesome writers to experiment with new forms is significant, for it augurs well of the future drama that the dramatist working within the frame of the one-act play should be anxious to broaden the scope of his material and to try to circumvent the rigid laws of his craft.

It is an undisputed fact that, for many years, the one-act play has been hindered by antiquated laws of construction, scene, and characterization. For some strange reason, undisclosed even to the initiate, the writer working in the one-act play form was compelled to pledge greater allegiance to some of its outmoded laws of craftsmanship than the writer working with the three-act play who, almost invariably, was allowed more freedom to experiment and develop new technical devices. In order, therefore, to keep pace, even in a small way, with the advanced work being accomplished in the longer play, the progressive one-act playwright was constrained in many instances to abrogate some of the effete technical formulas encumbering the short drama, formulas which, if adhered to closely, invariably circumscribe action and compress movement into one scene (an obvious mistake, for a one-act play does not necessarily mean a one-scene play). He thus strove by revision and, in some cases, cancellation of old rules to substitute a more athletic technique, and this helped to facilitate greater elasticity in characterization and exposition.

"A one-act play that has any pretensions to literature," writes Miss Helen Louise Cohen, "must be looked upon as a law unto itself and should not be expected to conform to any set of arbitrary requirements."

Read any orthodox textbook on the technique of writing one-act plays (there are, to be sure, several volumes which encourage experimentation and the pursuit of originality in expression) and you will be astonished to perceive the preponderant emphasis on either dogmatic or arbitrary requirements which, when applied, have made the one-act play for a long time a stilted, precious, and frequently tedious vehicle of dramatic interpretation. Indeed, it has been this inexorable stress on established dogma that has aroused either rebellion or distaste in the creative dramatist towards working in this medium. He has been taught, with almost clerical severity, that any deviation from or experimentation with this form was tantamount to inviting critical abuse by the diehards and courting disaster by "tampering" with the "fragile" craft of the short play.

No license, little freedom allowed! These, in effect, were absolute edicts hurled forth by rigorous instructors, conservative writers of textbooks, and certain graybeards writing one-act plays. Fortunately, there were some, like Strindberg, Pirandello, O'Neill, and Odets, who loved the one-act play more than they feared a boycott and who proceeded to challenge these apparently inexorable precepts by showing all the wonderful possibilities in the flexible one-act play. As a result, their own plays, when considered as models of innovation, brought the short drama another step nearer to the bounds of our own responsive contemporary theatre.

Hence, it was imperative that the "experimenters," in order to participate fully in the expression of our rich, pliant life, should invade the academic citadel of preciousness, clean house, or, as an alternative, introduce a new set of forms and devices closer to and more expressive of our own times. These particular gentlemen, among others, found it necessary to include even more variety of material in order to avoid the traditional monotony. This is a rule which applies as forcefully to the writing of poems and plays as to the composition of quartets and symphonies.

This variety—of characterization, incident, plot, episode, exposition, scene—sprang from the need to reveal to the audience certain factors in the action which until now were invariably implied but hardly ever shown. It was, from the spectator's point of view, singularly illuminating and exciting to know more about certain characters; to see subsidiary forces brought adroitly into view, exposing conditions and incidents which used to be mentioned in passing or signalized by innuendo but hardly ever presented factually before our eyes. Obviously, with quick-moving devices—such as, for instance, black-outs—this additional material, when used, did not tend to obstruct the movement of the play. Instead of being, as it often was, leisurely and slow, the one-act play suddenly became swift and agile, flexible and responsive. Instead, too, of concentrating, as heretofore, on one or two crucial episodes, the larger breadth of form and elasticity of technique enabled the dramatist to show more than before (without destroying the inherent form of the one-act play) and introduce, if need be, related problems of plot and character, all of which tended to bring to the content of the short play a new kind of theatrical excitement.

The one-act play was, as I have already mentioned, found especially suitable by many of our young dramatists for the dissemination of social propaganda, wherein a series of episodes—complete in themselves yet related to the central theme—were projected swiftly on the stage, and the play, with its several subplots, continued to move on, as a unified dimension, to its inevitable climax. The social dramatist discovered the one-act play, as it has been discovered by other persons in different endeavors, to be indispensable to his special needs. In this kind of play, with its use of multi-scene, he found the perfect answer to his needs. It was a swift medium, almost like that of a motion picture, with which to project and heighten his message; and the audience reacted to it with enthusiasm, for it was not only exciting and vibrant, but realistic and authentic.

Some writers and critics may disavow the purposefulness of this kind of drama and resent the uses to which these "brazen" men and women have put the one-act play. But none, I am certain, can deny that these uses, when once introduced and proven to be valid, have helped bring fresh excitement and vigor to the contemporary theatre. What is more important: these devices are now an integral part of our dramatic technique. They are as modern as electricity. The one-act play cannot return to its outmoded forms, for now it has become, in the hands of these advanced writers, a flexible instead of a rigid and sometimes sluggish medium.

II

We know what place the one-act play occupies in the present scheme of the theatre. What, briefly, is its future position? If the seeds of the future are usually sowed in the present, then we need not go far afield in our speculation to determine its ultimate place.

Radio and television—the latter, at this time of writing, still in its experimental stages—will have even greater need of the short play form, primarily because of its brevity, concision of movement, swift characterization, and economy of production.

The movies, too, will discover in the one-act play a rich source of story material. All films, curiously enough, are one-act plays (directors, I am told, could not possibly screen an actual three-act play, with its three different curtain climaxes, because it would take too long), but owing to some deeply ingrained prejudice the film companies are loath to use the regular one-act play, which is, as can be seen, ideal for film purposes. This reluctance to tap a rich

7

dramatic mine will soon give way, I feel, to an enthusiastic desire—and a profitable one, too—to film one-act plays as they were originally conceived, i.e., as one-act plays.

Little Theatres, university and church theatres, amateur and industrial dramatic groups will continue to present regular bills of one-act plays as they have always done. First, because of more variety in dramatic fare and, second, because of economy in staging and production.

We arrive now at the one-act play in the professional theatre. Its position, in the eyes of many managers—who have long been proven to be somewhat myopic—is still that of an illegitimate child. This is curious, for if they were to study the records of history they would find an immediate answer: we know that the plays produced by the ancient Greeks and those presented by the *Commedia dell' Arte* were all one-act plays in one form or another.

Two dramatists, Clifford Odets and Noel Coward, have done much to make Broadway audiences one-act play conscious. Odets aided the movement by contributing *Waiting for Lefty* and *Till the Day I Die*, two one-act plays which were produced by the Group Theatre and which ran for many weeks on Broadway, thus doing much to dissipate the legend that short dramas—especially of a social nature —would make no money. Noel Coward and Gertrude Lawrence, in *Tonight at 8:30*, brought the one-act play, as it were, into high society. Refuting the Broadway "experts," who considered the short drama to be an amateur drill exercise, a sort of romping, frivolous, precocious adolescent whose outpourings were intended for the delectation of a small, high-brow audience, Mr. Coward helped dignify the one-act play by presenting it with a pair of long trousers and a cutaway.

Mr. Coward, of course, has not been the first to recognize the artistic and commercial benefits of producing, acting, and writing one-act plays. He has had notable predecessors. We can cite such pioneers in this field as Eugene O'Neill, George Middleton, Percival Wilde, James Barrie, St. John Ervine, Susan Glaspell, Percy MacKaye, Paul Green, Holbrook Blinn, and many other distinguished names.

Commercial managers, usually hailed as astute fellows, have not yet revealed that proverbial sharpness for tracking down a hot tip by starting to produce one-act plays in the Broadway theatre.

Despite their attitude, for or against, however, one-act plays will continue to be written, not as exercises for the dramatist but as a precise and mature dramatic form. The time is not too distant—this is not intended to sound like an oracle—when the one-acter will be used as solid grist for the theatrical mill.

One great advantage which a bill of one-act plays has over a single three-act play is variety. This is something not easily to be despised.

Ivor Brown, leading English critic of the drama, asks in some dismay:

Why is it that people who are paying for their seats at a professional show resent the idea of getting three separate one-acters instead of three acts of one play? . . . They will take the triple bill from the hand of Mr. Coward, but his example is not followed.

And anticipating the usual vocal objection, Mr. Brown continues:

9

Is it that readjusting yourself to three new starts is a strain and that playgoers are so lazy that they will not face even so small an effort? After all, if you reckon up your chances of entertainment, the three one-acters is really the safer investment. In the case of a three-acter, you may realize before the first scene is over that the show is "not your cup of tea" and has no likelihood of becoming so. In that case, your evening and your money are wasted. In the case of three one-acters, dislike of the first effort need not utterly dash your expectations for the evening. You may heartily enjoy the other two. In a variety bill, however feeble the start, there is always hope of something turning up, and it usually does. The evening of one-acters applies the variety principle to the legitimate stage.

The maturity and growth of this brief form does not necessarily mean the decline of the other. Dramatists will persist always in writing long plays. The mistake has been that, with the gradual relegation of the one-act play to amateur circles and its decline as an appropriate curtain raiser, professional writers have evinced indifference to the form. These dramatic gentlemen saw in the one-act play only small lucrative returns, only one future, and that, it appeared, was somewhat blighted. Like canny race-horse bookies they refused to play on what seemed to them to be a foregone loser. Therefore, by turning away from the one-act play, they took with them a certain professional dignity, and it was left, in many instances, to the amateurs—the shock troops of the theatre—to continue writing one-act plays, keeping these alive and exciting by interesting experimental productions within their own immediate circles.

In many other cases, however, professional dramatists have turned completely to writing one-act plays for the amateur or little theatre stage.

As Ivor Brown says:

For the dramatist, this market may prove lucrative: it is creating authors of its own who rarely, if ever, write three-acters for the "pros." Mr. Harold Brighouse, for example, seems now to be concentrating mainly on the amateurs, and Mr. Sladen-Smith, Mr. Sydney Box, and Mr. Joe Corrie, the Scottish miner-playwright (and Mr. Percival Wilde in America), are among the first favorites whose work is eagerly awaited and taken up by the various groups and societies. . . . In any case, the author of a short play, if unluckily it does not earn much or make a large appeal, has wasted far less time and effort than if he or she had toiled over three acts. I am not despising the one-act drama if I describe it as a good field for graduation. Rather am I putting its value very high. Its technique is not easy: brief exposition, concentration of effects and quick reaching of the vital point are essential. (Barrie is here a model.) Of course, the rewards of a long play, if successful, will be very much greater; but it is a big "if."

Industry, no doubt, will be, as it has been, the major force compelling a change in the writing and production of short plays. Radio, for one, has done much to revive the one-acter, helping at the same time to devise new technical forms. For radio shapes drama to its own special circumstances, and, as it increases its cultural range and extends its influence, it will create a new era of specialists working in dramatic composition.

After radio, we will have television, which is discernible already on the horizon. If, therefore, these new industrial and mechanical innovations—and there will inevitably be others—create change, then it will be that, from these powerful influences, the one-act play will begin with a renewed and extended lease on life: encouraging young talent, insisting upon new technical standards and forms of expression and challenging established dramatists to master these forms.

The outlook, then, on the whole is most encouraging. One would hesitate to place implicit trust only in the radio and television, for these are only two new outlets, and the one-act play, as a dramatic form, belongs to the theatre; but where there are impetus and encouragement and profitable returns, there are bound to be favorable results. If we can be certain that the short play will come into its rightful domain, then we can be assured of plentiful productions and profitable consequences. From present appearances it seems that it has come into its own. It is now engaged in the process of proving how lucrative it can be to its writers and its producers.

III

A word about the present volume.

This book emanates from the current need to consolidate in one volume a multiplicity of professional opinions about the scope and function of the one-act play, as well as constructive advice to the young playwright who wishes to employ this form. The opinions, which reflect various authoritative points of view and interpretations, have one thing in common: they are written by men who regard with enthusiasm the one-act play as a vital, breathing form of art. The fact that these men—each a specialist in his field—are represented by contributions is a manifest admission that, to them, the one-act play must be and is not something intended for relegation to the library shelf or for the delectation of the historian, but an active, contemporary dramatic form designed for the playwright, amateur or professional, and for the general reader interested in dramatics.

My work as editor of a one-act play magazine has brought me face to face with certain major problems confronting those who write short plays and those merely interested in them as another significant phase of contemporary drama. It has occurred to me, therefore, that a single comprehensive volume—not too academic to dismay the amateur and not too general to discourage the student —containing all the vital information necessary to the writer and to the playgoer would be welcome and instructive.

I had one purpose in mind when collating the material for this volume: to do away with the cumbrous necessity of having to go to several books for what the reader should be able to find in one. In fine, to include everything purposeful and essential about the one-act play in a single volume.

There are numerous books on the one-act play, some covering in greater detail what has been so thoroughly epitomized in each of the present chapters. But, and I am in this instance thinking specifically of the writer, the man who is impatient to get to work on the composition of plays has little time to peruse all the lucubrations dealing with the various problems of his craft. I subscribe to the belief that, if he is to be a competent or even an informed writer, it is imperative that he be acquainted with all the angles of his work. Familiar not only with the principles pertaining to the technique of the one-act play but also with its scope and its history. Familiar not only with the most outstanding one-act plays but also with the men who wrote them.

It is obvious that, welcome as such knowledge is, it is not often a writer has the time or the leisure to indulge in long reading or study. Therefore, a book that would give him all that he wishes to know about his work is a book, I believe, of timely value. Part of the aim of this volume is to enable him to glean all the technical and historical information essential to his creative development, and, if he wishes to extend his knowledge, to go from here to larger and more detailed appraisals.

I must insist, with some emphasis, that this book has no intention of serving as a short cut to learning. Its purpose is to consolidate rather than to displace, to concentrate rather than to generalize. I can state with certainty, however, that each of the chapters is complete in itself, touching upon one or more important angles of the one-act play.

A man familiar with all the ramifications of his craft can easily compend a complete essay on most of his major problems, that is, technical errors, problems of construction, history, criticism, relationship of one form with another, uses of the one-act play, all of which are treated usually at length and in divers books. By eliminating parenthetical discussion and avoiding profuse illustrative exposition of what is or what is not correct (all of which can be summarized to touch the very marrow of his appraisal), much can be stated in a comparatively brief chapter.

I have tried also to look ahead regarding the role of the one-act play (as in the movies, radio, and television), and I hope that my foresight will be rewarded by making this book not only an indispensable item for study to the contemporaneous playwright, but a timely reference book to the playwright of tomorrow.

I feel particularly fortunate in having been able to se-

cure the services and collaboration of all the present distinguished contributors. No evidence is needed to show that
it is really their book, not mine, for it is they who give this
collective volume authority and distinction.

If this book succeeds in stimulating greater interest in
and understanding of the one-act play, if it helps to ex-
pand the technical knowledge of the student, the writer,
and the playgoer, then all of us will find ample reward in
our gratification. For underlying the technical plan of the
book was a manifest desire on the part of every contributor
to inculcate a greater love for, encourage a more intelligent
reaction to, the short drama today.

WILLIAM KOZLENKO

New York City

PART I   TECHNIQUE AND FORM

THE CONSTRUCTION OF THE ONE-ACT PLAY

PERCIVAL WILDE is the author of over one hundred one-act plays, which have been performed all over the world and translated into almost every language. He has also written *The Craftsmanship of the One-Act Play*, considered one of the best textbooks on the short play, and has edited the recent anthology, *Contemporary One-Act Plays from Nine Countries*. Mr. Wilde has established himself as one of the unquestioned leaders in the one-act play form.

He was born in New York in 1887, and was connected with the banking business from 1906 to 1910. He began writing as book reviewer for the New York *Times,* the *Evening Post,* and other publications. When his first story was published in 1912, Mr. Wilde received many requests for dramatic rights, and he thereupon turned to playwriting. Except during the War, when he served as an officer in the United States Navy, he has continued to be active in writing plays, novels, stories, and essays.

THE CONSTRUCTION
OF THE ONE-ACT PLAY

by Percival Wilde

LET us reason together.

We are about to write a one-act play.

We are "moderns," meaning by that that we dedicate our work to our contemporaries and (we hope) to posterity, exactly as did Shakespeare, Molière, and Aristophanes. For us "rules" of playwriting survive merely as curiosities. An inductive psychology based on a study of our own times and conditions leads us to results that square with some of the "rules," which we therefore tolerate; but it leads, also, to direct conflicts, hence we jettison whatever "rules" disagree with our first-hand investigations. We do so with excellent precedent: Aristophanes, Molière, and Shakespeare did the same.

We may begin by disregarding tradition; but we cannot begin without setting up, even if they are only targets at which to shoot, identifications of some kind. They serve to assure us that we are discussing the same subject, and the reader is at liberty to reject what he pleases.

A play is an orderly representation of life, arousing emotion in an audience. A one-act play is characterized by superior unity and economy; it is playable in a comparatively short space of time; and it is intended to be assimilated as a whole.[1]

These are broad definitions, intended to be interpreted even more broadly; and the second, particularly, is but an effort to identify for the sake of convenience a form so various that it defies anything short of the most generalized description. The one-act play, therefore, may be almost anything that its authors, critics, and students desire it to be—a few minutes or a full hour in length; ended by the only fall of the curtain or punctuated by a series of curtains; in one scene or in many—but that its gesture is toward unity, that it can run no longer than the period of time during which an audience can give it steadfast, uninterrupted attention, and that it dispenses with the lengthy intermissions whose psychological function in the full-length play is so important are characteristics so self-evident that they may be granted.

A play on the stage, where alone it reaches its full stature, differs from other forms of literature in its use of interpreters. The poem, the novel, the story, may be read aloud, and that reading may or may not increase the listener's enjoyment; but the play and only the play is spoken and acted by two or more individuals who, for the time being, are identified with the characters they represent. The play is storytelling by impersonation. The actor speaks, when he is most interesting, in the first person, and he is not merely relating a tale but is living it.

---

[1] While Mr. Wilde's essay is entirely new, especially written for this volume, some of his definitions and summations of principles are quoted from his *The Craftsmanship of the One-Act Play*, sixth ed., with the permission of the publishers, Little, Brown and Company, and from his article on "Playwrighting" in *The National Encyclopedia*, with the permission of the publishers, P. F. Collier and Son Corporation.

That immediacy of portrayal brings with it both gain and loss. There is vividness of a kind which can be obtained in no other manner; there is, according to the abilities of the actor, his director, and his author, a high degree of persuasiveness; there is an appeal to the emotions, frequently so overwhelming that logical discrepancies are overlooked or forgiven. The audience knows that Gielgud is playing Hamlet, that Gielgud is Gielgud, that Gielgud is also Hamlet, that he is at one and the same instant himself and somebody else; and it surrenders to the fact which, for an hour or two, is even more important: that the play is on the boards, and that actor and audience are co-operating in a fine, spiritual adventure. When the curtain rises Gielgud has stepped out of today into the Middle Ages; when it falls he steps back. That is the miracle of the theatre.

The gain does not end here. An audience will react in a manner more extravagant than would any single member of it. It will weep openly; it will laugh to excess; it will shout mass approval or disapproval in fashions more pronounced than those possible or appropriate for solitary individuals. Its emotion is contagious, for mob psychology is compelling over the units of a multitude: Gielgud cannot be Hamlet, yet he is; and his auditors, knowing what fate is to befall him, knowing by heart many of his speeches, comparing his performance, perhaps, with those of Howard and Sothern and Forbes-Robertson, find themselves nevertheless stirred. They see men and women die and not die. They see catastrophe approaching and they do nothing to avert it. They see it eventually crush a being who has no being, and they experience that pleasurable discharge of emotion which Aristotle, so many centuries ago, called "catharsis."

CONSTRUCTION

Immediacy of portrayal imposes limitations. Whatever cannot be convincingly shown or suggested is beyond the scope of the play. The time factor is important: while the speed of action may be accelerated or retarded, it must not be so far from that of life, as conditioned by the mood of the drama, that it is wholly rejected. Since the auditor, unlike the reader, cannot turn back to a page whose content is obscure, dialogue, while progressing at a natural pace, must possess such complete clarity that it may be understood as rapidly as it is spoken. The play itself must "build," becoming more interesting as it develops, or the audience will be bored; and it must end, finally, at a moment which is neither too early nor too late, and with a state of affairs which is psychologically correct and satisfying.

There are implied obligations. Since the stage does certain things superbly well, it is the duty of the craftsman to make use of its capabilities from one end of the keyboard to the other: to appeal to the emotions, since that is its natural gesture; to be vivid, powerful, and direct. He has chosen the play form because it can cope with his material; it is for him to exploit it with the touch of the artist who commands his instrument.

II

Technique may be defined as the art by which the playwright adapts his play to the conditions of his times. The conventions which his living audience accepts or can be made to accept are useful; those which it rejects are dangerous ground. An old-fashioned convention may be accepted for the sake of a play seeking to create an old-fashioned atmosphere, exactly as a new-fashioned convention, not known before and not likely to endure, may be accepted for similar reasons; but no device which suggests only inept playwriting ever has a place in the drama. The play is to produce a certain effect. Technique, shaping its action into a form which may produce that effect, dictating construction, so that the story may unfold persuasively, co-ordinating details so that the whole may be well knit and unified, and, as a final step, effacing every trace of itself, is the means to that end.

The audience cannot pay intelligent attention to a story if it is not first acquainted with the antecedents upon which the story is based. They are dealt with in an initial exposition, made so interesting and so natural that it may be accepted for its entertainment value without arousing the suspicion that it has other functions as well. It concerns itself with the setting, making clear whatever is not self-explanatory. It fixes time and place. It introduces the characters, identifying them and indicating their relations to each other. It sets forth such facts as must be known at the beginning.

The initial exposition, in a solid play, is likely to be brief and to the point: the action is to rise to such a pitch of interest that the audience will resent its interruption by footnotes. In a work either of lighter vein or of more subtle character it is frequently extended, built upon, and interwoven with the fabric of the play. When a piece depends upon charm, delicacy, fine shades of meaning, psychological distinctions, footnotes may be inserted almost anywhere provided only that they are in key.

Any sound exposition is less an art of answering questions than one of making the audience ask the questions one wishes to answer. The modern dramatist does not thrust information upon his auditors. He does not raise his curtain on servants, who simultaneously dust the furniture and the family skeletons, nor upon visitors, who tell what they know and disappear. He uses his actors and his scene to create curiosity. By placing on the stage one person who shares that curiosity and acts as a temporary representative of the audience, he is able not only to tell what he pleases, but simultaneously to suggest further questions which will permit him interestingly to proceed with the action of his play. If he selects characters who are not equally well informed upon every subject with which he proposes to deal, it is obvious that he may use any of them or each of them in turn to convey the information he desires.

Simple principles, demonstrable psychologically and evident when we study examples of sound, effective writing, suggest themselves when we consider exposition.

The exposition being necessary for a right understanding of the play, action should not be allowed to accumulate too great force before the former is complete.

If an action is to rise early to a high plane of interest, exposition should be compact and rapid or should be accomplished through the beginning episodes of the action itself.

If an action is to rise deliberately and if the expository material possesses or can be made to possess great interest, action and exposition may be closely interwoven, the latter terminating at a point comparatively late in the play.

Finally, in order to exposit interestingly, it is preferable to convey first not the fact itself but a question to which it is an answer. If the audience can be made to demand the exposition, it will be interested in it.

III

The exposition, looking backward no more than it must, has set the stage: the arrival of the dramatic situation, indicating that the present state of affairs, whatever it is, is transitory and that the coming change will be expressed in terms of human happiness, faces the audience about and sets it to looking forward with mingled apprehension and suspense. Plot has come into being, and plot means only an action which moves.

The audience is flesh and blood. It is interested in flesh and blood because it cannot respond emotionally to any other subject. Whether farce or tragedy, melodrama or the politest drawing-room comedy, it is the destiny of human beings which counts. The writer has suggested that a "dramatic" situation may be defined as any state of affairs that arouses concern for the happiness of the persons involved in it. It is a definition so flexible that it applies to dramatic literature of every variety, from the humblest "black-out sketch," which, if good, succeeds in giving its audience uneasy moments before it explodes, to productions as unconventional as *The Living Newspaper* (Works Progress Administration, 1936), whose sponsors proudly declared that it violated all possible principles of playwriting, yet overlooked that the audience, instead of being filled with concern for the happiness of one or two individuals, was merely filled with concern for the happiness of an entire nation.

A state of complete happiness, free from every threat, is desirable in life. Because it is not a "dramatic" situation it is not desirable at the beginning of a play. The curtain may fall upon it, dismissing the audience with the assurance that the characters will live happily ever after; but if a happy home is the scene upon which the curtain rises, the dramatist must introduce menaces to its peace if his audience is not to lose interest. His characters must face problems; it is only when they do so that the human beings on the other side of the footlights can worry about them.

For exactly the same reasons, a state of complete unhappiness, lacking every hope, is no "dramatic" situation. "Drama" conveys with itself the thought of change. Where the state of affairs is fixed, once and for all, where the happy are secure and the wretched are hopeless, the interest of an audience finds nothing upon which it may lay hold. Both heaven and hell are void of the "dramatic": the playwright—and his audience—would troop to purgatory for entertainment. It is apprehension for the future, the certainty that change is to take place and the assurance that it will be expressed in terms of human happiness and human destiny, that make the "dramatic" situation engrossing.

A dramatic situation which too obviously carries its solution within itself lacks interest; hence complication, the impact of a second situation, a second point of view, a second theme, is introduced, intensifying the interest of the audience, causing the initial situation to press for solution, and, incidentally, making that solution less apparent, hence more entertaining. In homely terms, situation and complication are the roots of the plot and the subplot; from a more dignified point of view, they are a look at life, a recognition of a situation to be found in life, and then a second look which takes account of, and brings into the play, consideration of one or more of the crosscurrents which impinge upon the central subject.

This is no trickery. On the contrary, if an author, having recognized a dramatic situation, does not also recognize other angles from which it can be studied and other actions and forces which will arise by their own power and enmesh themselves with it, then he lacks penetration and his play or story will be thin.

Life is a great organism. Situation without the background of life, without regard to the multiple secondary situations which entangle themselves in any one that may be cited, results inevitably in cheap, one-dimensional writing. The majority of the newspaper comic strips illustrate the dramatic situation which lacks complication, hence can produce neither the semblance of life nor a powerful, lasting effect.

IV

Through a development, a logical working out according to the mood of the play, the action rises to a crisis—the point at which solution can no longer be delayed; and to a climax—the most emotive point, wherever it occurs; and closes in a resolution—a recasting which satisfies the interests aroused earlier. In any survey so brief as this little attention can be paid to suspense, the quality in a play which compels the audience to look forward with growing interest and anticipation; to "preparation," the art by which the dramatist answers in advance the questions which will be asked later, thereby increasing the persuasiveness of his action; and to the minor but extremely important details which suggest how the dialogue may be used to accelerate or to retard, so that each scene may give the audience as much as there is in it.

The beginning erects a situation. It is added to, developed, made more interesting, and treated in such a manner that the final solution, be it happy or tragic, brings with it satisfaction and a sense of correctness. If that solution merely consigns the unmarried characters to the bonds of matrimony, considering that the end of all things, the degree of satisfaction to the audience—and the quality of the play—cannot be high. By extension, if it merely brings its actors to deaths which lack inevitability and dramatic fitness, it can be no better. It is only when the solution brings with it satisfaction and illumination, the realization that it has been given to the dramatist to see keenly and revealingly into life, that the play is worth while.

In the construction of the play the characters may be merely typical—superficially drawn, naturally diverting attention from themselves, because there is nothing new in them, to the plot, which promises better. But they may possess depth, indicating psychological study, and that study may be photographic, portraying what is plainly there, or it may be searching, lighting up the inner recesses of the soul. In the unambitious play the character is a cog in a story, conditioned by it, and without motive power of his own. In more serious writing the story evolves from the study of character, arises directly out of it, and acquires superior validity. In one form of dramatic writing a killing is the most important action that can take place on a stage; but in the forms that are more likely to endure, to kill a man is an accomplishment less notable—and less interesting—than to cause him to change his mind. Violent action has natural interest, attracting the curious, the simple-minded, and the ingenuous, both as author and as auditor; but the dramatist who has only violent action to offer necessarily conveys the impression that his observation of life has been haphazard and superficial. The things that are permanently interesting do not lie on the surface. They are to be found only by the student who looks deeply, attentively, and sympathetically into himself and into his fellowman.

At all times the mental attitude of the writer is important. Is it his object to write a play, whether or no he has anything worth while to set on paper? Or has he discovered something which demands to be told, and can be told best in the play form? If he can and will honestly answer that question before he begins to work, he may achieve the feat which ranks second only to writing a good play: he may stop himself from perpetrating a bad one.

Notes on the Technique of a Few Contemporary Dramatists

EUGENE O'NEILL: Commencing with *The Moon of the Caribbees, The Long Voyage Home,* and *Bound East for Cardiff,* the one-acts show extraordinary technical skill. "Preparation" is used boldly and with virtuosity. Exposition is usually in the first person and is accomplished at length by making the character so interesting (*Ile, The Emperor Jones*) that he can talk about himself. Backgrounds are established with power. *All* of the one-acts deal with variations of the same theme: conflict between an individual and an environment.

O'Neill's weaknesses are to be noted: (1) educated women, when not engaged in violent action, are unconvincingly portrayed (*The Hairy Ape*); (2) there is never a vestige of humor; (3) the longer one-acts are overwritten, a fault which becomes more pronounced in the full-length plays.

PAUL GREEN: Faithful depiction of a locale which the author knows thoroughly. Green's approach is nearly always that of the poet, both in his conceptions and in the language

29

in which they are expressed. Few living writers are so sensitive to the audible quality of their dialogue or so successful in creating speech that is both natural and musical.

As a body, Green's plays give the impression that he has lived with his themes a long time before venturing to set them on paper. One result of that process of incubation is that his actions become so real to him that technical problems almost solve themselves; another is that the persuasive quality of his writing, because of its complete fidelity to life, is high.

J. M. BARRIE: No writer has made more use of visible stage business, both as expository material or as the substance of the play. The eye is never forgotten. The characters possess degrees of picturesqueness, and their pantomime is important. The plays, therefore, give talented actors scope and are difficult for less able interpreters.

His approach is frequently that of the novelist, and the extremely lengthy stage directions indicate how much expository and descriptive material that would be detailed in a story version is flung at the actors, to be conveyed by them as best they can.

The actions are delicate, hence the expositions may be—and are—lengthy. The resolutions are invariably based on a reorientation with life, hence the endings are quiet but impressive.

G. B. SHAW: In the one-acts the technique is inclined to be sloppy, studded with false preparation, dragging in references to subjects which are the reverse of helpful to the play.

Shaw is a natural-born orator, who talks well but too much. The dialogue is consistently interesting and quite as consistently untrue to life: the person who lacks an education is likely, in a Shaw play, to speak with more brilliance, wisdom, and wit than his employer. Shaw's mentality is visibly behind every character—a serious fault.

Exposition is profuse, inclined to become tangled with

verbosity. There is probably no Shaw play which could not be improved by cutting.

NOEL COWARD: A satirist whose skill in writing dialogue that possesses the natural tick-tock of life is astonishing. His construction is extremely sound, but it is marred, often, by the introduction of songs and dances which have no place in the play and which were written in to please the actors.

His psychological insight is profound, and his understanding of human nature and human reactions impressive. Because of his extraordinary dialogue he is able, sometimes, to make much out of weak initial situations. He is far more successful at writing comedy or satire than when preoccupied with "dream" plays whose composition calls for a temperament more poetic than his.

As satirist, as student of psychology and in particular of abnormal psychology, he is possibly superior to all other living dramatists.

HAROLD BRIGHOUSE: An excellent technician who uses simple themes. His point of view is direct, his stories well digested, his insight keen. He is at his best in his dialect writings, making adroit and successful use of visible stage business.

His actions are likely to rise slowly. His construction is solid. His endings sometimes possess much force; sometimes, however, his development fails to carry through, and there is danger of anticlimax.

His use of dialect to enhance the effect of his situations and to achieve a natural quality is masterly.

CLIFFORD ODETS: The actions are violent, hence are introduced by brief expositions. The developments are extensive and are used to "build" with great skill. The steady increase of interest in *Waiting for Lefty* and in *Till the Day I Die* indicates how effectively the author exploits his material.

The dialogue is extraordinarily harsh and grating: it is almost

31

intentionally nonmusical. It possesses great vigor and is altogether suitable to the violent character of the actions portrayed.

Outstanding among recent one-act plays are *The Valiant* (Holworthy Hall and Robert Middlemass), a fine, poetic vehicle for a "star," lengthier than it would normally be because of oratory; and *Bury the Dead* (Irwin Shaw), a work with a splendid initial situation, a powerful complication, a development which is repetitious, long-winded, and none too skillful, and a glorious ending.

WHAT ARE THE CHIEF FAULTS IN WRITING ONE-ACT PLAYS?

WALTER PRICHARD EATON has been since 1933 Associate Professor of Playwriting at Yale University, succeeding the late George Pierce Baker as instructor of the famous "47 Workshop," the pioneer course in playwriting from which Eugene O'Neill, Sidney Howard, George Abbott, Philip Barry, and many more were graduated. Mr. Eaton began his work in the theatre shortly after his graduation from Harvard, as assistant to William Winter on the New York *Tribune*; he was later dramatic critic of the New York *Sun*.

Mr. Eaton has published three collections of criticisms and a volume of historical papers called *The Actor's Heritage*. In 1923 the Actors' Equity Theatre produced in New York a play by him, in collaboration with David Carb, called *Queen Victoria*. He has also written several one-act plays, one of which, *The Purple Door-Knob*, has been acted in almost every state in the Union. He is a member of the advisory board of the Dramatists' Play Service and a former secretary of the National Institute of Arts and Letters.

WHAT ARE THE CHIEF FAULTS
IN WRITING ONE-ACT PLAYS?

by *Walter Prichard Eaton*

IT often seems to me, in reading or witnessing the one-act plays which get published and produced, that their chief fault is insignificance. No one can say of the short story that it is insignificant because it isn't of novel length. A considerable number of short stories are written every year which impress the reader as significant. But the number of such one-act plays is lamentably small. The reason for this may be, in part, that the editorial standard for the short story is in general higher than the standard set by those who pick and produce one-act plays. I very much fear it is. But the reason in part may be found in the technique of the medium; and that is all which can concern us here.

First let me make clear what I mean by significance. In a letter to Henry Arthur Jones, Shaw once said, "The best established truth in the world is that no man produces a work of art of the very first order except under the pressure of a strong conviction and definite meaning as to the constitution of the world. Dante, Goethe and Bunyan could not possibly have produced their masterpieces if they had been mere art-voluptuaries. It may be that the artistic by-product is more valuable than the doctrine; but there is

35

no other way of getting the by-product than by the effort and penetrating force that doctrine braces a man to. Go straight to the by-product and you get Gounod instead of Wagner."

These words should not be taken as a plea for propaganda in art; and certainly I don't mean that. What I take Shaw to mean, and what I mean, is that the significant artist is thinking about life, trying to say something about it, and the entertainment values of his work are a by-product of his putting what he has to say into dramatic form. In the significant one-act play, no less than the long play or story or novel, we are ultimately more aware of the world behind and beyond the play, in its envelope of life, than in what actually has taken place on the stage. The insignificant play may be amusing for the moment, but it has no envelope, it exists in a vacuum. And most one-acters are in just that condition.

Consider a few short plays which will generally be admitted to have significance: *The Old Lady Shows Her Medals* and *The Twelve Pound Look* by Barrie; *The Shewing Up of Blanco Posnet* by G. B. Shaw; *Waiting for Lefty* by Odets; *Bury the Dead* by Irwin Shaw; *Riders to the Sea* by Synge; yes, that good old war horse of the young American amateurs, *The Valiant* by Middlemass and Hall; *White Dresses* by Paul Green; or for comedy almost any of Lady Gregory's plays or *Neighbors* by Zona Gale or Noel Coward's *Fumed Oak*—if it is a comedy—the one of all the nine in *Tonight at 8:30* which, in the summer theatres, without Coward's own acting, has most effectively reached the audiences. Here are plays of totally different styles; some are propaganda, some are completely without any remotest idea of propaganda. But each, in its way, looks

36

forward and back, each has an envelope of life which gives it significance. Behind the fooling of *The Twelve Pound Look* is an infinite pity for all wives of such men as this about-to-be knight, and the play creates in imagination the entire drama of this particular wife's past. What is behind Odets' brilliant *Waiting for Lefty* is obvious. Behind such a comedy as Lady Gregory's *Workhouse Ward* is a smiling recognition of a phase of Irish character; we translate the actions of these two old men into a thousand human relationships. Behind that hushed and moving tragedy *Riders to the Sea* is the hard life of an island people, seen through the lens of a temperament which disclosed its simple and pathetic beauty, as Robert Flaherty did in his Aran Island photographs. (For Flaherty is an artist who puts an envelope of life around his pictures.) In *Fumed Oak*, in spite of the fact that Coward to some extent indulges in the ancient trick of building up a straw man for the purpose of joyously knocking it down, audiences recognize, wistfully perhaps, sometimes, the revolt of the hungry human spirit against the dullness of routine and nagging domesticity and lower middle-class intellectual and emotional poverty. The play lingers in memory not for itself but for what it represents in human society.

To see any such play as one of these well performed is to experience satisfaction, a satisfaction quite as complete, in its way, as that experienced at a long play. We sense the envelope of life which encompasses the little drama and, sensing that, we have, actually, a greater drama stirring in our imaginations.

Now it is not enough to say, and certainly no help to say, that we don't have more such plays because such plays are only to be written by men or women with strong feelings and convictions about life. A good many people who have, I am positive, strong feelings and convictions about life write piffling one-act plays. Others, who attempt to use the form deliberately to express those feelings or convictions, make a mess of it and write plays which are not successful on the stage. There must be an explanation in the form itself.

Rip Van Winkle is a short story, and one moreover which contains hardly two hundred words of dialogue. After more than three decades, in which many attempts were made to convert it into a play, it was at last successfully dramatized by Boucicault and Jefferson, becoming one of the most popular plays in our entire history. But in no case was the attempt made to keep it a short play, in conformity to the short story form of the original. In less than ten thousand words Irving covered a time span of twenty years, with atmospheric suggestions of antecedent and subsequent years as well, and in his narration gave us the meat of no less than three obligatory scenes—i.e., scenes which our curiosity would demand to see on the stage; namely, the expulsion of Rip from his home, the meeting with Hendrik Hudson's crew, and the scene which contains, of course, the eternal stuff of the story—Rip's return after his long sleep. Here, then, is an eminently successful short story which cannot be converted into a short play. Even the short story can have a range which the short play does not possess. I have seen many attempts made to convert the Book of Ruth into a one-act play. It is one of the shortest of classic short stories, but so far, in my experience, has defied all student attempts to dramatize it. A one-act play, we may safely say, presupposes a single set, even though (like Mr. Coward) you don't play quite fair and drop your curtain to indicate a time lapse. Suppose you choose the barn for your set—almost a necessity if you are to dramatize the major situation of the story of Ruth. If you bring in Ruth in the darkness to lie at the feet of Boaz, without the proper amount of explanation, you run into all kinds of danger with an audience. But how are you to manage the necessary explanations or exposition? The obvious suggestion is for Naomi to bring Ruth to the barn in advance and tell her what to do. But that is not only clumsy—it takes away most of the suspense that might be in the play could we see poor Ruth come creeping into the dark stable alone and unsupported. As a matter of fact, we need to see Ruth, sick for home, standing in tears amid the alien corn, in order to establish the necessary emotional background for the climactic scene. And we come to the conclusion that it cannot be accomplished in a one-act play. Not, at any rate, by a beginner.

The one-act play, by its nature and the rigid restrictions of the medium, has to confine itself to a single episode or situation, and this situation, in turn, has to grow and develop out of itself. To be sure, it is characteristic of all drama that it must grow and develop out of itself; that is just as true of a long play. But in the long play there is time for exposition to make the past clear and room for a series of episodes, covering perhaps years of time and miles of space. The one-act play must be relatively devoid of exposition and confined in time and space. The first problem which confronts the would-be author of a one-act play, then, is the selection of an episode, or situation, which when put upon the stage will be at once largely self-explanatory, or in which explanation can come during, and without delaying, the action; and which, secondly, can by its own growth and development create suspense and emotion. Whether or not such an episode, when chosen, will make a *significant* one-act play is dependent on how truthfully and deeply it fits into a larger life pattern.

The Old Lady Shows Her Medals, though the curtain is dropped twice to indicate two time lapses, may be classed as a one-act play. It needs very little actual exposition, even today with the Great War more than twenty years behind us. Four old charwomen are taking tea; one of them, who we soon guess has no son, displays the letters her "son" has written to her from the front. (She has written them herself.) And then the "son" appears! Here is a situation. The poor old lady never banked on this when she began her heart-hungry deception. The growth of this situation, in characteristic Barrie fashion, is the play; and behind it are smiles and tears and the sense of all England bravely at war. The situation fits into a larger life pattern and is so nearly self-explanatory that the story gets under way almost at once.

Riders to the Sea has complete unity of time as well as place. It is half an hour in the lives of certain Aran Islanders. The sea and the perils of the sea are around it, behind it. When the play begins the two girls are opening a bundle of wet clothes to see if they belong to their lost brother, Michael. One sister, examining the stitches in a stocking, cries out, "It's Michael's, Nora!" and you have in that heartbroken cry all the antecedent information you require. Anyone can grasp it instantly and be moved by its emotional implications. The situation now develops; a second son must, through the hard necessities of existence, undergo the same perils, though his old mother tries to restrain him. And the outcome is tragedy. Man against the sea. The drama, of course, owes a great debt, for its effectiveness, to the beautiful and haunting rhythm of the speech and its folk metaphor; but structurally it is sound and it would be a significant one-act play were the dialogue much less poetic.

At first glance, *Waiting for Lefty* may seem much more complicated and indeed may not seem a one-act play at all. But certainly it is a short play, and there is no curtain. It contains a series of extremely brief plays, or episodes, each concerned with one of the chief characters in the major play. A number of men are on the platform at a labor meeting, debating whether or not to strike. Several of them make speeches to set forth, by their personal experiences, the need for drastic action. And as each gets into his personal confession, as it were, the general stage illumination goes down till the half-circle of men on the stage is dimmed to vague shadows, and in a pool of light on the forestage the speaker and the necessary other characters (who have slipped in from the wings) enact the episode which has made a potential striker of him. No exposition is needed. The few preliminary words of his actual speech to the meeting have supplied that; besides, we know this is a labor play, and we have the necessary background from the start. The accumulated weight of these several acted episodes makes the emotional power behind the climax of the play, when everybody on the stage (and many actors planted in the audience) are crying, "Strike! Strike! Strike!" as the curtain falls. Actually the play is not at all complicated. But it is significant because it fits into a life pattern which, we feel, is passionately accepted by the author.

Let us now assume that the would-be author of a one-act play has realized the necessary limitations of his medium and accepted the fact that his play must be concerned with a single episode or situation, that he cannot indulge in any considerable exposition, and that his situation, easily and quickly grasped, must be one which can develop out of itself, by a process of internal growth. He wants, we also assume, to make his play significant. What happens? In nine cases out of ten, in my experience, he discovers that most of the situations which come to him, and are recognized as potentially significant, require much more exposition than is possible, or at any rate theatrically effective, in a short play, and probably also call for variations of time and place in order to bring out their significance. They are too complicated for him to handle. He either tackles one of them, and fails, or turns to some situation which can grow into a theatrically effective climax, can have a beginning, middle, and end, largely because it has no significance beyond itself and is therefore free from complications. Such were hundreds of the old-time "afterpieces" which used to cap every bill, even *Hamlet,* before the audiences would go home. And such today are hundreds of one-act plays published by the houses which supply amateurs. I well recall a farce in which I used to act more years ago than I like to confess. It was called *A Pair of Lunatics,* and I think was originally produced by George Alexander as an afterpiece or a curtain raiser. A man and a girl, each normal, met in a lunatic asylum, and each thought the other was a patient. You can perhaps imagine what silly asses they made of themselves before the final discovery of their mistake. And do you also surmise that ultimately they supposedly fell in love? Gentle reader, you are right! Well, in its day, this was a theatrically effective one-act play. It amused hundreds of audiences in the English-speaking world—and it was totally devoid of significance.

How is the ambitious young dramatist to avoid, on the one hand, the mistake of developing a situation which tempts because it is complete and can be effectively handled but which really leads nowhere, has no significance; and to avoid, on the other hand, the mistake of selecting a theme which seems to him important, which has an envelope of life, but which cannot be made effective in the theatre because it calls for too much exposition or too spreading a canvas?

The difficulty is perhaps not so great as it seems, if the dramatist, when he selects his theme, will at once ask himself, first, "Is it of some significance?" and, second, "Is it of such general interest or does it so chime in with general knowledge that the background is created for me before I start?" The background for *Bury the Dead* was created for the author by the horrors of the Great War and two decades of peace propaganda which followed the war. It is doubtful if his play would have succeeded prior to 1914. But in 1936 he was able to assume not only a complete understanding of his basic situation, but immediate emotional sympathy. He could at once let his situation begin to develop out of itself, out of the refusal of the dead men to lie down in their graves and be buried. The background for *The Twelve Pound Look* is not primarily an English social background, but a domestic one readily grasped by anybody. The stupidly tyrannical husband is, when the curtain rises, doing a silly rehearsal of his knighting ceremony, and that gives us all the social background we need, while diverting us by its humor, and it sets the characters of the couple so vividly, by action, that we sense at once the gulf between them and know that because of it something is going to happen. Our sympathies are with the wife—as any woman, not merely as the wife of a *nouveau riche* knight.

But I must warn the reader against taking anything but the *start* of *The Twelve Pound Look* as a first model. The start is admirable to follow; amusing pantomime which both sets the characters and gives us needed background information, while so diverting the eye that we are not aware of it as exposition. Thereafter, however, the little play becomes almost Ibsenesque in technique, because the wife does not reappear until the very end and the actual drama of the husband and the stenographer took place long ago and is brought to us through their conversation. Only a skilled dramatist can hold an audience by this retrospective method. Do not, at first, attempt the retrospective method. If you find you need even one of those "Do you remember" speeches, go back and try again. Keep your play moving in the present.

To get back now to the simple situation and the wide and readily understood implications. In a certain playwriting course the first assignment is always the adaptation of a short story, and almost invariably at least one student chooses that vivid and moving *conte* by Prosper Mérimée, *Mateo Falcone*. This, you may recall, is the story of a Corsican patriot who shoots his ten-year-old son because the boy, tempted by the bribe of a watch, has betrayed a Corsican refugee to the soldiers. The story is simple, vivid, and direct; it seems highly dramatic and tempts the beginner. But he runs at once into two grave obstacles. The first is, of course, that what is pathetic on the page can be shocking on the stage. While it is quite possible to tell about a father shooting down his ten-year-old son as a sacrifice to family honor, it is terrifically difficult to show him doing it in the flesh without causing revulsion. The other obstacle (and it *must* be surmounted before there is any chance of surmounting the first) is how to put your audience into an understanding frame of mind regarding these people. What do most of us know about the Corsica of a hundred years ago? What audience knowledge can the dramatist assume about the fierce prides and codes of honor belonging to these alien people? Very, very little. The short-story writer can sketch it all in a paragraph, and the reader gives intellectual assent. The playwright cannot. Nor is mere intellectual assent ever sufficient in the theatre. In the theatre seeing is believing. But the young dramatist, reading this story and sensing the drama to begin when the father and mother depart, leaving the boy to tend the house, nine times out of ten there begins his play. As a result, we do not really know a thing about this family, we have no idea what fate the boy is storing up for himself when he later betrays the fugitive (hence there is no *emotional* suspense in the scene), and above all we are bewildered and revolted when the father returns, discovers what the boy has done, and kills him. Here, then, is a story which does not have, after all, readily understood and easily grasped implications and background, to make it effective for an audience here and now. It needs full and enormously persuasive exposition. The first job of the dramatist is to supply this exposition; that is, to invent a start for his play which he will not find in Mérimée at all.

There is excellent practice to be had in dramatizing short stories or studying such dramatizations. I spoke a moment ago of the lack of emotional suspense in the dramatization of Mérimée, because the audience did not realize in advance how seriously the small boy's fault would loom in his father's eyes. Many short stories, particularly by O. Henry, Saki, and the writers of "short shorts," depend for effect on a surprise ending, and it is a common error of beginning playwrights to suppose that surprise is equally effective in a short play. It is not. Quite the contrary. Surprise in the theatre is worth very little, ever; and in most cases can be achieved only at the sacrifice of far more important values. One of your primary values, of course, is a situation which will rouse emotion. The play which does not rouse emotion is a dead thing. Now, to take a crude situation, suppose you saw a man teetering on the edge of a hole which you had no reason to believe was more than a foot deep. You'd be quite unmoved by the sight. You might have a shock of horrified surprise if he fell and the hole turned out to be a hundred feet deep, but the preliminary teetering would have had no emotional suspense. Your character in a play is teetering on the brink of some act, but whether the consequences will be serious or not we, the audience, have no idea. Indeed, you may perhaps deliberately have led us to assume they will be trivial. Do you suppose that the audience is going to be emotionally excited as they watch the character becoming more and more involved? Certainly not. And if you ultimately fool them, they will probably be resentful.

Take *The Old Lady Shows Her Medals*. If you in the audience did not know clearly, in advance, that the old lady has been pathetically bluffing, that this hulking Scotsman who suddenly appears is not really her son but has come to demand a showdown and spoil her little game, do you think for one instant that you would have the tingle of expectation you now have as you watch impatiently the departure of the other characters and lean forward to see the first clash between these two? There is no surprise here for us. *We* know. The surprise is for the old lady and the soldier, and the dramatic excitement for us comes because we *do* know more than they do, and hence can understand and sympathize with every move they make. The emotional suspense comes from our great desire to see the old lady win him over, our wonder how she will do it, our recurrent chuckles as we watch the process. The beginning dramatist too often does not realize that suspense in the theatre does not consist in keeping your audience in the dark, above all not in fooling them. It consists in giving them the fullest possible knowledge of how the land lies, and then letting them enjoy the spectacle of the characters working themselves out of their predicament.

Avoid the trick ending. Avoid the "short short" technique. Never think that surprise is of any value on the stage. As Dunsany once said, after the solution of a play, short or long, we should not exclaim, "How surprising!" but rather, "Why, of course!"

A word about dialogue. If, like so many novices, you start your play by seizing pen, ink, and paper and commencing to set down dialogue, you will soon discover that you have consumed half your space to accomplish what your play should do in the first three or four minutes; and your dialogue, moreover, will not only be prolix and much of it irrelevant, but the chances are that much of it will be "literary." That happens over and over. You have a painfully small number of words with which to accomplish a large effect—for effects must in general be large on the stage. Therefore, every word must count. You must first have, either in your head or in a scenario, a clear, definite skeleton of structure worked out for your play, in which the line of progression is never lost and in which the *relative* importance, and hence the length and weight, of each little scene is predetermined. To that pattern you cut your dialogue, using nothing which is irrelevant, nothing in excess, paring down your speeches to the minimum, and making each lead inevitably to the next. And yet your characters must all seem to speak naturally and in their own idiom! It is a hard task, not lightly to be undertaken. That so many one-act plays are full of speeches without dramatic meat, without emotional bite, without contributing to the march of the play, is too often the result of the "literary" approach, the failure to build the play first and to regard dialogue not as the fundamental of the drama but as the final clothing of the essential frame. Get your frame built first, for you cannot very well tack on dialogue where there is no stud to nail to.

It would be tempting to go on, and talk of writing dialogue for the actor, patterning it so that he can give it variety, break it up with motion, "let the play come through." That is vastly important, but perhaps only to be learned from actual practice in the playhouse. However, space does not permit me to discuss it. Doubtless others will. I shall close by reiterating that the significant one-act play should have a simple situation, with a wide and easily grasped application. The theme, or situation, may be serious or comic or ironic, but it must be simple. The beginner is only too likely to believe that simplicity means insignificance and to think that because he cannot compress a social theory for ending depressions, say, into a short play, therefore he must sink to a farcical skit. Nothing could be more mistaken. On the contrary, simplicity and strong emotion in the theatre generally go together. Establish two or more interesting characters in an easily understood situation, which requires little or no explanation, and whether that works out, grows, into a significant short play pretty much depends upon the truth, the applicability to life, of the situation. Of course, if you are not interested in writing significant plays, but only actable plays, you won't bother to ask whether your situation is true—only whether it is workable. But if you have somewhat higher ambitions, you will inevitably ask yourself that question, nor will you be satisfied till your conscience has answered it.

There is, to be sure, no crime in writing insignificant one-act plays. But neither is there any credit, or probably much cash. The one-act plays which endure and have many profitable productions are usually the work of conscientious authors, who at the least are trying to illuminate character and give you a sense of life outside the theatre. George Kelly, author of such long comedies as *The Show-Off*, began his career as a writer of one-act plays for vaudeville. They were popular and successful—and the situations which they developed were humanly true. O'Neill began his career as a creator of one-act plays, plays of the sea, chiefly, and the very first criticisms spoke of the enveloping atmosphere, the brooding sense of something above and beyond the stage. Yet their themes were simple, their characters uncomplicated. In *Ile* a dogged whaling captain drives his ship on into the arctic for another year, in order to fill his hold, though his wife who is aboard pleads to be taken home. What will come of this? She goes insane. That is simple enough. Years later O'Neill saw her wandering through the streets of Provincetown

49

and conceived his play. He needed five hours to tell the story of the Mannon family, but this story could be compressed into less than half an hour. It is no less significant and moving on that account—not so long as in this world the self-willed and fanatic ambition of one person can bring misery to others.

We cannot go on laboring the point with illustrations. Let the beginner read for himself a number of successful and significant one-act plays and study for himself the speed with which the author gets his story going, with the minimum of exposition, because his situation is simple, readily grasped by an audience, and recognized by them as humanly true. Then let him ask himself, "Is the situation *I* have chosen simple, can I, too, begin to let it develop without the need for complicated exposition and explanation, and will my audience feel it to be humanly true and hence respond to it emotionally? Do I, myself, respond to it? Do I really care what these people of mine do and say, how they get out of their predicament, because I like them warmly as people or because their predicament seems to me of social significance?"

If the beginner answers these questions right, he will at least start his one-act play with a good one-act situation. What he does with it thereafter, I very much fear, is more dependent on the gifts God has given him than on anything he can learn from a book.

THE TECHNIQUE OF THE EXPERIMENTAL
ONE-ACT PLAY

SYDNEY BOX is one of the best-known writers of one-act plays in England. In an article, Mr. Box says: "I am really a bit of a Jekyll and Hyde. . . . In the early morning, when the dawn is yawning dismally over the roof of the rabbit hutch opposite, or late at night, when the candles are guttering like drunken men, and drunken men are guttering, I write those brilliant plays that have graced so many stages and disgraced so many societies. In the more conventional midday hours, I am by way of being a commercial doctor.

"Nothing, be it noted, to do with medicine. My job is to diagnose the deep-seated ailment which is causing a newspaper circulation to decline, a company's turnover to decrease, the sales of a product to drop. Diagnosis complete, I prescribe amative or preventive treatment—and often dispense the medicine I prescribe."

THE TECHNIQUE OF THE
EXPERIMENTAL ONE-ACT PLAY

by Sydney Box

TO begin with, I must disembarrass the reader of the hope, perhaps inspired by this chapter's title, that there exist laws of technique which apply only to what is loosely termed the "experimental" one-act play. It would be dangerous, indeed, to let pass the assumption that there is such a thing as an experimental play. For it is obvious that today's experiments in technique, if proved successful, are tomorrow's commonplaces, and that those which miss their mark are either quickly forgotten or lie in that limbo which it is the curious historian's occasional delight to disturb.

The audacious medieval playwright who first introduced the vernacular into his Church Latin "mystery" was certainly an experimenter in his day—and was equally certainly rewarded by the malediction of authority for his pains. The Elizabethan author who was first to see the dramatic possibilities of the penthouse on a fixed stage, and wrote his drama accordingly, was an innovator of great moment. Some theatrical diehard of the seventeenth century must have bubbled with indignation when he took his seat in the theatre and found that the newfangled apron stage had considerably altered the technical presentation of his plays. And Tom Robertson's now disregarded comedies of manners were highly successful simply because this author accommodated his technique to the up-and-coming demand for realistic sets in which doors slammed, windows opened, and a ceiling overtopped as faithful a reproduction of a drawing room as the stage carpenter could put together. Innovators all, to this day: but experimenters only so long as their innovations were untried or open to argument.

Any experiment in presentation is, therefore, nothing more than an *accommodation* of existing technique to changing ideas, twists of taste, and improvements in stage machinery (this last, of course, the most fertile source of successful innovation). For the practical playwright, whatever the form of his inspiration, is bound to take into consideration two things over which he has little control: his audience and his theatre. Unless he is content to write his plays for the printed page alone or (to quote a currently fashionable tag for an old disease) is satisfied by the personal idiom of surrealism, he knows that his first job is to make himself understood to his potential listeners. He must speak a communicable language in a communicable idiom. He must obey certain conventions which make that communication possible. His innovations should be made not only with reason, but with some regard for the fact that since they are innovations, his audience should be given the chance to assimilate them easily. The playwright must, in fact, obey the technique of his craft. He must learn the elements of his job: must know how a play is put together, why it is put together in such a way and in no other, and where and why he can dispense with any one trick of his trade when occasion arises. It doesn't matter whether he is experimenter or traditionalist; the playwright must have a profound working knowledge of his craft. The same rules of technique apply to all, and the same opportunities of developing them.

Therefore, before noting a few examples of experiment in the technique of the one-act play, it is necessary to have some idea of those elements of craftsmanship which must be mastered if the author is to produce sound, actable work. Mistrust at once the superior person who tells you that a play is "an act of inspiration," or is too frightfully bored for words by the mention of the word technique. Unless he *is* a genius, you may safely write him down as knave or fool. In all probability he possesses a drawerful of rejected manuscripts which he reads over lovingly to himself behind closed doors. For playwriting—even one-act playwriting—is an act accomplished only by blood and sweat and tears. It is a craft which has to be mastered by considerable practise; its principles must be learnt just as the plumber's mate must patiently experiment on his workshop waste pipes until he is competent to repair those of his neighbors. Judging by the annual output of published one-act plays, this last principle is almost universally ignored. Technically, the majority of plays which see the light each year are of such poor quality that their authors appear to imagine that the craft of playwriting, like their inspiration, is vouchsafed from above. True enough, in some fortunates it is. But in very, very few.

In a preface to one of his plays, Percival Wilde has written of the one-act play: "Unity is its inspiration; unity its aim; unity is its soul."

The unskilled writer of one-act plays could absorb no

better first principle than that. For inherent in it is the practical corollary: discipline your inspiration; discipline your objective; discipline your construction. There is no time in the brief passage of a one-act play to follow up this or that incidental issue, however profitable of exploration it appears. No time for the five or ten minute byplay with telephone or cocktails in which authors of three-act plays may excusably indulge themselves. The maid and the butler have no place in the short play for those brief interludes of cushion patting and table clearing in which they either fire off a few of the author's best epigrams to ease the tension of a dramatic scene or expose the fact that their mistress is deceiving her doting husband. Such a trick is well enough for playwrights who know that half of their audience invariably arrives ten minutes after the curtain has risen and lingers in the bars after each interval. But the one-act playwright, with some forty minutes of playing time at his disposal, must forgo all such temptations to pad. Once his curtain is up, he must write in no line and may create no situation that does not carry his chosen theme or plot forward to a resolution. Nor, be it added, is he at liberty to display the many-sidedness of character by evolving various situations which will test the reactions of his characters. The one-act play form is not one which lends itself easily to much subtlety of characterization. It is essentially concentrated and single of purpose, and for this reason imposes the strictest discipline upon the playwright who makes use of it. Characterization is the touchstone of all drama, whatever its scope or intentions. A play is as effective as its characters are credible and may not rise above the degree in which the audience is ready to be convinced by the characters presented to it.

Therefore, the one-act play, which may never be discursive, must weld characterization and situation most firmly together. Through situation essential to the forward movement of the play alone is it possible for the playwright to bring his characters to life.

It is for this reason that singleness of purpose is the one-act playwright's first principle. If it were asked, "What are the qualifications of the one-act play?" the answer might well be that it should have singleness of theme, should aim at making a single impression, should possess singleness of situation, and should concentrate its interest on a single character or group character.

Inspired by his theme, a dominant character, a strong situation, or a ready-made plot, the playwright tackles the job of putting his play on paper. He has come to grips with the problems of applying his knowledge of play construction to his inspiration and probably wishes that it was all as simple as Lewis Carroll's instruction to "begin at the beginning, go right on to the end, then stop."

If hitherto I have appeared dogmatic about certain aspects of one-act play construction, I must ask the reader to forgive me on the ground that a short essay allows of little scope for the niceties of precise definition. But in considering the play's construction, there need be no apologies for laying down certain rules which must be followed.

All one-act plays may be divided into definite periods, each with its own technical problems. They may be named as follows: (1) opening; (2) exposition; (3) development; (4) climax; (5) ending. These periods may, of course, vary in length, may coincide one with another, and may be further subdivided on a more detailed examination than I have space to give them here.

The chief, perhaps the only, quality of the short play's opening is that it must capture the audience's interest. This does not imply, as is commonly stated, that the one-act play should plunge without more ado into its story. On the contrary, some short plays (i.e., those whose chief interest is in characterization) need careful preparation before the plot may safely be got under way. It means simply that the moment the curtain is up the audience must be brought into the world of the author's imagining. In a play where plot is all, a violent attack may serve, in which no sooner is the opening made than the playwright has passed on to his exposition. He may choose to create his opening effect entirely by the directions he has given to scene-designer and stage-manager, leaving it in their hands to build the atmosphere necessary to his exposition. Again, he may begin with pantomimic action or spend several minutes in building his atmosphere while he is also getting on with the job of exposing his characters and his situation. About his methods in beginning the play there are no laws: about his employment of these methods only one—that he claim the audience's immediate attention and direct that attention so that it is attuned for what follows.

Having made his initial attack, it is the playwright's task first to sustain it, secondly to make his premises crystal clear to an audience which knows nothing about his characters and is always apt to care less! Before undertaking any development either in his characterization or in his story, the audience must be made aware of every detail of character and situation that has any bearing on his ultimate resolution. It is here that the author first invites his audience to ask questions, prepares the way for the quickening of his action, raises in the minds of his listeners a desire to know "what happens next."

Only then can he move forward to the principal period of his play—its development. Here it is necessary to note that what most commonly wrecks the novice's work is the tendency to digress and to work out what appears to be a profitable side issue. Nothing should take place in the play's development that does not arise directly from its opening and exposition. But, it may be objected, this is a confinement of inspiration beyond reason. It is a negation of the casual disorder of events as they occur in real life. The answer to that is that it is the dramatist's job to make order out of disorder: to select precisely those incidents from the mass of material available to him which satisfy the logic of cause and effect. If he presents on the stage an effect for which he has omitted to provide good cause, his audience will quite rightly reject it.

Out of development, the climax. Here the craftsman is summing up the conflict, spiritual or physical, that he has stated in his exposition and has argued in his development. It is the moment at which his audience is closest to him, waiting for his resolution. It is to this point that he has been patiently building throughout the play, and the point at which all the threads of his action are drawn firmly together. Then follows the last phase: the play's ending, its resolution of all the questions and problems the playwright has asked. The playwright, having claimed the audience's attention, must now reward it with a satisfactory explanation. It may not be "logical" in a common sense of that much misused word. That is to say, it may not be a conclusion that everyday life would lead us to accept as valid. But one thing it must be: it must be true to the author's own logic and must complete the proposition that he has, with a considerable display of ingenuity, led us to accept in the early stages of his play. It is worth noting in this connection that the so-called "surprise ending" is not, as some imagine, a sort of knockout blow directly at variance with all that has gone before. True, an ending may surprise the audience, but if it merely astonishes, the playwright is in error—not his audience. The dramatically unexpected resolution again must be inherent in the preliminary stages of the play, and, while it surprises, must satisfy the audience's sense of reason no less than the ending which is accepted at once as inevitable.

So much for the elements of craftsmanship. How, next, can the playwright apply these elements to plays which introduce novelties of technique?

The one-act play is a form of drama particularly suited for technical experiment, since it is almost entirely the province of amateur players and producers—rather, of those whose interest in the theatre is not bound first and last to the problem of making profits. The professional theatre, being what it is, does not take kindly to experimental playwrights: it has to consider dividends first and experiment a long way after. Since it is almost exclusively in the Little Theatres that the one-act play is produced, the playwright with new methods has every reason to make his experiments in the one-act play form.

Again, the one-act play is brief and soon told. The author who desires to introduce some novelty of technique is therefore at liberty to use the one-act play as the architect does his small-scale model of an important enterprise, or the artist his preliminary sketches. If his experiment fails, it has failed with a considerable saving of his labor—

and of expense to the management which supported the enterprise.

The one-act play has no such heavy burden of precedent and convention laid upon it as has the longer play. The professional critics (and the one-act playwright may return thanks for it) have not endowed it with a literature of conventions. On the contrary, they have for the most part left it to its own devices. In its modern shape still a youthful form of dramatic writing, those audiences which have come to look upon it with as much affection as on the longer play are catholic enough in their tastes to encourage the writer of one-act plays to experiment.

It is an intimate form of drama. It asks of the audience not only that they associate themselves more closely with its author, but also that they should bring a keener perception to bear upon it during its brief recital. Therefore, since forty minutes of close attention is all the playwright asks, he is given an ampler freedom to draw his audience with him along unfamiliar paths. An unsuccessful innovation in technical presentation would drive the most patient audience out into the night were it billed to continue for three hours; but the most impatient audience will endure a failure when it knows that the agony will only last for some forty minutes.

A playwright's inspiration may come to him in a variety of ways. For instance, he may be inspired by a theme (money is the root of all evil); a character (an old lady with a gift for clairvoyance); a situation (a concentration camp commandant recognizing in a new prisoner his younger brother); an atmosphere (a dictator's vision of hell)—and so forth. Whatever the inspiration, it must then be given shape through character, situation, and plot. And then follows the technical problem: how may this shape most effectively be presented on the stage?

To take a concrete example. We will suppose that the playwright decides that there is promising material for a short play in the proposition: overweening ambition sooner or later overreaches itself. By itself the statement contains little hint of dramatic action. It must be restated in terms of the particular, embodied in character and situation.

Sooner or later the character is evolved in the playwright's mind—a newspaper seller who is determined one day to be the financial genius of the skyscraper at whose foot he now sells evening papers. So far, so good. It is now necessary to know something more about this character, so that the most effective moment of his career may be portrayed in action. A chain of events suggests itself.

We will suppose that the newspaper seller works his way into the skyscraper as a junior clerk, advances rapidly, makes himself first master in his own office and subsequently the biggest manipulator of shares on the market. He overreaches himself, gets caught in a slump, goes mad, and is finally released from a lunatic asylum to return to his original pitch as a newspaper salesman where—last act of all—he is knocked down while running across the road to greet one of the men he knew in his boom days—still dreaming of a conquest in high finance.

In considering how this mass of material may be presented as a one-act play, a score of possibilities will present themselves to the playwright. Obviously, in using conventional methods of construction only one phase of this character's life-story may be presented, and much of the original chain of events must be scrapped. It might be most profitable to show him at the moment when his world is beginning to crash and, perhaps, to illustrate the tragedy of his ambition by introducing a wife who married him only for his money. One might see dramatic possibilities in the lunatic asylum episode: the character tortured by the uneasy ghosts of his past and the specters of his future. At any rate, rigid selection must be made if this character and the chosen theme are to be presented with success within the limits of the conventional one-act play.

At this point the playwright sees that with a good switchboard and the use of simple, representational scenery, he need jettison nothing of his original material. Instead, he may make the experiment of writing an episodic play in which every significant phase of his character's career is displayed within the space of forty minutes. The use of the black-out and a spotlight or two has left him free to concentrate attention entirely on his chief character, on the drama of his rise and fall, and on illustrating his theme by the most economical of means.

Such is the outline of a simple experiment in expressionistic technique. It formed the basis of one of my own experiments with the one-act play form—an episode play entitled *Self-made Man*.

The episodic play is liable to failure on the grounds that interest in a rapid succession of short scenes is easily diffused. In the case of *Self-made Man* this danger was to a certain extent overcome by focusing all interest upon the central character. Not a very simple problem to solve, I might add, when costume changes and scene shifting have to be taken into consideration. Therefore, I will examine in more detail a similar play—Cedric Mount's *Twentieth Century Lullaby*—which, while it is essentially an episode play covering the life-story of one man from cradle to grave, satisfactorily solves the problem of creating unity of time and place.

The scene is a nursery. In the firelight a mother, Mary Smith, rocks a cradle and sings a lullaby to her sleeping child.

(*Presently she begins to talk to the sleeping infant as mothers will.*)

MARY: There's my precious! Sleep well! And soon you'll grow up into a fine big boy, won't you, my darling? And everyone will say: 'Look at Peter Ulric Smith—isn't he the bonniest boy you ever saw?' And then you'll go to school and the master will teach you all sorts of clever things. And you'll learn them all so quickly! 'Peter Ulric Smith,' he'll say, 'you've got a brain in a million. If all my pupils were as easy to teach as you are, my job would be a pleasure,' he'll say . . .

(*At this moment another voice—a man's—starts speaking from the other side of the room, and in a patch of light among the shadows we see the schoolmaster standing, dressed in mortar-board and black gown. He seems to be talking to someone we cannot see, and Mary takes not the slightest notice of him, but goes on whispering to her baby. The only difference is that now we cannot hear her because of the schoolmaster's loud and rather sarcastic voice.*)

SCHOOLMASTER: Peter Ulric Smith! There's a name to give a boy! Did you ever hear anything like it?

(*He pauses for a moment with rather a sneering smile on his face, and in that second we hear* MARY *saying to the baby* . . .)

MARY: It's a very nice name, really—but you needn't tell the other boys what the 'U' stands for if you don't want them to know.

SCHOOLMASTER: I could forgive the name if you had any

64

brains, but really you seem to be even more woolly-witted than most boys of your age—and that's saying a great deal. God knows why I should spend my life teaching you and a hundred other brats like you, when I might have been doing something really useful—sweeping the streets or coal mining, for instance. How I'm going to cram enough knowledge into your brain-box to get you through your beastly little examinations, I can't imagine. . . .

MARY (*still talking to her baby*): And my clever son's going to pass all his examinations—right at the top of the list—isn't he? Eh?

Technically, this is a most interesting opening. The scene is set. Lullaby and flickering twilight arouse the audience's interest at once. The brief passage of opening dialogue is capable of introducing anything, but with the repetition of the name of the child the audience is being guided towards recognizing it of importance: the unusual second name raises a question in the listeners' minds. Then with the entry of the schoolmaster the situation of the play is at once made clear with the utmost economy of means. By skillful manipulation of the dialogue we are at once launched into the future, while our eyes still hold us to the present, where Mary whispers her dreams for the future over the cradle. The playwright has hinted at his theme, impressed us already with the tragic irony of a situation familiar to all of us, and has carried us straight into his exposition in three or four passages of dialogue. Furthermore, he has prepared us for a succession of episodes which do not take us out of this half-lit nursery and which already imply a climax and a resolution when Mary's dreams clash with reality.

In a similar way, a series of ironic scenes pass. Peter

Smith's baptism, his first job and his first glimpse of modern business ethics, his marriage.

Here the playwright, by this time certain that his audience is following his method, has no need to emphasize it as he did in his opening scene. He can now make a more audacious leap, demand more participation from his audience in the narration of his play.

The brief marriage scene is ending:

CLERGYMAN: Till death us do part—

BRIDE: Till death us do part—

ANNOUNCER: The number of marriages solemnised in churches during the past six months has declined by forty per cent., states a report—

CLERGYMAN: Judith and Peter, you have just taken the most solemn vows a man and a woman can take. You have sworn in God's house to love and cherish one another till death parts you. I hope you realise sincerely the true significance of that vow, and that you will fulfil it, come what may—

ANNOUNCER: On the other hand, the report records that the total number of divorces granted during the same period was more than sixty-five per cent. above the figures for the previous six months.

(*During the last six or seven speeches,* MARY *has been humming Mendelssohn's Wedding March. Now she breaks off and speaks to the sleeping baby.*)

MARY: Then you must be very kind to her—but you must try and be firm, too. Remember, a man must always be a hero to his own wife—

(*The* BRIDE *has taken off her veil and orange blossom, and now she bursts into a tirade of abuse.*)

BRIDE: A hero! My God! A fine hero you'd make. Why on earth I was fool enough to tie myself up to you for life I can't imagine. Look at the Robinsons—they've got a car. Look at the Browns—they've got a radiogram. Look at the Joneses —he takes his wife to Brighton every week-end.

In a few significant flashes the tale of Peter Smith is carried forward. Here the playwright is using precisely the technique of the movie camera which establishes a scene or a lapse of years with three or four well-chosen shots. And the simile is not without its significance.

The play continues with the consummation of Peter Smith's divorce. He is dismissed from his job, the politician appears making demagogic speeches calling on the unemployed to fight another business-man's war, and Peter Smith joins up to the concerted applause of schoolmaster, business man, and clergyman, who have hitherto regarded him with either contempt or indifference. His death is announced over the radio—and at once the playwright's climax is upon us.

A long passage of declamatory speeches closes in this way:

SCHOOLMASTER: Peter Ulric Smith! Write his name on the war memorial! What a tribute to the training of the old school! Fourteen of our boys have laid down their lives already—

CLERGYMAN: Peter Ulric Smith! Greater love hath no man than this: that a man lay down his life—

BUSINESS MAN: Peter Ulric Smith! He used to work for me, but this is the best day's work he ever did. I mean to say, look at my dividends—

ANNOUNCER: The Royal trumpeters will now sound the Last Post . . .

(*During these speeches* MARY *has risen to her feet and she is now standing, facing the other characters. She is trembling and suddenly she shouts:*)

67

MARY: No! You shan't do it! Stop, I tell you! Stop it!
ALL: What?
MARY (*shrieking*): Stop!
ALL: Stop?
MARY: Yes, stop! It mustn't be like that! It mustn't! Is that what I've suffered agonies for? Is that the best you can give my son? If that's all the world can offer, then I'd rather kill him now—before he's had time to learn what a mockery it all is. I'd rather kill him, I tell you, than let him grow up for that! I won't have it, I tell you. Do you hear that? I won't have it. (*All of the other characters begin to laugh derisively. MARY listens hopelessly for a moment. Then she shouts despairingly.*) Stop it! Stop it! (*The baby in the cradle begins to cry.*) There! Now you've wakened him.
(*She turns and picks up the child. Holding him in her arms, she turns again—to find that the others have all gone.*)

Here is the climax, in which nightmare reality interrupts the dream of the future. It is the moment towards which the playwright has been working throughout the play and which now demands a resolution. Cedric Mount ends his play by introducing the figure of the Madonna in the place of the figures which have vanished, who brings to Mary Smith a message of comfort saying that the secret of motherhood is hope: hope that every child is a potential savior of mankind. And the play closes, as it began, with the mother singing a lullaby to her child in a half-lit bedroom.

In some ways the resolution is unsatisfactory, since it conflicts with the bitterness of the satirical scenes. At the same time, it is true to the author's own logic and follows naturally from the first peaceful scene and from Mary's subsequent lines, which continually interrupt the bitter picture of Peter Smith's probable future.

68

l have dealt with this play in some detail because it does illustrate very clearly the point I made at the beginning of this essay: that the construction of all one-act plays is essentially the same and that certain laws of technique apply to all, whatever their form. *Twentieth Century Lullaby* is an experiment in presentation—episodic, making use of cinematic technique, introducing in the Announcer an equivalent to the Narrator or Chorus of an older form, and successfully—even audaciously—mingling realism with fantasy. But it is faithful throughout to the elements of good craftsmanship that I have already noted.

Today the observant playwright-innovator has a wealth of new ideas and technical improvements in stage machinery to make use of. As regards such innovations as the revolving stage and recent improvements in lighting systems, it is noticeable that in the professional theatre technical equipment is at least thirty years in advance of most of the drama it is exercised upon. Go to any large theatre which possesses a revolving stage, and you will see that it is merely used to send the same old scenery decorating the same old situations a little faster round the stage. Yet here is one outstanding instance of a technical improvement which, used by a playwright-innovator, could considerably alter the presentation of the drama and could infuse new life into worn-out modes and conventions.

But writers of one-act plays have themselves hardly begun to take advantage of all their opportunities. For the most part they are content to work to the convention of the picture stage with its fixed fourth wall and its conventional pattern worked out from curtain rise to curtain fall. But improvements in stage lighting have dissolved the fourth wall, if only playwrights had the sense to see it.

The intimacy of the Little Theatre has given them the chance to restore the vitality of close contact between audience and players; to draw the audience into the action, if need be, as Odets has done with such success in *Waiting for Lefty*. With this intimacy, the soliloquy is once more a natural and powerful part of the playwright's equipment. It can make its direct appeal without appearing unreal. The cinema is daily teaching a score of technical tricks that the playwright could well adapt to his own medium. And there is the radio—at once the least used and most opportune of mediums for the craftsman who wishes to accommodate his technique to new materials.

In the preface to his brilliant verse play *The Fall of the City* (the only play, to my knowledge, whose theme and technical presentation could have been put over by radio and through no other medium, and one which is packed with extremely interesting technical innovation) Archibald MacLeish argues eloquently in favor of the verse dramatist's use of radio as a new stage. His argument is that, in the first place, the word alone must convey atmosphere, setting, color, gesture, mood, and even costume, and in the second that since the foolish prose writers have merely used the radio as they would their platform stage, it is up to the poets to show them that radio has perfected new tools which need revolutionary methods of application. Radio drama is, of course, the poet's great opportunity. But there is no reason why the prose dramatist should ignore it or treat it (as did the first films in silent days and as the majority of English films still do) as just another "vehicle" for conventional theatrical methods. The radio makes its appeal to ear alone. There are no extraneous aids to imagination such as the theatre provides in abundance. Through the spoken word alone can the imagination be captured, held, excited, and satisfied. When one considers the appalling poverty of language to which the prose playwright has been reduced by more than sixty years of the "realistic" play, there emerges a strong argument in favor of the study of radio technique by any playwright who wishes to experiment. Radio will never wholly compensate the prose dramatist for the loss of color and the loss of contact between the players and a vigorous and responsive audience. But mastery of its technique should assist the dramatist in evolving new forms for his theatre and will certainly help to bring back to the stage the color and vitality of language it has so long lost.

THE CONSTRUCTION OF THE SOCIAL
ONE-ACT PLAY

MICHAEL BLANKFORT, who is in his late twenties, is a graduate of the University of Pennsylvania and was formerly associated with the Psychology Department at Princeton. His activities in the theatre have been numerous. He was one of the organizers of the now defunct Theatre Union; directed *Stevedore*, and adapted Friedrich Wolf's *Sailors of Cattaro*, both Theatre Union productions; wrote lyrics for *New Gulliver*, contributed to the Theatre Guild's production of *Parade*, and is the author of *The Crime*, a one-act play produced by the Theatre of Action, and *The Brave and the Blind*. He is co-author with Michael Gold of *Battle Hymn*, which was presented by the Experimental Theatre (WPA). Mr. Blankfort was, until very recently, an instructor in playwriting at New York University. He is the author also of the successful novel, *I Met a Man*.

THE CONSTRUCTION OF THE SOCIAL ONE-ACT PLAY

by Michael Blankfort

TO the average critic, a social play is something he can write an extended Sunday column about.

To the hot, ardent, and newly fledged social critic, a social play is something that calls for the directing genius of a Piscator, Stanislavski, and Lee Strasberg. He demands a revolution in form as well as in content. A proletarian horse needs a proletarian stable. There used to be a time when anybody who thought of writing a social play —a revolutionary play—with a first and last curtain was considered as conservative as Clyde Fitch.

In short, there has been a lot of wholesale nonsense written about the construction and purpose of the social play. It is a sprightly subject, and a few additional dicta more or less cannot hurt the dramatist who, at this moment, in coal camp or New York apartment is writing the next great social play that will do what it wants with construction.

If you are looking for blueprints in these few pages, stop here. It would be far better if you studied the headlines and a few choice social classics, statistical as well as dramatic. The social world is exciting enough for you to

75

write your social plays with such heat that the form will almost take care of itself. New material will make its own demands for new construction. Whenever there was an addition to the timeworn, rutted conventions of play construction, there were additions to timeworn, rutted conventions. That is the way it works: the world changes and so does the drama. The theatre and Bourbonism are mutually exclusive.

There are still tolerably intelligent people who, whenever the subject of the social play arises, hasten to put on a Lazarus act and raise from the grave the decomposed corpse of an old controversy—art versus propaganda. It has never been my purpose to aid and abet such vandalism. However, inasmuch as I am writing about the construction of the *social* one-act play, and someone else is writing about the construction of any old one-act play, social, antisocial, a-social or bi-social, some effort must be made to separate the propaganda wheat from the artistic chaff. The corpse has arisen; let the responsibility be on the head of the editor.

Among the choice bits of nonsense written on this subject, none has been so meaningless as the statement that all plays are propaganda. Meaningless only because not everybody walks around with a dictionary, and it is a waste of energy to define your terms every time you use a good word. (I must state here that in articles in the *New Theatre* magazine and elsewhere, I have written my share of the above nonsense.) "Propaganda" is a nasty word used to describe what you do not like. In all truth, it has been knocked around so much it will be no good for another twenty years. Let us leave it where the New York *Times* dropped it.

Nor is there much more light in the statement that only those plays which reflect their times are social plays. Noel Coward is one of the best reflectors of his times; he is not what I should call a writer of social plays. All plays, like all newspapers, reflect the times in which they are written. The question is—how?

The third bit of critical lackluster which ought to be got out of the way is the opinion that only social plays have something to say. Other serious plays, I suppose, are written because the author has nothing to say.

Let it be said that every serious playwright thinks he has something important to say. That is the only way you can distinguish serious playwrights from those who write in order to buy a home in Beverly Hills. Every serious playwright believes in what he has to say even if, like Maxwell Anderson in *Winterset*, he believes in the futility of the belief that anything can be said.

The simple mark of difference is this: what does the belief consist of? what is the playwright saying in his plays? Any other standard is painting stripes on zebras; they will come off in the first rain.

Some beliefs, or doctrines, if you will, are basically out of touch with the reality of the situation in the play, as well as the framework of the world in which the play is written. They run counter-clockwise to the movement of their social epoch. We laugh when Glenn Wilbur Voliva says the earth is flat. But we seem to take seriously Mr. Anderson's statement that men are helpless before an unjust world. (I do not want to appear to strike unreasonably at an able play and an abler playwright. I agree with John W. Gassner who in a considered piece, "Catharsis and the Modern Theatre," appearing in the August, 1937, issue of *The One Act Play Magazine,* said: "For two acts *Winterset* is a stirring indictment of injustice; then the third act resolutely fronts the verities in a lather of bathos.")

There are other beliefs and doctrines, however, more understanding of their epoch, more realistically appraising of the forces of their times, therefore, more progressive, truer, broader. They are the ear to the ground and the heart to the heart of the movement of peoples and classes, of wants and wishes. Those who hold such beliefs are not merely men of good will; they are men of active will. These men are the social playwrights of their times; they reflect their society and their years in a *progressive* way; their beliefs are progressive in every sense of the word, economic, philosophical, and political, frightening as the last is to most Americans who look on art and politics somewhat the way the Archbishop of Canterbury looks on the ex-king Edward.

II

There are a few other misconceptions with which the mind is burdened; that is, the mind of novices in the social playwriting field and of Joseph Wood Krutch.

No one has said that social plays are necessarily good plays. A progressive idea in the hands of an incompetent or semiskilled playwright turns into an incompetent or semiskilled play.

Social plays can deal with other things than strikes; they can be written about other heroes than strikers, workers, farmers, slum children; they can incorporate other ideas than unionism, anti-fascism, and William Randolph Hearst. There are no horizons of character, situation, or ideas beyond which the social dramatist is forbidden. He can, if he is able, handle material that would make Noel

Coward's seem positively proletarian by contrast. He can, as in *You Can't Change Human Nature* by Philip Stevenson, write a broad farce about the 1776-ers or a fine poetic and symbolic masque as in Archibald MacLeish's *Panic*.

Social plays have more in common, by way of construction, with other plays, present and past, than they have differences.

Social plays are not necessarily simple plays. Unfortunately plays are only as rich as their authors.

Social plays can and must deal with *values* as well as events.

Social plays demand a social mind. *The social mind of the playwright is the key to the construction of the social play.*

On this last point, John Howard Lawson has an eloquent paragraph in his book, *Theory and Technique of Playwrighting:*

If the playwright's scheme of thought is irrational it distorts the laws of the drama, and inhibits the will to create meaningful action. He must either conceal this weakness by obscurantism or pretense; or he must overcome it by the slow labor of thought.

Clarity is as necessary to a social playwright as conflict to the social play.

III

The hardest thing in the field of playmaking is to write a social play. The reason is that you have to have a genius for *clarity*. Well, at any rate, you should have a taste for it. The playwright's social mind, quite unlike other minds, has to be replete with clarity. He has to be clear about the world he lives in, the world he writes about, the world he

79

writes for. Then, and only then, will he be clear about what he wants to say. Such clarity is indissolubly linked with the plot action of his play, his characters; in short, the construction of his play will not be taken for granted, but will, I hope, be satisfactorily illustrated later in this piece.

In addition to dramatic logic, the social writer must be possessed by a remorseless social logic and a realistic eye to the world. The reader may ask, "What will he see?" My answer to the curious interrogator—I am limited by the function of this book—is to study carefully the implications of the plays mentioned in this article.

Social clarity is a pure and simple technical demand of the art of social writing. Why?

"A dramatist," wrote George Pierce Baker, "must study his characters until he has discovered the entire range of their emotion." A social playwright must study the environment of his characters until he has exhausted every possible use to which it can be put, for the social play is based on this truism, that drama is the result of a change in equilibrium between people and their environment, which includes, of course, other people. Just think of the drama implied in a man working in a factory which he once owned. Or see where a lack of such study will lead, if you want to write a social play about coal miners without ridding your mind, so carefully cultivated in university sociology, of its romantic reformism, in which the substitution of plumbing for outhouses will transform a company-owned town into a proletarian paradise.

Social clarity is a technical demand.

Starting from one or more disparate experiences, a play needs a *unifying idea* to give it meaning. (I cannot help it if you have seen the unifying idea called by other names, "the spine" or "the theme" or "the root idea." Without their own vocabulary critics and dramatists are lost.) The unifying idea affects the construction of the play; it is the daughter of social clarity and the mother of the play.

An example: A dramatist feels strongly about war. He wants to write a play about how and why wars are made. His general intention is clear. Perhaps he has some characters in mind, a good scene or two, and a curtain that will bring the audience to its feet. Consciously or unconsciously his mind reaches out for the conception or idea which will bring unity to his intention and his material. He sits down at his desk with a copy of McDougall, the psychologist, at his left hand, and perhaps Karl Marx on his right. McDougall is easier to read than Marx. Thus, after some study, our playwright is persuaded that wars are the result of the combative instinct in man. Ah, a conception that will unite everything in his play. Suddenly, he feels that his exposition is clear. He will have some young men talking about the last war. They will pledge themselves never to go to war again, for they are convinced that wars are made for the profit of a few rich men. He jumps, naturally enough, from exposition to climax. A new war has come and the same young men forget their wise pledges and, carried away despite themselves and their hatred for war, join up. They are victims of an instinct to fight, of the combative urge.

In this rather extreme example, based vaguely on the play, *Men Must Fight*, the tightly knit correspondence between social clarity—or rather unclarity—and the unifying idea is visible. Did the unclarity affect the play? Certainly, for nowhere, in play, platform, or laboratory, can an instinct to fight be credibly established. But the author based his entire play on it. Certainly, that is why it had no validity, neither incidents nor characters nor climax.

IV

The old dramaturgic saw that the action of a play must advance the story is true, of course, for all plays. But in social plays it has to do more than that; it has also to advance the unifying idea.

The social play is interested in boy meets girl. It is a situation which no one can or wants to avoid. But the social playwright has to decide whether boy meeting girl best illustrates, in a dramatic way, what he wants his play to reveal. In that way, the writer of social plays has a principle of economy all his own.

In Irwin Shaw's *Bury the Dead*, for example, the unifying idea is to expose the fundamental insanity of war. A brilliant dramatic action was selected by the author to dramatize his idea—the refusal of dead soldiers to be buried. There are, however, several scenes, well written in themselves, which tend to choke up the play. The average audience entranced by *Bury the Dead* must feel a slackening or diversion of interest in several spots, notably the scene with the prostitutes and one or two of the colloquies between the soldiers and their women. It was precisely these scenes which were not at all integrated with the unifying idea. "The slow labor of thought" would have eliminated them.

Stevedore, although a full-length play, is an even better example. More clarity brought to the play would have resulted in a construction far more economical. The play tried to say too much. It had several themes, each given equal importance: (1) Negroes should fight back against their oppressors; (2) white and black workers must unite in order to win security for themselves; (3) unionism rather than individualism is the way out for workers.

The fact that the resultant confusion misled critics as to the authors' exact intentions is less important than the fact that the overabundance of themes, each given major emphasis, made it impossible within the time of the play to develop the characters with sufficient roundness and depth.

To sum up: social clarity in the playwright's mind helps —does more than help, determines—to a large extent the selection of his unifying idea, the incidents and actions, and, therefore, characters which dramatize this idea; and, finally, it assists him in bringing forth his drama in the most economical and in the most effective way.

Without dramatic logic, any play is a bad play; without social logic, a social play is confused, misleading, and sometimes unintentionally reactionary, i.e., not a social play.

v

There has been a singularly modern development in the social play which has worried most social playwrights— worried their sympathetic critics as well. It has been designated by some unknown hero as "the call to action." The need for a call to action grew out of the situation of our times in which the social artist felt called on to do more than expose the cruelties of modern capitalism. He was impelled to do something about them. He demanded that his audiences do something about them. He wanted not merely individual rebellion but organized social protest. And he wanted to incorporate a call for that protest in his plays, whether it be a call to join a union or to organize against war or to stand up with your fellows against moral corruption or to revaluate life with new and humane and revolutionary values.

Unfortunately—but as was to be expected—the call to action in the early plays took the forms of slogans without much integration to the play and therefore without much human warmth. But they were exciting. The audience, itself, brought the excitement to the slogans—not the playwright. The early calls to action were very explicit and concrete, but see how they have developed from such mass chants as *Dimitroff* (Kazan and Smith), *Newsboy*, *Angelo Herndon*, and *America, America* (Alfred Kreymborg) to *Hymn to the Rising Sun* (Paul Green). They have developed from the explicit to the implicit, from the call to concrete action as in Odets' *Waiting for Lefty* to the call for a revaluation of the conception of the heroic in *The Brave and the Blind*. And yet . . .

The call to action, technically, may still be used to describe the *final curtain* of almost every well-known social play. It is Agate's last speech in *Waiting for Lefty*. It is the victory of the longshoremen in *Stevedore*, the turning out of the power plant in *Marching Song*, Rubin's summary in *They Shall Not Die*, Gruber's answer to the priest in *This Earth Is Ours*, the triumphant march of the dead soldiers in *Bury the Dead*, the last eleven speeches in *Private Hicks*, the clarification of the meaning of war by Benda in *The Trumpets of Wrath*, the proselytizing of Zets by Reynolds at the end of *Transit* ("Reynolds: *Organ-eye-zation . . . I'm tellin' you*"). It is the surprise speech from the audience in *The Crime*, the last three speeches in *Give All Thy Terrors to the Wind*, the lights going out in *The Secret*. And when *God's in His Heaven*, an exception to the above plays, was published, a foreword suggested that the play be supplemented by a program note outlining the ways and means of combating the conditions exposed in the play.

There is a very good reason for the fact that the most recent plays have the most implicit calls to actions, relying not on slogans nor on program notes but on the indigenous quality of the play to make its point. The last seven years have been years of vast education. The newness of organized protest is no longer new. The audience knows how to act, or, at least, its isolation from action has been broken.

There is a second reason. Social playwrights, new ones as well as old, have increased their command over their craft. They do not have to be crude and oversimple to say what they want to say.

There is also a third reason. The call to action, explicit and sloganized, was part of the very honest and necessary compulsion of the social writer to look at his plays and characters dynamically. He saw movement in the world around him. He saw his heroes and heroines (although there were too few of the latter) moving forward from one environmental relationship to another; being converted from scab to striker, from pacifist to revolutionary, from do-nothing to do-something. He wanted his audience to do the same—his prime object in writing social plays—and wanting it, he gave birth to the conversion play, the modern equivalent of the old moralities.

The foremost and best example of the conversion drama can be found in *Waiting for Lefty*.

That the simple conversion play, rich and satisfying and exciting as it was, contained the seeds of its own destruction (from a construction point of view) may better be illustrated when we talk about characterization.

The conversion play after a while gave justice to the charge that the social playwright was building his plays by rote and formula. But what was really meant was that the social playwright was still cutting his teeth, still crude and unsure of himself.

There is a great past as well as a great future to the conversion play. Society has not slowed down in the last decade. Men are still moving. But hereafter where a playwright *chooses* to deal with conversion material, he will not be awkward and sometimes beyond credulity, and he will deal not with slogans but with human values no less dynamic.

In the last sentence, I used the phrase, "where a playwright chooses." The phrase was deliberate. I believe the time has passed when a social playwright feels that he has to deal with conversion material and have a call to action or be less a social playwright. On the other hand, it must not be understood that such dramatic elements as conversion or call to action have anything to do with a social playwright's being more or less an artist. That such a misconception is still widespread is shown by an essay on *Hymn to the Rising Sun*, which appeared in the August issue of 1937 of *The One Act Play Magazine*, written by Percival Wilde, an otherwise discerning and sensitive critic.

It has, I think, everything that a great play should have. Its theme, man's inhumanity to man [I wonder whether Paul Green would agree that this was his theme], is broadly conceived. It is dealt with objectively, calmly, massively. Its suspense is created at the rise of the curtain. It is increased by masterly touches. Its action is terrible, but utterly logical. It

86

marches to tragedy with the resolute step of a Greek classic, but it does not end there; it asks the question, "What are you going to do about this?" *and with a final touch of artistry, it offers no answer.* (Interpolated comments and italics are mine.)

The quotation speaks for itself as well as for me.

VI

It is not my intention—it is not the scope of this essay—to analyze the ways and means of characterization. Undoubtedly, the question will be raised in other parts of the book. Lawson has a brilliant chapter in his *Theory and Technique of Playwrighting* on this subject. There are, however, certain special problems in characterization which the social playwright has to face. These problems have been so considerable that, up to the present, the one major technical fault of the general repertory of social plays has been their schematic and inadequate characterization.

First of all, the social playwright has been and is a pioneer. Not until *They Shall Not Die* and *Stevedore* in a full-length play or *Mighty Wind A'Blowin'* (Alice Holdship Ware) in a short play has the Negro been shown on the stage other than as a servant, comic relief, or a spiritual singing stepanfetchiting levee loafer. Taxi drivers were minor gangsters until *Waiting for Lefty*. Who knew a chain gang and a chain-gang boss until *Hymn to the Rising Sun?* Or the C.C.C. campers until *The Young Go First?* Or a sharecropper until Bernice Kelly Harris's *His Jewels?* Or the inside of the mind of a young National Guardsman whose father is a worker until Albert Maltz's *Private Hicks?* Or the pain and sacrifice of an underground worker in Nazi Germany until Clifford Odets' *Till the Day I Die?*

Where on the American stage can the American sailor be found, the farmer, the white-collar worker, the small tradesman, the industrialized backwoodsman, the miner, the steelworker, the immigrant, the bindle-stiff, the unemployed, the American hero of the past, and the slum child, except as they were poeticized or lampooned or were stooges for a laugh and a gag? They can be found characterized with varying degrees of success in such plays as *Give All Thy Terrors to the Wind* (the Siftons), *Black Pit, 1931—, Ingot City, Transit,* and *God's in His Heaven* (Philip Stevenson), *Battle Hymn, Money, Let Freedom Ring* (Albert Bein), *This Earth Is Ours* and *The Trumpets of Wrath* (William Kozlenko), *The Cradle Will Rock* (Marc Blitzstein), *Dead End* (Sidney Kingsley).

I have not even scratched the surface of that new cast which the social playwright introduced to the American audience. The playwrights, themselves, have not even begun either. And the importance of this pioneering is self-evident when you realize that these characters represent ninety percent of the population.

Pioneering had its own headaches. Bringing new people to the stage in new situations was enough to engulf the playwright. Because he had to learn about even the most external aspects of their lives, he forgot, for the moment, that workers are first of all human, that even bosses love their wives and children. It is a strange fact that the social playwright, above all people, took a long time to find humanity in his characters. And a social play cannot live by melodrama alone.

The writer of social plays became aware of his deficiency. He had to face the fact consciously that his job was not merely to entertain his audience, not merely to give it

88

pleasure—necessary as both these elements are—but also to instruct it. He began to see that instruction or "enlightenment," as John W. Gassner has put it in a splendid piece in *The One Act Play Magazine*,[1] must be translated into human terms. For only in this way could credibility be established. If, for example, Paul Green wanted to expose the cruelty of a chain gang, he did not make the cruelty unbelievable by making his "villains" inhuman. Nor did he make the cruelty palatable by glossing over or blunting it with crude melodrama. But by an understanding insight, Green made it sharper, believable, and dramatically true. To his villains as well as to his heroes he brought a profound human sympathy. One derived the feeling that there are deeper and more fundamental sources for the insensate barbarism of the chain gang than the bestial whims of any particular chain-gang boss.

Here is an example of such characterization from *Hymn to the Rising Sun.*

CAPTAIN (*to the convicts*): That's right, boys, you remember how Runt liked to hear the trains blow. What you say? Shall we take him up there and bury him? (*The convicts look at him with dull cold eyes.*) Well, I don't blame you for feeling bad over it. I do myself. All right, we will. It's his last wish and the wishes of the dead are sacred. We all know that. (*Now standing over* RUNT *and looking sorrowfully down on him.*) You know me, Runt. I didn't have no grudge against you. It was the law said to do it. (*With sudden blinding rage.*) Yeah, the law!

Pioneering had still another headache. The social playwright was, for the most part, a newcomer into the realms of social clarity. He had not yet integrated the fresh and

[1] August, 1937.

Balboa-like discoveries of his world—the outside world—
with his own interior philosophy of life. Everything was
good, that is, progressive, or bad, that is, reactionary. He
became a great classifier of things and men and deeds . . .
and history. Justly, he disliked the tortuous, "there-are-
two-sides-to-everything" attitude of the liberal. He failed
to realize that his job was to illuminate the high sources
of human action in a complete way and in a human way.
In short, he overlooked that most obvious fact (obvious
to him now) that the eternal conflicts of life—birth, death,
love, fear—are closely and indissolubly tied to the temporal or topical conflicts of classes and nations and that the
greatest realistic illumination of the headlines comes via
the heart lines.

There is no wonder, then, that his characters were
merely schemed out and sketched. It is no wonder, then,
that frequently his plays were mere pendulum plays in
which halfmen, albeit for the time sympathetic and exciting men, swung pendulum fashion from one extreme to
another without fully revealing, in human character as
well as environment, the reasons for the swing.

The marriage of the playwright to his social material
was, contradictory as it sounds, first a divorce.

The great importance of this is clear when you realize
that the author's ideas are real to the audience only when
they are stated through character and not merely through
the hanging participles of dialogue, if I may borrow a
phrase from English grammar.

Lawson, in referring to Agate's last speech in *Waiting
for Lefty*, says, "One is swept along, swept by Agate's call
to action at the end 'Stormbirds of the working class.' *But
the development which leads to this speech is not cumu-*

latively logical, not based on flesh and blood realities."
The fault, he points out later, "springs from the gap between the immediate impulses of the characters and the
wider frame-work of events."

The social play demands such a cumulative logic. Without it the force of the playwright's ideas is nullified in
the drama; it is incompletely realized. In characterization, this means that there must be no obiter dicta, no
Charlie McCarthyisms, nothing spoken or done which does
not flow immediately and truly from the logic of the character and his relation to the environment. Otherwise, the
audience will feel justifiably that the play has stopped
and the author has stepped onto the stage to give a preach-
ment—and that does not work unless you are George Bernard Shaw.

A social playwright demands that his ideas be effective.
Let him write pamphlets, if he is incapable of dramatizing
his ideas in the medium of the theatre, which means in
the heart and humanity of his characters.

VII

The one-act play used to be invariably a one-scene play.
Today the one-act play, more accurately described, is a
play which runs anywhere from five minutes to an hour.
The shift in definition may be traced to the new freedom
given to this form by the social playwrights. *Bury the
Dead* has the fluidity of a movie; so also *Waiting for
Lefty. Till the Day I Die* is a compact three-act play, yet
taking a third of the time. *The Brave and the Blind* is
composed of several scenes; so are *The Crime, The Young
Go First, This Earth Is Ours,* and *The Trumpets of
Wrath.*

This "cinematic technique," as it has been called, has its perils as well as its profits. Fluids sometimes run too thin to have consistency. The breadth of freedom in this form frequently leads to such diffusion that the play suffers. *The Crime* is an example of this. It has nine scenes, ten when produced. The effectiveness of *The Crime* was weakened because of its lack of compactness.

The social one-act play, I believe, will tend to leave behind the multiscened structure. Originally, this form was the result of new material in the hand of the playwright; new material that seemed to cry out for many scenes. But the playwright's vision is becoming more disciplined; his treatments are becoming more intensive. He is, as pointed out before, concerned with ideas through character rather than with ideas through slogan. It is likely that his new concern will call for compactness.

VIII

Social dramatists have a responsibility not only to themselves as artists, or to the ideas which enrich their view of the world, but also to the audience which comes to see their plays.

The social playwright is an artist, therefore he writes to please not only himself but also an audience. This does not mean that he writes Mother Goose tales because they happen to be popular. He writes for an audience in the sense that he is giving dramatic expression to the darkness and light of its life as lived in society. Without that he is not a social playwright. He is acting on his audience as well as being acted upon by it. His audience—a working-class audience, frequently—is seeing, for the first time, its hopes, frustrations, tragedies, and accomplishments set down before it. By its own immediate experience, it can test the truth of what it sees. It is an exacting audience. It does not worry about what form the play is cast in—poetic, fantastic, realistic, satiric—as long as it is conceived from a realistic and progressive philosophy of life.

But the social playwright does not necessarily have to write with a working-class audience in mind, nor, as pointed out previously, deal with working-class subjects. His audience, then, may shift from one class base to another. Being clear about whom he is writing for, the playwright realizes that the dynamics of the audience-playwright relationship has likewise shifted. He cannot expect a fundamentally sympathetic ear. He must compensate for that by the way he writes the play. His wit, his talent for theatrics—the conventional attractions for this kind of audience—may negate an antagonism.

Too long has the art for art's sake objection to writing with an audience in mind prevailed. The social playwright has helped break it down, for his vision is meaningful; he has purpose and direction to his work.

IX

Without entering into a discussion of the mechanics of dramatic conflict—the heart of play construction—there are a few things that can be said.

The social playwright has brought to the stage new and rich variations on old human conflicts. In *Private Hicks* he has dramatized the struggle between a boy's will to do the right thing for the sake of his integrity and the forces of a world which would forbid him that. To as old a dramatic conflict as that of brother against brother—how many Civil War plays there have been which utilized this—

Waiting for Lefty has given new meaning in the scene, short as it is, between the striker and the stool pigeon. The same play has given another kind of meaning to the fight for the right to love—as old as *Romeo and Juliet*, if not older—which places that conflict irretrievably in our own times as much as Shakespeare's play was in his. The eternal philosophic conflict of life against death can be found in such different plays as *Bury the Dead* and *The Brave and the Blind*.

The conflict between loyalties, the struggle for the right to live, to think freely, the conflict between men for power are all old human conflicts. The social playwright has used them too, but he has translated them, in a sense, and given them, fittingly, the meaning of our times. Love versus duty, as theatre-worn a dramatic conflict as there is, becomes revived and renewed in the hands of a playwright who sees, as in *Black Pit*, that in our world love and duty are not inimical to each other's interest. Rather, it is possible that one can be satisfied only by the satisfaction of the other. Joe Kovarsky must inevitably and tragically lose the love of his wife when he forgets that he has a duty to his fellow-men.

The social playwright looks upon conflict in the theatre with a dynamic vision. He is not content to accept the tradition that certain loyalties and values are by nature the antithesis of each other. He has brought to these old conflicts a synthesizing touch which derives from this acceptance of a unified, progressive, and humane world point of view.

PART II   SCOPE

THE ONE-ACT PLAY AND THE RADIO

VAL GIELGUD is Drama Director of the British Broadcasting Corporation, and as such especially qualified to write on the subject of "The One-Act Play and the Radio." He has himself written several one-act plays which have been produced widely in England, and is the author of a technical book on how to write for the radio. Besides his professional connections with wireless and playwriting, Mr. Gielgud has written a number of detective novels.

THE ONE-ACT PLAY AND THE RADIO

by Val Gielgud [1]

TO the writer of one-act plays, the radio has opened a new and in many respects a very fascinating field. At the risk of seeming to insist upon the obvious, I feel that any article dealing with this subject must begin by emphasizing one fact: that playwriting for the stage and playwriting for the microphone are two very different things. The broadcast play is, of course, the Cinderella of the drama. In comparison with the play of the theatre, with its honorable lineage stretching back to Aeschylus and even beyond, or even with the cinema, which has crammed birth, adolescence, and at any rate quasi-maturity into something like forty years, the broadcast play is an infant in arms. Indeed, it is doubtful whether it can be claimed to have had any serious existence at all for more than four years at the outside. It would therefore be ridiculous to pretend that the moment has yet come either to compile a history of broadcast drama or to lay down a code of hard and fast rules for its writing and production.

The author who is looking to the stage is dealing with

[1] Although Mr. Gielgud, being English, naturally relies on the British Broadcasting Corporation for statistics and on English plays for examples, what he has to say about the short radio drama in this chapter is basically applicable to the American scene.—*Editor*.

an audience in mass, essentially susceptible to mass reactions of emotion. The author who is writing for broadcasting is dealing with an audience infinitely larger—but an audience mainly composed of individual units. His approach therefore must be far more personal, more intimate. He cannot count on the help of his audience to do much of his work for him, as a stage author, for example, can count on one or two members of his audience to start his laughs for him. And this qualification must continually be borne in mind with regard both to subject and to technique of construction and dialogue.

There is the further point that the radio audience covers every section of society. The radio play must cater for the tastes of a potentially nationwide audience; as opposed to the very limited potential audiences of theatregoers, whose tastes can pretty easily be gauged and summarized.

The principal problem of the would-be radio playwright is of course how he shall overcome the fundamental handicap of being deprived of his audiences' eyes. People are accustomed to the idea of "seeing plays," as opposed to hearing them. Therefore it is essential that the attention of listeners should be immediately caught at the opening of the broadcast play and their curiosity aroused.

It is doubtful whether the broadcast play—leaving television possibilities for the moment out of account—can ever have the widespread popular appeal of the film, for the simple reasons that people find it easier to use their eyes than to use their ears and that a medium which appeals to two senses simultaneously can achieve its object more simply than a medium which can only appeal to one. Nevertheless, there is plenty of evidence to show that the invisible audience for radio drama is steadily increasing;

and—what is the primary motive of this chapter—there are apparently sufficient people interested in the question of writings plays for broadcasting for an average of some forty plays a week to be submitted to the British Broadcasting Corporation for production on the air.

The radio play can afford no "padding." It must make its points clearly and distinctly. It is probably elementary to insist on such points as the need for limiting characters in number to a minimum and for differentiating them as strongly as possible in type to give scope for easily distinguishable voice casting by the producer and for the fairly frequent insertion of the names of the characters in the course of their dialogue to make sure that the audience is not growing at a loss over the various speakers' identities. These things are the A B C of writing for the microphone.

If the author begins with the assumption that his work can be given to the microphone either because, although written for the stage, it has failed to achieve stage production or because he wants practice in writing for the stage and thinks that writing for the microphone will keep his hand in, he is strangling his work at birth. There is, of course, a place in radio dramatic productions for the adapted stage play. But such adaptations are quite a different type of work from the original play written for broadcasting. It is on one common ground only that the stage and the microphone meet. That ground is, of course, a vitally important one. Both demand that the author should be able to write and have something to say. But in technical methods they have nothing in common. The stage has one set of limiting conventions; the microphone has another and a quite different set.

If a play is unsuitable for stage production, the odds

are a hundred to one that it will be even more unsuitable for studio production. It is possible that the theme may be unsuitable for the stage and yet suitable for the microphone. But if that is so, the theme should be treated a second time strictly from the microphone point of view. It is, practically speaking, useless to submit a rejected stage play for broadcasting.

The newcomer to writing for radio is only too often misled by a curious legend that has grown up on the subject of "sound effects." For some years, in Great Britain at any rate, a quite disproportionate importance was given to the activities of the Effects Staff at Broadcasting House, with their specially surfaced tables, their electric resistances, their mixing panels for phonograph records of effects of all kinds, their tin baths and roller skates. It has been proved by harsh experience that the best radio plays are far from being those which employ the greatest number of sound effects. On the contrary, the fewer sound effects there are in a radio play the better. And any experienced radio producer will point out that while one good effect will, in the true sense of the word, be "effective," a multitude serve only to confuse the listener and fog the outline of the play.

Radio should come sympathetically to the experienced writer of short plays because of his training in handling the limited time. It is true that in England the average length of the radio play tends to be considerably greater than the length of an ordinary one-act play. This is partly because the British Broadcasting Corporation has always maintained a considerable proportion of adapted full-length stage plays in its dramatic output—adaptations whose average length works out at an hour and a quarter.

VAL GIELGUD

I understand this is not the case in the United States, where the normal length of a radio dramatic piece is half an hour. And even in England it has been fairly convincingly proved that the best original radio plays written for the microphone take from forty to fifty minutes.

It is, on the whole, true to say that the ideal length for a broadcast play has tended to grow steadily shorter, experience showing that an audience finds listening to the spoken word for more than an hour and a half at the outside too much of a strain. An exception can be made in the case of adaptations of full-length novels, such as *Carnival* or *Jane Eyre,* or in the case of familiar classical plays such as those of Shakespeare, but if the original radio dramatist aims at a length varying from forty minutes to an hour and a quarter, he will probably not be very far wrong. Listening to a radio play has not yet become an automatic habit, and the radio play runs without intervals. A play cannot be appreciated from the loud-speaker with that vague sense of lazy entertainment so widespread amongst theatrical audiences. People are not used to relying on their ears alone, therefore the radio dramatist demands an extraordinary degree of concentrated attention for his work, and this quality of concentration must not be unduly or unreasonably strained.

The writer of one-act plays is therefore at an advantage as compared with the ordinary playwright, who is accustomed to his three acts of preparation, development and climax, and explanation or retrospection. He is used to a choice of subject which can be handled within a comparatively brief time limit; to the need for a rapid establishment of essential characterization; to the requirements of strong and simple plots. Not only this. He is freed from one of the greatest problems of the writer of the one-act stage play. He is not hampered by having to get along without changes in time and space. The radio theatre has the freedom of the cinema, perhaps an even greater freedom, in regard to changes of scene and sequence.

This leads us immediately to the consideration of the next practical point. For precisely the same reasons that the radio dramatist cannot afford to be too lengthy or too verbose, he must also avoid obscurity of treatment. He must never forget that his listeners, while having eyes, are yet for his purpose blind. Development of plot, careful distinction of characters, even limitation of number of characters, and definite stamping of time and place must all be emphasized without being stressed to absurdity, or labeled to monotony.

For this essential clarity of treatment, two methods can be employed. The simplest—a method more frequently used a year or two ago than at present—is the use of linking narrative to form, as it were, the spinal cord of the play. This has the great advantage of solving the problem at a single stroke; but it brings with it almost equivalent disadvantages of tending to a certain unreality and crudeness of construction. It cannot hope to satisfy a really conscientious dramatic craftsman, although, again in the case of radio adaptation of novels, it is occasionally justified, and will probably continue. But where this slightly pedestrian method is not employed, the author must continually bear in mind that he has nothing but his dialogue with which not only to tell his story clearly and unmistakably but also to indicate changes of scene, physical traits of his characters, and the essential details of their background.

It is obvious, therefore, that the simple plot, involving few characters, and those few characters of a type to be simply and immediately distinguished by innate differences in their individual voices, is the best for the dramatist's purpose. The fact that much has been written of the technical complications of radio production has led a good many people to believe that the best radio play is also the most elaborate radio play; that the simultaneous use of many studios, various ingenious effects, and a quantity of music are the essential ingredients of the ideal broadcast play.

This is simply not the case. The somewhat elaborate machinery which can be placed at the disposal of the producer must be the servant of the play and not its master. Complication for its own sake is as bad in the case of radio drama as it is in the case of anything else. Both for author and producer the golden rule is that a complicated method should never be employed where a simple one can achieve the desired result. Mere ingenuity has covered far too great a multitude of sins in the history of the broadcast play. There may be occasions when such technical ingenuity is both desirable and necessary. Such occasions should be the exception and not the rule.

But, as in all playwriting, two things are essential to the microphone author. He must have something to say, and he must be able to say it. In other words, he must have the gifts of imagination and of dialogue. And I fear that these gifts are literally gifts. I doubt if they can be acquired, though it is a pathetic belief of the organizers of the scenario departments of various film organizations that dialogue can be achieved as it were synthetically, if only enough mixed brains are put onto the job. An exhaustive knowledge of the technique of microphone production is by no means necessary. It is of course helpful. But the microphone is like any other medium. It should be the servant, not the master, of the artist. The play that is written merely to exploit the tricks of the radio producer's trade will be a second-rate play. The limitations of the medium must of course not be neglected. But with that qualification kept firmly in mind, the actual bringing of the work of art to the listener can safely be left to the professional radio producer, whose daily business it is.

II

In entering upon the vexed and difficult question of suitable subjects for the radio dramatist, it should be established that authors should in the first place write microphone plays round subjects rather than attach subjects painfully to microphone plays. More explicitly, because the machinery of radio offers the dramatist certain particular advantages and attractions, it is a mistake to make use of them regardless of whether the subject is suitable for this type of treatment or not.

While it is true that, as compared, for example, with vaudeville programs or concerts by military bands, broadcast plays are program items of relatively minority appeal, nevertheless, the mere fact that a play is broadcast as opposed to being presented in a theatre makes it necessary that its basis be, from one point of view or another, a popular one. This is not entirely to shut out from approach to the microphone the play which appeals to a strictly limited audience. There is, and should be, a place for such plays. To attempt to broadcast nothing but plays that would please every listener would result only in failing to please any listener.

The best that it could be hoped to achieve from a policy of broadcasting nothing but entirely popular drama would be to avoid hurting anyone's feelings: an ideal conflicting seriously with the classic definition of the value of drama— the purgation of the emotions of its audience by arousing in them pity and terror. Nevertheless, it is absurd for the radio dramatist to think of his audience in anything approaching the same terms as does the author who hopes that his work may face an audience in the West End of London.

First of all, he must remember that his audience is not in the strict sense of the word an audience at all. It is not a corporate body, it is a cross section of society made up of individuals, for the most part by their firesides and in the company, not of strangers interesting or irritating as the case may be, but of their relatives and friends. Secondly, it is an audience comprising all sorts and conditions of men and women. It would be absurd to carry this second point too far. Unless he is an author of the first rank, in which case he can certainly dispense with these various well-meant hints, the dramatist cannot hope that his work will appeal equally to children and grownups, dukes and dustmen, clergymen and charwomen, philistines and intellectuals. But it is a great mistake to forget the vast size of the target aimed at and to ignore the implications of that fact; and this particular point may perhaps be summed up in the axiom that on the one hand the subject of a broadcast play should be as broad based as possible; on the other that such subjects must be limited by considerations of tastes and common sense, from the point of view of what can desirably be broadcast for one and all to hear.

Needless to say, this question of subject has not yet been finally solved. It has gone through various phases parallel with the development of the broadcast play. At one time, for example, it was considered that owing to the peculiar facilities offered by its machinery, abolishing limitations of space and time, the most promising field for the radio dramatist was in the fast-moving story of adventure, covering miles of country and years of time, and involving every type of mechanical sound device to give variety and diversion. There probably remains a place for this kind of broadcast play, the play of colorful action and adventure, particularly if music is one of its essential ingredients. Perhaps the most successful example to date is the play written by W. Rooke-Ley and Christopher Martin on the subject of the composer Chopin's tragic love affair with Maria Wodzinska.

III

It is, incidentally, almost impossible to overemphasize the importance of music to the broadcast play. It stands to reason that as people are trained by habit and custom to listen to music, while they are not so trained to listen to plays, the addition of music to a play which is heard but not seen is bound to make it more varied, more pleasant, and easier to listen to. But this is not all. If music is used as one of the ingredients of a broadcast play, it cannot by any means be regarded as "incidental" music. The conventional overture and indifferent entr'acte, which we all know so well as being the signals for the male members of a theatrical audience to leave hastily for the bars, have no counterpart in radio drama. Any music which is used immediately becomes *ipso facto* of the first importance.

I do not think that it is too much to say that the music of a broadcast play is quite as important as its actors. There may be much of it, there may be extremely little; but whatever its quantity, it is always an essential and never a mere accessory. It is difficult to put limits to the various ways in which it can be used. It may be employed merely for emotional purposes, as in Mr. Marvell's *Across the Moon*, when various tunes, impregnated with the strongest sentimental associations, were deliberately wedded to various parts of the play and produced an astonishing effect; an effect rather cheap and easy, perhaps, but none the less perfectly legitimate. Again, it may be used, as in Mr. Harding's special broadcast version of *The Tempest*, to indicate changes of scene and to stamp clearly the entrances of different characters by providing them with musical themes, almost after the fashion of a Wagner opera.

It may be used, as was the case in *Chopin*, as practically the central core of the play. It is unnecessary to multiply examples, but the dramatist who neglects the musical question when he is deliberating the problems of subject and method is simply tying one hand behind his back. Prophecy is seldom a grateful or successful pursuit, but in this connection I feel that the first radio playwright who can do for the microphone what René Clair has done for the screen, by the combination of the rhythms of music and of the spoken word, will win a high place for himself. And unless theatrical production entirely distracts his attention, I should be inclined to point to Tyrone Guthrie as the most likely individual to succeed on these lines, if he fulfills the expectations that were aroused by *Squirrel's Cage* and *The Flowers Are Not for You to Pick*.

IV

This consideration of the problem of subject could obviously be expanded at indefinite length, but perhaps it will be sufficient to conclude here with a few words on one more point: the question of suitable characters. This question of characters must be immediately related to a proper sense of the audience for whom broadcast plays are written. As I mentioned before, this audience is essentially a cross section of individuals. It is not like an audience in the theatre, susceptible to mass influences and mass emotions. It is not even primarily expectant of entertainment, and therefore prepared for the sake of entertainment to dismiss most considerations of common sense and reality. Therefore the author, whose invention produces characters who from their essential humanity convince listeners of the real existence of themselves and their circumstances, starts at a tremendous advantage. In this sense, perhaps, the radio dramatist can borrow from the technique of the novelist rather than from that of the playwright.

The characters in a broadcast play are much closer to their audience than the characters in a play or a film. There is no visual barrier of silver screen or golden footlights. The radio audience is at the actor's elbow. If that actor is a marionette or a dummy and if the circumstances and the scenes in which he moves are composed of the painted "flats" of stage convention, the listener will be unconvinced and apt to grow first disappointed and then exasperated.

The truth of this is very clearly demonstrated by the

fact that while the plays of Shakespeare in the theatre are most magnificent examples of classic tradition and must be watched in a certain conventional manner somewhat comparable with the way in which a reader turns the pages of Milton or a traveler regards the Parthenon or the Sistine Chapel, a Shakespeare play broadcast becomes an intimate thing, a thing less severely majestic, less esthetically dignified, but one, from the point of view of the average man, far more immediately comprehensible, even more—dare one claim it?—absorbingly interesting.

And while in the theatre the play about the common or garden person, the play of the mean street or the suburban villa, is apt to be rather a bore and to achieve merit in proportion as it is related to somewhat pseudo-Russian symbolism, the same type of play from a microphone and loudspeaker has an immediate and unqualified appeal.

v

In conclusion, I would add one last practical piece of advice in relation to the question of subject. If he is wise, the radio dramatist will not choose that type of subject which most readily springs to his mind as being suitable for a broadcast play. Such subjects as deal with remarkable scientific inventions, monstrous natural cataclysms, and in general the type of thing of which H. G. Wells wrote so brilliantly in the days of *The Invisible Man* and *The War of the Worlds* are more easily conceived as radio drama than written—also, there have been too many of them. At first sight they are attractive. They offer unlimited scope alike to the imagination of the radio dramatist and the ingenuity of the radio producer. They fulfill one of the canons that has been laid down in this article, in so far as such subjects are quite outside the capacity of the normal stage.

But the dramatist who knows his business and who prides himself on being craftsman as well as artist should to some extent aim at supplying a demand. There is at present a great demand for the writing of comedy for broadcasting. So far the demand has not even begun to be met. It is probably not an exaggeration to say that the most successful humorous dramatic writer who has been broadcast (in England) is Oscar Wilde. It has occasionally been made a reproach to the Productions Department of the B.B.C. that their tendency has been to produce plays either morbid or sensational. Unfortunately, it is impossible to manufacture humor synthetically, or by formula, and make a good job of it. A wireless Wodehouse, a broadcasting Barry Pain would be beyond price, could they be found. Miss Constanduros and Gillie Porter have proved in their several ways that it is perfectly possible to write humor indigenous to the microphone, but so far no one has emulated them in the field of the broadcast play.

This field of broadcast comedy lies practically virgin before all aspirants to honors in writing plays for broadcasting.

THE ONE-ACT PLAY AND THE FILMS

ISAAC GOLDBERG, distinguished essayist, translator, and critic, was born in Boston in 1887. He evinced an early interest in the arts and for a time was seriously determined to become a composer. But, at the behest of his parents, he entered Harvard, paying his way through the university with annual free scholarships and prizes, and specializing in languages. Music, drama and letters remained, however, an absorbing and vital fascination. He received his Ph.D. in Romance Philology.

Mr. Goldberg is a varied and prolific writer. He has written books on Gilbert and Sullivan, George Jean Nathan, Havelock Ellis, George Gershwin, H. L. Mencken, Spanish-American literature, drama and many other subjects. His forthcoming books are *The Wonder of Words*, a popular treatment of linguistics, and *American Drama Today*.

THE ONE-ACT PLAY AND THE FILMS

by Isaac Goldberg

IT is always useful, in discussing an art and its products, to keep in mind the materials out of which the product is made. It is especially useful for those to whom the sound of the word "product," in connection with art, vibrates with overtones of sacrilege, or, at least, of gross materialism.

Art is made not by angels for God but by man and woman for men and women. It is made, to be sure, in the travail of the spirit; but it must find, for that spirit, an expression in terms of concrete material. It is a great triumph for the human soul to hack away marble and release from its depths an inspiring significance for humanity. We must not forget, however, the hand that does the hacking and the marble that is hewn. We speak poetically of "releasing" significance from the depths of the marble. What we are really doing is sculpturing ourselves, not the marble; the significance comes, not out of the marble, but out of our sculptured selves.

The essential nature of the marble or the granite, nevertheless, has a determining influence upon the form that our expression is to assume. This is natural. One cannot do in stone what can be done in wood. One cannot do with music what can be done with poetry. This is not to say that a certain amount of interfusion cannot take place among the arts; Wagnerian opera—or, to be more precise, Wagnerian music drama—was a brave attempt at such an interfusion that sometimes resulted in confusion. There is far more music in poetry, for example, than many poets and many musicians seem to discover. Poetry and music blend very naturally, since it is possible—indeed, unavoidable—to sing and speak at the same time. Speech and song probably began together and have never become truly separated. That is why the conventions of opera achieve so ready an acceptance. Speech-song is not altogether a "convention"; it is fundamentally natural. It is more primitive, of course, than the relatively songless speech of such languages as English; Chinese, on the other hand, and not Chinese only, incorporates the pitch of words as an essential phase of their meaning.

Opera, again, moves at a slower pace than drama. This is necessary because in opera the duplex nature of the dialogue (at once song and speech) requires more effort from both singer and spectator-auditor than does the concentrated nature of dialogue upon the stage of the playhouse. Too much action in an opera can be as troublesome as too little. Often it is hard to choose between the nervous tempo of an Italian opera and those long-drawn episodes in Wagnerian music drama that only a too too perfect Wagnerite can endure without weariness of the flesh and the spirit. The one is irritating; the other is exhausting. Neither represents the most effective use of the material at hand, nor the most subtle appreciation of what is called the psychology of attention.

All of this has its pertinency to the problems of the short play as contrasted with the long, and of the short play on the stage as contrasted with the short play in the movies. Perhaps that last phrase is fantastically optimistic. The movies really have no short plays; maybe they will never have any. Maybe the "short," as we know it on the screen, will always remain short—of reason, of sense, of anything that has appeal for a half-civilized spectator. However, if I really believed such a thing I should not be writing these lines.

Oh, yes. . . . I have heard the statement, and have re-peated it, that the movies after all are made for persons with a mental age of thirteen or fourteen—or was it twelve? I dare say that most of them are. It does not hap-pen to be "most of them" that I am interested in. Nor is it the part of a critic to accept the lowest standards of an art. (You see, I regard the movies as an art, and as a most important art.) I was the more astonished, then, to read in the New York *Times* (September 26, 1937), shortly after the broadcast of a half-hour play by Maxwell Anderson, the following comment from an anonymous writer:

In 1937 noted dramatists have recognized "the ether" as a dramatic medium as never before, with their experimental broadcasts revealing deep thought and preparation. They have yet to discover, however, that simplicity is the key-note of success; that they are aiming at an audience the average intelli-gence of which is estimated at the thirteen-year-old level, the same which Buck Rogers and Bobby Benson strike.

This is discouraging. For it shows that the radio critic has taken over from the movies a dangerous half-truth. I do not deny that the movies aim, generally, at the thir-teen-year-old audience or at the adult audience in its thir-teen-year-old moments. Surely, however, the radio is in somewhat different case. And that difference is important, especially for the Andersons and the MacLeishes who are trying to establish a new dramatic form.

To clarify this issue will help to clarify the particular problem that suggested this chapter.

In the first place, the radio deals in presentations that range from fifteen minutes to one hour in length, with the half-hour as the favorite period. The movie demands an hour as the minimum—that is, the feature picture does; frequently it runs beyond this length. It may be offered in rejoinder that the radio, concentrating upon sound alone, demands more in the way of attention than does the movie, with its wide variety of sensuous appeal. There is something to the point. It is not conclusive, however. One may switch from this program to that on the radio; we have to take our movies as we find them.

On the radio there are special programs for the symbolic thirteen-year-old. There are programs, too, that seek to appeal only to this symbol's father, mother, and elder brothers and sisters. Only the other day a Hollywood director was discussing with an interviewer the advisability of having certain showhouses specialize in certain types of film, so that persons with special tastes might know just where to go for the kind of product that they felt like seeing. Maybe this is a dream, but it is the dream of a hard-headed Hollywood director, not of a soft-headed, high-brow critic. It may also be a mere coincidence that at the very time this director was being interviewed, the proprietor of a New York movie theatre was announcing that thenceforth his house would specialize in the showing of horror films and Westerns.

The age level of the radio, then, is not so constant as is

that of the movie. It fluctuates, which is a contradictory thing for a level to do.

Now, nobody could convince me that Messrs. Maxwell Anderson and Archibald MacLeish are aiming at a thirteen-year-old audience or that they should be doing so. Indeed, they have come to the radio, they have been asked to participate in the establishment of a new form, just because the radio companies wish to appeal to an audience distinct from the characteristic audiences of the commercial programs. If we are to continue indiscriminately to appeal to the thirteen-year-old mentality, why trouble the MacLeishes and the Andersons, when the regular script-writers are doing well (that is, ill) enough?

If the writer in the New York *Times* cannot see the point, how are we to expect better of the radio listener? It is somewhat discouraging. The more so, indeed, as the anonymous writer, in the course of his comments, pronounces Amos 'n' Andy not only "tops among radio actors" but "master playwrights." One had thought that Ibsen, with whatever faults his writing may show, was a master playwright. One had reserved such extravagant phrases for Shakespeare, Goethe, and few others. Now, because Amos 'n' Andy can appeal to child mentalities with their "simple, common, and homely" material, the MacLeishes and the Andersons must not aspire to complexity, uncommonness, and beauty for an adult audience.

Such comment is not criticism. It is lack of discrimination; it is even corruption by the very medium that one is called upon to improve.

I am not undervaluing such virtues as Amos 'n' Andy may possess. Myself, I find these men dull, or, rather, meaningless. That is simply a matter of personal interest.

Amos 'n' Andy haven't the slightest desire to appeal to me. Why should they have? They probably laugh themselves into knots over their masterful playwriting, but not on radio time with the microphones turned on.

Why Anderson and MacLeish should have to go to school to these pseudo black men, I fail to understand. It was a very proper question that Sir Toby asked: "Dost thou think, because thou art virtuous, there shall be no more cakes and ale?" But one might have asked of Sir Toby, "Dost thou think that because there are cakes and ale there must not therefore be virtue, on occasion?" In other words, if Amos 'n' Andy have their place, must there on that account be no place for Maxwell Anderson and Archibald MacLeish?

I discuss this matter at length because I am visionary enough to look for an improvement of "shorts" in the movies; so impractical, indeed, as to look forward to a time when, even on the screen, there will be a place for the Andersons and the MacLeishes.

Yes, what I venture to suggest is the adoption of one-act plays, whether singly or in groups, by the movies, as part of their regular offerings.

Is the idea so fantastic, after all?

The short film supplies a need, in the movie programs, that is quite similar to the need for short stories in the magazines and the newspapers, to the need for short plays in the amateur and the commercial theatre, to the need for short plays that has begun to be felt by the radio. It is not merely that brief tales are required to fill odd spaces in the dailies, weeklies, and monthlies, or that brief material is required to fill odd time in cinematic programs. Certain material simply does not lend itself to long treatment, just as other material demands a broader canvas for its most effective presentation.

We used to hear a great deal about the reason for the vogue of the short story. We were a hurried people, ran the explanation. We had little time for long tales, such as the Victorian three-decker. Then along came *Anthony Adverse* and other mastodon fictions, reaching a climax in *Gone with the Wind*. I fear that *Gone with the Wind*, regardless of its deficiencies as fiction, must have buried the old short-story theory deep beneath the sod of Gettysburg. Dost thou think that because thou art in a hurry, no one else shall have leisure for long fiction? Or that because thou hast plenty of time everybody else must read books a thousand pages long? No. It takes all kinds of people to make even the world of the movies, and some of them have stopped being thirteen years old.

It is too bad that none of the short afterpieces of the Greek theatre was preserved. Had any been saved for posterity, brief forms would have achieved precious academic sanction, together with the comedies and the tragedies. As it is, the one-act play is still a left-handed sister of the longer form, and brevity, in general, seems by a queer psychological twist to imply inferiority.

If this is still appreciably true of the theatre, despite the efforts of a Chekhov, a Lady Gregory, a Synge, or a Schnitzler, what can we say of the radio and the cinema? Yet the cinema has had, from the beginning, a marvelous opportunity that so far has been neglected sadly.

The opportunity still points, like a many-armed Hindu deity, in a number of directions. It might even be seized upon to solve some of the problems associated with the curse of double billing, and that strange habit movie people have of setting out, with deliberate intention, to create an inferior, class B, picture. I shouldn't be surprised if another classification appeared, to take care of "bank-nites." So that the grammar of the cinema would recognize, as its scale of positive, comparative, and superlative values, the terms Class A, Class B, and Bank-Nite: positively terrific, comparatively colossal, and superlatively pediculous, respectively.

It has been the custom, up to now, to regard "shorts" as stopgaps, as irresponsible fillers, devoted either to cheap slapstick, to vaudeville, or to melodramatic nonsense. First-class actors and actresses would be insulted—and rightly, under present conditions—if they should be asked to take part in one. The "shorts" are made with little conscience and are received, generally, with as little pleasure.

They add up, thus far, to so much waste. Yet this need not be. The proper exploitation of material for "shorts" could serve a number of valuable purposes, altogether aside from the chief purpose, which is entertainment for semi-civilized creatures.

There is no reason—and at this point I shall probably be accused of unreason—why even the top-notch stars should not take part in the one-act films that I have in mind. Greatness in acting is not synonymous with length of footage; besides, a happy idea for a cinematic action might actually prove more effective when presented as the brief impression it is than when dragged out to fill an hour or an hour and a quarter.

I remember, from the days of the old Yiddish Art Theatre, a performance of Andreyev's *Seven Who Were Hanged*. A certain gifted actor—he was a star even then—had been entrusted with the role of an army officer who comes to bid farewell to his son on the eve of the boy's hanging. The officer was on the stage for but ten minutes, but into those ten minutes he distilled the concentrated essence of hapless, hopeless good-by. Those ten minutes became a play within a play—the tragedy of misunderstanding between father and son, between generation and generation, between old regime and new, the tragedy of final parting. The name of the actor was Muni Weisenfreund, now known to the films as Paul Muni.

I do not suggest that our leading players go *en masse* into short cinematic plays. However, when a first-rate short play is written for the movies, a first-rate cast should go into it. I do not suggest, either, that the proposed one-act plays for movies (with their naturally more varied backgrounds, more elastic action, and cinematic tempo) should be regarded with condescension, or as a corner into which to throw material discarded from longer films. Yet the briefer form could make an excellent training ground for players on the way to deeper abilities. It could provide, so to speak, a "little-theatre" department of the cinema. It could employ minor talents—but talents, nevertheless— in a sort of school for finer things. It could serve the same purpose for directorial talent. It could offer opportunity, too, for the kind of experimentation that could be applied profitably, in time, to the film of regular length.

These are all side issues, however, and secondary to the chief purpose: the presentation of the best material available, not as Class B or Class C fillers, but as Class A material of naturally restricted scope.

Is this really so fantastic? Is it any more fantastic than *three* series of one-act plays on three different nights in the theatre, during a single week? But, I seem to hear

someone say, it was Noel Coward and Gertrude Lawrence who drew the public to *Tonight at 8:30*. I'll not
deny that it was the stars, not the plays, that attracted the
patronage. This makes all the more practical my proposal
for the movies, since it is the star rather than the play that
attracts the chief attention from the movie public. An evening of one-act plays in a movie house may sound altogether insane, until somebody has the courage to try it
out and make a success of it.

Let me consider but one technical problem of many
that the cinematic one-act play could help to solve: the
matter of numerous scenes. It is not a rare experience to
discover a long play with a single set and a short play
with many. In the long play, when the single set is not
dictated by the action, it is a measure of practical economy.
In the short play, more often than not, the plurality of
visual scenes is a confession of dramaturgic inadequacy. It
corresponds to excessive words in writing and to inept composition. Unity of impression, of course, takes precedence
over such a shallow unity as that of location; a play with a
single set may be badly disjointed, while a short play in
several scenes may possess a very tight unity. I recall a
notable epigram by Manuel González Prada, a Peruvian
libertarian whose spirit should be better known in our
own country. "One may be concise in a volume," he said,
"and garrulous in a line."

The movie has its own way of dealing with scene and
tempo and impression. It has its own way of dealing even
with subtle, introspective, subjective material—a way impossible to the stage. Many of the plays written for the
stage appear to have been thought out in cinematic rather
than in dramatic terms. Nor do I refer to those dramatists

who write with both eyes upon eventual purchase of their product by the movie studios. The classical stage of England and Spain, for example, is far more cinematic in this sense than is the French.

Madness, in cinematic terms, could be made much more mad than the stage makes it; battle scenes, pageantry, magic, lend themselves admirably to treatment on the screen.

The screen is more contrapuntal, so to say, than is the stage. It has a command over time and space, which it can telescope at need, that the stage can never hope for. This does not mean that the dramatist must always hope for such a command, or that his values are the values of the screen. They are not. It does mean, however, that the screen supplies, for the nervous tempo and the subjective matter of much contemporary writing, a remarkable medium. It does mean that many of the polyscenic short plays that we read could achieve their maximum effect as movies, where the unity of impression (with the proper direction, naturally) could be made to persist despite the shifting of scene from one locale to another.

This must not be misread as a suggestion that the stage go out of business and that all aspiring dramatists become, instead, aspiring scenarists. It means only what it says: that in the movies there is a remarkable opportunity for the presentation of brief material in highly effective, artistic fashion and that a time may come when even the movie people will discover in the one-act play a profitable staple of popular entertainment.

When some of the sentiments in the preceding paragraph were first printed in my department of *The One Act Play Magazine* (issue of July, 1937) a commentator upon

Hollywood replied cheerfully that my criticism of Hollywood "shorts" was quite justified. They were, indeed, "junk," but, he went on, in this business you can't junk junk so easily. Irving Hoffman, who writes the "Tales of Hoffman" column for the *Hollywood Reporter*, knows his junk. The whole matter, he agreed, had begun to smell like a corpse concealed somewhere on the premises. In simple Anglo-Saxon, the average movie "short" smells. Who is to blame? Oh, yes . . . that thirteen-year-old scarecrow, who takes all the whippings for the industry.

Well, the thirteen-year-old seems to bear up pretty well under such films as *The Informer* and *Pasteur* and *Zola* and *Mutiny on the Bounty* and *Captains Courageous*. He responds quite nicely to the Walt Disney animations, many of which are one-acters of a highly fantastic sort.

Now that vaudeville has returned to the screen in the shape of Big Broadcasts, Vogues, Scandals, Follies, and what not else, how about trying out a real one-acter as part of such a long entertainment? By a real one-acter I don't mean a slapstick sequence devised in impromptu fashion in the studio. I mean a dramatic narrative (tragic or comic) composed by a dramatist with a flair for the movies. The public does not need to be educated for this type of entertainment. The newsreels, the travelogues, even the fashion "shorts," have paved the way from the beginning. These all contain elements of the one-act play. I am not a mind reader, but it seems to me that many a first-rate performer would prefer an appearance in a strong brief film to an appearance in one of those dreary full-length affairs that adds nothing to the actor's reputation, the enjoyment of the audience, the prestige of the studio or the contents of the box-office till.

I'll wager that right now the Noel Coward pieces in *Tonight at 8:30,* which are hardly examples of the dramatic art at its best, could be filmed to run several in succession, as a single bill, making altogether a film of slightly more than average length and appealing successfully to the typical film public. It would be more like Hollywood, however, to buy the whole nine and make full-length films of each.

Before doffing my prophet's robes, let me repeat: Hollywood one day will discover the finer possibilities of the short play. When it does, it will be a happy day for all concerned, except the bad dramatist. Who knows? We may even discover that the thirteen-year-old has added cubits— or, at least, a year of I.Q.—to his stature. To tell the truth, I don't believe that the mythical creature exists. I know many thirteen-year-olds. But I know, too, that they have elder brothers and sisters, and fathers and mothers.

In the movie house there are many publics. The short play could be made to appeal to all, or most, of these. And if, as compared with other films, it had no other virtue to recommend it, it would at least be shorter than they.

And, yes . . . that thirteen-year-old public. . . . The problem is so bound up with numerous considerations of class rule, censorship, theology, and politics that it would take a book to elucidate. I have never believed that it was the public who dictated to the manufacturers of the movies. Not altogether; not nearly altogether. For those who have been deluded into thinking so, I recommend a reading of Horace M. Kallen's essay, "The Censor, the Psychologist, and the Motion Picture," which is to be found in one of his best books, *Indecency and the Seven Arts.* This is a book, incidentally, that I should mark as obligatory for all who are interested in the theory or the practice of the drama in any of its forms.

I recommend, especially, the final paragraph of Dr. Kallen's essay:

The responsibility is on the financial masters of the motion picture. The public does not know what will satisfy it. The public simply feels hunger and unrest. Any one of thousands of possible pictures, well-made or shoddy, may serve to allay that hunger, to still that unrest. The public has no initial power of choice. If its gratifications are provided through a poor picture, it will accept that for want of a better one. If a better one is provided, it will flock to that. The decision is not in the box office at all. The decision is in the makers of motion pictures.

THE ONE-ACT PLAY AND TELEVISION

GILBERT SELDES' talents are so varied that it is difficult to keep up with all his activities. He is reputed to be the only writer who has ever contributed steadily and simultaneously to both *The Dial* and the *Saturday Evening Post*.

Mr. Seldes was born in New Jersey in 1893, and was educated at Central High School in Philadelphia and at Harvard. In 1929 Mr. Seldes became dramatic critic for the New York *Evening Graphic;* in 1931, columnist for the New York *Evening Journal*.

His adaptation of Aristophanes' *Lysistrata* in 1930 was one of the high lights of the dramatic season. He is the author of many books, among which are *The Seven Lively Arts, The Movies Come from America, Mainland,* and *Your Money and Your Life*.

At present Mr. Seldes is director of Television Programs for the Columbia Broadcasting System.

THE ONE-ACT PLAY AND TELEVISION

by Gilbert Seldes

THE first impulse of anyone preparing to experiment in television programs is to fall down on his knees and thank heaven (and a few hundred dramatic writers) for the one-act play. Without being too sure of the ultimate nature of television programs, the experimenter assumes that the drama in one form or another will be an important element; and at once he shrinks back from the unpleasant necessity of compressing the contemporary full-length play to his requirements. He shrinks also from the physical and financial difficulties of producing a play with several sets and a large cast of characters, under conditions parallel in many important respects to those of stage production, for a run of one night. The one-act play relieves him of his troubles. It presents its own difficulties, but it is simple, compact, and complete.

Yet the dramatist who wants "to get in on the ground floor of television" and is already planning a group of one-acters against the coming demand, should be forewarned. No one can tell how much of its time television will be able to give to dramatic programs. So far as we can see now, a sight-and-sound program will have three major elements: direct transmission of events at the moment they occur (an inauguration, a tennis match, a riot); second, moving pictures—any movie can be placed before a film scanner and transmitted to the television receiver; and third, programs originating in the studio. This third section has to be subdivided because eventually it will include all of those programs now being broadcast which require or can easily use a visual counterpart, and in addition a certain number of programs which will be created because the television screen has enormously widened the range of available material. So that our studio work may include ballet dancing, lessons in cooking or higher mathematics (unlikely), symphony and jazz orchestras, demonstrations of gymnastics, musical comedy and the drama.

To balance this warning, there is the promise that television, like radio, will probably use up its material very rapidly.

Tentatively and almost timidly, I suggest that the use of dramatic material in television will be governed by an unstable factor—the intensity of attention which the television screen will demand. A year ago I made a sort of rule-of-thumb guess, as an operating basis, that you would have to be five times as attentive to television as you are to current broadcasting. It is not merely sight, but motion which catches and holds the eye, that has been added to sound. This precisely reverses the experience of the moving pictures when sound was added; we know in effect that sound slowed up the movies because directors had not worked out the correct principles governing the relation of microphone and camera. The moving picture still does not develop its material as rapidly as it did in the silent days, but of course it develops it far more completely.

In radio the amount of creative material used for each

quarter or half-hour of drama is extremely small. (I am, of course, not speaking of legitimate plays adapted to the use of radio but of material specifically written in the radio dramatic form.) The serial dramatic sketch has established a sort of norm or standard which is probably adapted to the capacity of the audience; that standard develops in fifteen minutes a tiny part of an episode which may take five or ten quarter-hour programs to be rendered completely; and that episode in turn is only a part of a complete dramatic action which may take half a year. (*The Rise of the Goldbergs* and *Amos 'n' Andy* are examples of this development; in the latter, one event, the breach-of-promise suit, was the sustaining interest of several months of broadcasting which consisted of five fifteen-minute periods a week.)

That television can make its points more rapidly is obvious from the nature of the medium itself. There will be no waste of time in making the spectator aware of objects (doors or daggers) which are used in the dramatic action. Moreover, the action itself, being visible, will be self-explanatory; as things seen are more impressive than those heard, less emphasis will be required, and to avoid being repetitious and dull a dramatic program for television will have to proceed more rapidly than one adapted to sound broadcasting alone; television will possibly approximate the tempo of a stage presentation.

I said above that the intensity of attention demanded by the television screen will be a variable factor. The reason for this is that I do not know how absorbing the action on the screen will be *after we have become accustomed to it*. At the beginning I should think it likely that the owner of a television set will sit before it and refuse to be distracted; but a good television program will have to include in its variety certain things which any particular spectator will not find of primary interest. He may be an enthusiast for sport and after the novelty of television has worn off, he may turn away from the screen when music is being played and merely listen; an enthusiast for dancing may not be interested in the visual portion of a program of current events. We have to face the possibility that since television will be received in the home (as opposed to the moving picture seen in a theater where there is no opportunity for distraction) it may get the variable attention which radio now gets. The difference will still be that when the attention is acute, the auditor-spectator of television will be receiving far more impressions than the auditor of radio. Even if people do not let their fascinated eyes cling perpetually to the television screen, the dramatic sketch on the screen will have to assume that they do.

I want to repeat that these judgments are still largely guesswork. Always in the back of my mind there are the two dangers of prophecy in this connection. I recall on one side the dogmatic assertion that Marconi's signal would never cross the ocean; and, on the other side, the fantastic promise made by a reputable scientist that by the end of 1938 we should be able to sit in our homes and watch the efforts of a mountain climber up Mount Everest or a deep-sea diver at the bottom of the sea. Between saying that television will never be able to handle a full-act play and saying that it will be able to offer the equivalent of a movie musical there lies the limited field in which we can judge by what has been done and make tentative projections into the future.

Actually a full-length play was produced for television for the first time on the eleventh of November, 1937, by the British Broadcasting Corporation; the drama chosen was *Journey's End* and it would be superfluous to dwell on the defects of that production because none, so far as we know, points to any permanent disability in the medium itself. The characters in the dugout seemed to jostle one another—that is because the range of the scanners is still limited; the scenes of the action in the trenches were more impressive—and they were moving-picture film. What we know in general is that in this early stage of development a full-length play was done and in the minds of many spectators was at least a praiseworthy attempt. On the other hand this does not prove that a full-length play is ideal material for television; it may be good material now and prove unsatisfactory later on, or new methods and new equipment may make it possible for us to produce even more ambitious long plays.

Nevertheless, at the beginning, the one-acter is peculiarly available for us. The dramatists who have learned to write in this form seem to have anticipated our requirements of compression and our capacities to present a sustained action in a brief time. Particularly during the experimental stage the one-acter relieves us of the necessity of building many settings and it reduces the variety of costumes; moreover, our players will not require too long a time to memorize their parts and will therefore reduce the number of rehearsals. Further, until the field over which the television camera can operate is extended, the comparatively small number of actors will be an advantage to us; we have worked out methods by which we can use larger numbers, but they are still expedients, and temporarily an action which is in the hands of only three or four people simultaneously in our visual field is ideal for us.

Oddly enough this limitation brings to us two entirely different types of material: melodrama and the play of intense psychological interest. Both of these, of course, are highly individualistic: they are based on an intense feeling of the value of private lives. The *Grand Guignol* type of melodrama, for instance, reflects our concern for our bodily safety in a world of violence and accident; and the amorous trifle or the quick study of a single powerful emotion reflects our interest in the sanctity of our own psychological processes.

There is nothing more private than a sprained ankle or an Oedipus complex, and the passion with which we regard ourselves has been nourished for long generations by artists in every field. This means that we have a sort of backlog of material available—from the delightful operettas, with three or four characters, of the late eighteenth century, down to Schnitzler and Noel Coward. But we note that our physical limitations exclude a theme which has become more and more significant in the past few years—the mass. In other words the social drama to be adapted to the use of television has to be personified and individualized—and certain theorists of both social and dramatic structure believe that this process of personification (which brings us back to the hero and the villain) corrupts the theme of mass action which it is attempting to express.

Since I have been so hesitant about the future of television, I am certainly not now going to say that we will be unable to use themes of great social significance. I am only pointing out to any dramatist aware of the questions of our own time that he will have to discover ways of using contemporary themes by placing people in a new framework. The moving picture, the radio, and the theatre (using new techniques in the last generation) have all been expansive. Dramatic presentation has broken through all sorts of limitations, some of them natural and some of them highly artificial. Now we approach with television a great freedom in some directions and severe physical limitations in others.

The dramatist who wants to create or adapt one-act plays for television will for a long time be compelled to study not television itself, but radio and movies, and he will have to guess in what proportion these two forms will influence the emerging techniques of television. I have suggested a sort of guide line in the tempo of the moving picture as compared to the speed of purely verbal broadcasting. Reducing this contrast to a practical principle would bring us back, I think, to some essential ideas about the theatre. Since the listener will also be a spectator, he will want movement; there the lesson of the motion picture will be important. The dramatist who still thinks that words are his principal instrument will have to discover ways of using speech and movement in counterpoint. There will be moments when the passion of his play can be expressed only in speech; yet it would be a fatality if the movement of the drama should stop while the speech is being uttered. (I recommend *The Life of Emile Zola* to students of these problems; the long speeches delivered by Paul Muni do not actually hurt the inner action, the essential movement of the picture, and there is just sufficient superficial movement to keep the eye of the spectator satisfied.)

The dramatic writer who has gone from the stage to the moving picture has seldom recognized the essential fact that the movies have presented to him a new way of expressing dramatic action; and in the rare cases where the dramatist has seen this, he has usually rebelled against it. The result is that our movies are woefully overwritten; the dramatist in Hollywood is still writing his dialogue for the tempo of the stage. Sometimes his infatuation with words cannot be curbed even by those good directors who, having had experience with silent films or laconic Westerns, know the actual requirements of the movies.

Because a great many items in the ordinary television program will be short, I think that we will have to develop writers who understand the true relation between speech and action; those who can invent a plausible but not too striking series of movements when words of great significance are being uttered and who can face the necessity of making the words themselves secondary at times to a sharply defined movement. The writer of one-acters is in a good position because his experience has already been with a medium which offers him more difficulties than opportunities. It is a hard saying of Goethe's that the master can only prove himself when he works within limitations; it is hard, but it is also inspiring.

VIRGIL L. BAKER is Associate Professor of Speech and Director of the University Theatre at the University of Arkansas. The University Theatre was organized by him in 1932 and has produced six plays each season besides a large number of one-act plays. During the last four years he has built up a group of playwrights who are centering their attention about folklore and historical and social material peculiar to Arkansas and the Southwest and who produce a regular schedule of original one-act plays.

Mr. Baker spent a year (1936-1937) at the University of Iowa, where he held a fellowship in playwriting. He is the author of a number of one-act plays, among which are *Ol' Captain*, *Witchin' Racket* and *Spanish Diggin's*.

THE ONE-ACT PLAY IN THE COLLEGE THEATRE

THE ONE-ACT PLAY IN THE COLLEGE THEATRE

by Virgil L. Baker

THE nonprofessional theatre in colleges and universities —the Theatre of Youth—like youth, is a challenging reality. There is much of the adolescent in it, with resulting confusion, maladjustment, and fumbling, but it must also be admitted that there is inherent in it the characteristics of a rapidly approaching maturity. It has already demonstrated its ability to solve problems and to achieve, and at present it feels that it commands sufficient insight and resourcefulness to assume creative leadership. In this vein it takes as its slogan "The Theatre of Youth, the Theatre of the Future." This goal, somewhat startling, may cause maturer and more conventional minds to fear that the gap between aspiration and realization is too wide for youth to bridge. Still, these same minds do not ignore this theatre and, usually, upon closer acquaintance encourage and counsel it.

That leadership is rapidly being created to meet the demands of this Theatre of Youth is attested by the phenomenal rise of dramatic departments and dramatic organizations in colleges and universities during the present generation. Barrett Clark summarizes the achievements of this theatre by saying:

> There are approximately 700 colleges and universities that offer dramatic work and make regular dramatic productions. . . . Every night of the year from October to May it is possible in almost any state of the Union to see plays of every conceivable kind; there is no part of the country where one cannot see some sort of performance of a play by Ibsen, Chekhov, Shakespeare, Molière, Shaw, O'Neill, Howard, Kelly, Barry, Anderson, Rice, O'Casey, Synge—to mention only writers whose plays were mentioned in one issue of a local magazine that lists a few of the current attractions in colleges for one month of the past year. . . . In the colleges and universities alone there are probably 35,000 to 40,000 students regularly enrolled in dramatic departments.[1]

Among the thousands of performances each year in this theatre, one notes a proportionately large number of one-act plays. The longer play, of course, is, and has long been, the featured form; but along with it in recent years the shorter play has come into general use, not because of its novelty but because it fills needs. The one-act play has become rooted in this theatre, for it amplifies the conventional program by supplying a flexible, varied, and streamlined type of recreation now increasingly demanded by college audiences; and it helps to solve the problem of combining theory and practice in classroom instruction.

The one-act play adapts itself easily to many semi-public and public production needs. One of these needs arises in the dramatic organization itself. Its organization is composed of a large number of students with their own

[1] Barrett H. Clark, "Some Reflections on the Nonprofessional Theatre," New York *Times*, October 27, 1935.

officers. Regular meetings are held to conduct the business of the society and also for entertainment. The one-act play fits well into this semipublic program. It is short and gives many members opportunities to participate, thus solving the problem of keeping its membership active. Such performances also serve as a training ground for a large number who are not yet ready for appearance before the public. It stimulates interest in the organization and helps to keep the morale at a high level.

The one-act play also, because it is short and dramatically intense, adapts itself readily to numerous public production situations. The "variety" or "amateur night" program, a feature of which is a short play, is proving popular in many theatre programs. Other theatres present matinee programs: a short program consisting of a single one-act play offered in the afternoon after the rush of school hours is over. Such programs fit well into the swing of collegiate life and offer a period of relaxation and stimulation attested to by the students themselves.

Bills of one-act plays, appearing periodically on the regular public production schedule, are widely used. In some theatres, audiences, after having become accustomed to the more conventional program of the long play, are slow to respond to the one-act bill of plays. As a rule, however, they accept it on its own merits, finding in it novelty, variety, and dramatic intensity. Programs of this kind may take a wide variety of forms and present stimulating projects for the producing group. The plays on the bill are often chosen to provide a variety of play types, such as comedy, tragedy, farce, or melodrama. Other bills are built around a theme which the plays carry out from different points of view. Still others provide not several plays, but one play produced in different modes, such as realistically and expressionistically.

Another need which the one-act play supplies is that of furnishing suitable programs for extension service. The theatre is often asked to provide programs for local groups, and sometimes it travels beyond the borders of its immediate community. These types of production promote good will for the theatre and at the same time motivate it to establish a program flexible enough to be both adaptable and serviceable to the community. They encourage a wide choice of plays and resourcefulness in production. The play must be fitted to the needs of the community group. The actors must learn to adjust themselves to varied settings, as the invitation often takes them to schools, churches, banquet halls, clubrooms, and now and then may even take them into homes. Many times scenery must be dispensed with and the actor must stand upon his own resourcefulness. Community groups, however, are far less interested in securing literal settings than they are in securing good plays; they show remarkable willingness to dispense with the externals of production.

Among the most recent and potential activities which the one-act play has made possible are tournaments and festivals. College and university theatres have taken the lead in promoting these activities and have as a result broadened tremendously the opportunities for the use of the one-act play. Beyond the educational advantages received by those who participate in tournaments and festivals, there are a broadening of outlook and a unification of aims which point the way to the realization of solidarity in this theatre. The fact that festivals encourage creative writing is also of significance in this connection.

The one-act play thus adjusts itself in many unique ways to production demands both in and out of its theatre. This, however, is only one of the needs which the one-act play satisfies. Another need, and a very vital one, is the educational need.

Dramatic theory and practice, particularly in relation to the one-act play, is accepted by educators as sound educational discipline; in fact, the educational philosophy now most generally accepted is one inviting to the arts on the grounds that they furnish active educational techniques which are basic in the process of individual maturation.

Contemporary educational objectives are, more often than not, stated in terms of activities; the learning process is defined as growth in the acquisition of knowledge, attitudes, and skills. It is recognized that there is apt to be no learning unless there is immediate expression in the individual's behavior. Emphasis is placed upon those activities which will produce an integrated personality. Culture is defined in terms of the level of refinement which the individual actually achieves in living. William H. Kilpatrick maintains that it is what the individual does and how well what he does actually works that educates him. He says:

What counts for most is what we do actively by reaction or, better still, by creative initiative. Experience fully considered has both a passive and an active side. Both are necessary. Both teach us. But it is in the active willing, doing side that we reach our highest living. . . . This active willing, doing side of experience is what we here demand. Only as it is practiced will it grow. In education properly conceived the growing use

143

of such experience is both end and means to end. This active experience the new school must supply.[2]

In the same vein Dean Max McConn points out the superiority of learning by activities over learning by reading. He states that the perusal of the printed page "is only one way of learning; it is not even the best way; the best way is undoubtedly by living with those who have learned and done. The book method comes off a bad third among the desirable ways of learning." [3]

If these educational methods are sound, and the director of a college or university theatre, through his direct experiences, has every reason to believe that they are, then this theatre program, in theory as well as in practice, is well grounded. The study and production of dramatic literature gives insight into experience, not only at its intellectual but also at its emotional best; it establishes truth and exposes shams; it provides both direct and vicarious experience and not theory and abstractions alone; it encourages art, not for art's sake nor because it is fashionable, but art for the sake of rounding out a fuller design of living. The tremendous student demand for this type of educational experience created this theatre and continues to maintain it and is, indeed, tangible evidence of the validity of the educational methods that underlie it.

Since in the majority of colleges and universities the theatre is closely allied, if not directly sponsored, by the department of speech, educational considerations become important factors in its activities. The productions of the

[2] William H. Kilpatrick, *Education for a Changing Civilization*, Macmillan Company, 1926, pp. 114-115.

[3] Max McConn, "The Problem of Going to College," *Our Children*, Viking Press, 1932, p. 247.

theatre become laboratories in which the theories evolved in the classroom are put into practice. Here the true learning process begins. Production is entered into purposively and sincerely. The day is gone, if it ever existed in this theatre, in which the cast approaches rehearsals as a holiday from work. Also the day of the director who attempts to be a dictator is gone. Results are gained by directors who have insight into the problems involved and who have the ability to suggest and to guide rather than to dictate and command. Both director and cast work toward a definite end, and the pleasure that comes from production is that of having reached a high standard of achievement. As Hallie Flanagan so aptly says of the work in this theatre: "The college theatre is no longer in the limelight, it is in the searchlight; the elocutionary manner, the arty pose, the stage-struck young lady—on all these manifestations of the Theatre Sentimental the curtain fell ten years ago." [4]

Since this theatre is founded upon educational principles, it centers its attention upon those activities at its command which will best fit the individual to take his place normally in the life of the community and to help him find a worthy use for his leisure time. It does not consider itself to be a direct training ground for the professional stage, but this does not mean that it tolerates inferior work or sets its standards low. Its work in the past has been at a sufficiently high level to make it possible for many of its actors and technicians to go either directly or indirectly into the professional theatre. High standards in this theatre are in line with the demands of

[4] Hallie Flanagan, "Theatre Experiment," *Theatre Arts Monthly*, Vol. XIII, p. 543.

modern youth. Actors themselves are becoming more and more critical of their own work. Audiences and the college press provide standards of criticism that are continually rising. Many stages are becoming so well equipped physically that they can match the best in production anywhere.

In this milieu the one-act play adjusts itself naturally. It is peculiarly adaptable to classroom and laboratory methods and as a result it has come into the theatre to stay. It has both practical and cultural values. The greatest of the modern dramatists have used the form repeatedly. It offers instantly intelligible lessons in design and vicarious emotional experience. In its unity and economy it embodies the typical and the representative; in its expressionism, the poetic; and in its bold strokes and vivid flashes, the universal.

The one-act play offers opportunities not only for a sound but also for a diversified training. It is short, usually the cast is small, and as a result many plays are studied. Any individual is given a chance to study many roles as well as to train himself in the techniques of different types of acting. Type casting is discouraged; the learning process encouraged. Furthermore, a large number of persons are given opportunities for training through the technical work which the production of a number of one-act plays provides.

The short play is the logical form for developing the dramatic powers of beginning actors. The tasks assigned and the tensions set do not overtax the abilities of the novice in their resolution. It is true that in many one-act plays a particular role may be more difficult than the average role in a longer play, but the very fact that the play is shorter gives the beginner more of an opportunity to key his nervous energies to the tempo of the part and to sustain it throughout than does the longer play. Experience has proved that the actor who begins with the one-act play is better fitted to take his part in the longer one with its more complicated plot and subtle character developments.

One of the errors many theatres make is that of offering publicly one-act plays which do not measure up in acting to a sufficiently high standard. There will always be individual differences in the capacities of actors. Some will never become proficient enough to warrant their appearance in public, and should, therefore, be allowed to appear only in classroom or semipublic productions. There is always the temptation to rush into public production too hastily, and when this happens injury is done both to the actor and to the status of the one-act play itself in audience acceptability.

The one-act play also serves an educational need in the training of directors and technicians. With the rapid growth of dramatic instruction in the elementary and secondary schools, constant demands are being made upon dramatic departments for directors and technicians trained adequately to carry on such work. In order to meet this demand, courses in acting, directing, and stagecraft have been multiplied in departments throughout the country. It has been found that under proper supervision student directors can be given heavy responsibilities, particularly in the production of one-act plays, and high standards still be maintained.

As a means of training technicians, the one-act play does not offer any particular advantages over the longer play which has several settings. Many modern plays, because of the playwright's attempts to extend the walls of the theatre by the use of a very large number of settings—the technique of the moving camera—tax every resource of the well-equipped stage and present technical problems impossible of solution on many average or poorly equipped ones. Such plays would be harder to set than any conceivable bill of one-act plays. Under average conditions, however, a bill of one-act plays will not present unsolvable technical problems but will present problems sufficiently difficult to provide excellent training.

By far the most important need which the one-act play can help to supply in this theatre is the need for creative writing. It is significant that the movement which resulted in the establishment of this theatre in practically every college and university in the country had its inception in playwriting. The theatre in its actual development, however, took a different course. It achieved its reputation, attracted its following, and developed its leadership through its revivals of plays rather than through its premières. That it did develop more rapidly as a producer than it did as a creator is both natural and logical under the circumstances.

Now that it has established itself through production, it is showing more and more an inclination to become a living theatre by developing its creative function. It realizes that it justifies its existence even though it does no more than revive plays, but it also realizes, or is beginning to realize, that it has within itself the potentiality to become creative in a more vital sense. It is showing signs of restlessness under conditions that would continue to keep it an absorbing theatre; it wishes to release its energies and become a radiating theatre. It believes that history may repeat itself: it points out that the Renaissance universities had their share in the establishment of the English drama, and it believes that it may have a hand in contributing to the establishment of an American drama. In the characteristic manner of youth it believes itself to be the theatre of the future.

This theatre has given serious consideration to creative work only during the last few years. Yet there are indications from many quarters that it is becoming conscious of its full powers and responsibilities and that it will, in the future, depend less upon popular revivals for its success and more upon its own playwrights.

In the conscious strivings of this theatre for a fuller expression, the one-act play has led the way. When it began to use this form it could not hope to capitalize on the popularity of the play itself in the same sense that it could capitalize on the popularity of the longer play. One-act plays have never been "hits." The professional theatre has only given passing attention to them. Thus in choosing its one-act plays this theatre had to depend almost entirely upon the merits of the play for success; but it had the courage to make this venture, and audiences accepted it. As a result, a great market for the one-act play has gradually been formed, and a number of new playwrights have been produced. Its venture into the use of the short play has been truly creative and has contributed to the enrichment of dramatic literature.

The emphasis upon the one-act play has encouraged the student playwright. It has opened up to him a new channel of expression and enabled him to see opportunities that he had overlooked with his eyes fastened on the revival of the long play. Thousands of one-act plays are being written each year by local playwrights in this theatre. Première productions of short plays have multiplied to such an extent that the movement can no longer be labeled as a fad. This movement is a definite indication of the development of the creative side of this theatre.

Conditions existing in this theatre are on the whole conducive to work that is experimental in nature. It is comparatively free from box-office worries; in many cases it is completely subsidized. Specialized leadership is rapidly being developed to direct its work. In many colleges and universities experimental theatres are being established for the sole purpose of giving trial productions to new plays. A large number of theatres conduct contests and offer liberal prizes to encourage playwrights. Once a playwright with talent is discovered, he is provided with a training ground, an actual living theatre in which his plays may be given trial productions, and if they prove to be of merit they are given public production. It offers guidance that stimulates his best achievement without pushing him beyond his powers. It usually advises him to begin with the one-act play. Walter Prichard Eaton says on this score:

Though, in all conscience it is not easy to write a good one-act play, it is easier than to write a good long play, because only one situation has to be handled and a single mood sustained. . . . It is still the form in which experience has proved the students of playwriting can best start their practice, indeed, so to start is almost essential.[5]

It throws around him a congenial atmosphere and provides him with healthy criticism, thus allowing him opportunity

[5] Walter Prichard Eaton, *Yale One-Act Plays*, Samuel French, 1937, Vol. II, p. vii.

to follow the bent of his talents no matter what turn they may take. All of these considerations, of course, will not make a playwright of everyone who may wish to become one, but they do furnish an environment in which he can mature and one that he cannot find elsewhere, and certainly one which he cannot find in the professional theatre.

Many college and university theatres are emerging here and there over the country that are already pointing the way to creative and distinctive work. Thus far, the contributions have been largely in the exploitation of the dramatic possibilities of folk materials of the section in which the theatre is located, but this development does not exhaust the possibilities for contributions to the American drama. Surely the conflicts that are fundamental in the lives of thousands of men and women in our country today suggest rich leads for the young playwright and for the building of a theatre with individuality.

THE ONE-ACT PLAY IN THE CHURCH

FRED EASTMAN, while attending Union Theological Seminary, used to slip away to Columbia University two or three hours a day to take courses in drama and sociology. He skimped on board money to attend theatres. After graduation he made sociological surveys for a year, directed a religious and social work project at Locust Valley, Long Island, for five years, did editorial work in New York for another five, and since 1926 has been Professor of Biography, Literature and Drama at the Chicago Theological Seminary.

He has written many articles and books on drama, motion pictures, and biography. His most recent works are *Plays of American Life, Drama in the Church, Books That Have Shaped the World,* and two volumes of short biographies entitled *Men of Power.* Three more volumes of the latter are in preparation.

During the past ten years he has been interpreting through drama some of the major social conflicts in American life. Dramatic groups in colleges, high schools, and churches have given more than three thousand productions of these plays. His favorite ones are *The Tinker, Bread, Our Lean Years, The Great Choice,* and *The Examination.*

THE ONE-ACT PLAY IN THE CHURCH

by Fred Eastman

IN three great periods in the history of the western world, the one-act drama has played an important rôle in the religious life of mankind—in ancient Greece, in medieval Europe, and in modern England and America. In each of these periods, religion sought to develop the imaginative and creative life of the people, to direct religious impulses toward ethical ends, and to challenge the will of human beings to make right what was wrong in the world. It tried to deepen the understanding of the spiritual forces that struggle in men's souls. It called drama to its aid because, of all the arts, drama has most to do with the struggles of the wills and emotions of men.

In ancient Greece the tragedies of Aeschylus, Sophocles, and Euripides were all essentially one-act plays. They were produced in the Temple of Dionysus—the most sacred spot in Athens. They were presented at the most sacred season, the one corresponding to our Easter. They were done in honor of Dionysus, the god of fertility. During their production the poets who wrote the plays, the actors who took part in them, and the managers who directed them were all counted as ministers of religion and their persons held inviolable. The State paid the bills [1] for the plays and religion sanctioned them and made them the most important event in the religious calendar of the year. While these dramas were being presented all places of business were closed. Law courts were adjourned. The jails were opened and the prisoners led into the temple so they might receive the ethical and spiritual stimulus of the plays. The audiences were almost incredibly large. The population of Athens was only about thirty thousand, but twenty thousand of these attended the plays. The chief seats in the Temple were reserved for the priests and the leading citizens of Athens, and the statue of Dionysus was placed in the center of the orchestra so that the audience and players alike might do him honor.

The themes of the plays were distinctly religious. Through all the dramas of Aeschylus runs the emphasis upon righteousness. Those who break the moral law will suffer even to the third and fourth generation. Those who keep it will ultimately be justified. Sophocles stressed the same themes and applied them more specifically to the social and ethical problems of the day. For example, in *Antigone* he centers the action of the characters around this eternal question: In time of war when loyalty to the State

[1] In an old book, *The Tragedies of Sophocles*, published in 1788 by Thomas Francklin, "late professor in the University of Cambridge," I have just come across this astonishing statement: "All the expenses of the theatre were defrayed by the State, and were indeed so considerable, that nothing but the purse of an opulent republic, could possibly have supported them, as it is confidently affirmed by historians that Athens spent more in dramatic representations than in all her wars. . . . This assertion which seems rather hyperbolical, is notwithstanding supported by the grave Plutarch who, speaking of the Athenians, assures us, that the representation of the Bacchanals, Phoenissae, Oedipus, Antigone, Medea, and Electra, cost them more money than the defence of their own liberties in the field, or all their contest with the Barbarians."

and loyalty to the gods come into conflict, which shall the citizen obey? His answer is: He must obey the gods rather than the State, for upon loyalty to the gods all other loyalties depend. Euripides went further in the direction of humanism and concerned himself more with the relations between man and man and less with the supernatural, but he was still reverent and never let his audience forget that man's ultimate destiny is with the gods.

Through all these tragedies the dramatists looked at life from the standpoint of eternity. They saw man as infinitely small and yet infinitely significant. They portrayed life as a moral struggle in which man's victory had cosmic importance. They saw strife in the heart of man's moral life and insisted that the very essence of the heroic consists in man's power, even in the midst of conflicts that threaten to destroy him, to stand "outside of the prison of the material present," and to merge himself "in some life that is the object of adoration or desire." [2]

Again, as Gilbert Murray says:

What is really characteristic is that from the very beginning the tragic conflict has in it an element of mystery derived ultimately from the ancient religious conceptions of *Katharsis* and atonement. The contest takes place on a deeper level of reality. It is not to be estimated in terms of ordinary success or failure, ordinary justice and injustice, but in those of some profounder scheme of values in which suffering is not the worst of things, nor happiness the best. [3]

The character who ultimately triumphed in these Greek plays was always the one who adjusted himself to this profounder scheme of values.

[2] Gilbert Murray, *The Classical Tradition in Poetry*, Harvard University Press, 1927, p. 51.
[3] *Op. cit.*, p. 66.

The chief result of these one-act plays of ancient Greece was twofold: they developed the dramatic form to a perfection seldom, if ever, surpassed; and they stimulated the inner life of their audiences until the very name of Athens became synonymous with spiritual sensitivity. The little town of Athens, with its population of thirty thousand, produced more great poets than America has produced with a population of a hundred and thirty million. Does that seem a trivial thing? In the last analysis, the only enduring thing in any civilization is poetry. A people may build its temples in stone and its machines in steel, and they all crumble in time to dust. But when a man can be so true a poet that he can capture the hope, the courage, the spiritual insights of his generation and imprison them in the poetry of words or line or color or music, he may be sure that the everlasting hills will melt away before his poem dies. The material civilization of ancient Greece has crumbled, but the dramas of Aeschylus, Sophocles, and Euripides are as vibrant with life today as they were twenty-four centuries ago. Long after the last American skyscraper and steel mill have decayed and blown away in some future dust storm, mankind will still be repeating the poetry of the Greek dramatists.

The second period when religion called the one-act play to its aid was during the Middle Ages in Europe, particularly in England. There, in the ninth century, the priests found themselves in this peculiar situation: they were allowed to use only Latin in the service of the Mass. The common people of England did not understand Latin. The priests wanted to make clear to them the story of Jesus and his challenge to a better way of life. So they dramatized the story. They began first with a simple dramatiza-

tion of Good Friday and Easter. On Good Friday they
took the crucifix from the altar and hid it away in a tomb
while the choir sang Misereres. Then, on Easter Sunday
morning, they brought it out from the tomb and put it
back on the altar decked in flowers while the choir sang
Alleluias. Thus they taught the people that Good Friday
and Easter had something to do with this man who had
been hung on a cross by human hatred and been buried as
if he were done for, and then had come out of the tomb,
somehow triumphant over death. His triumph meant that
they, too, could conquer hatred and death.

The people wanted more of the story. So the priests
dramatized other incidents in the life of Christ: his birth,
his trials, his parables. Still the people wanted more, so
the priests went back into the Old Testament and dramatized the story of the creation of the world, the Garden
of Eden, Cain and Abel, Noah and the Ark, the lives of
the patriarchs and prophets, and on into the New Testament and the lives of the apostles and saints. Folklore was
mixed in considerable quantities with biblical material.
Each of these dramatizations was a little one-act play in
itself. Ultimately, they were strung together in cycles,
twenty to fifty plays to a cycle, dealing with the whole
history of God's relation to man. The cycles centering
around scriptural events were originally known on the
Continent as mystery plays; those around the lives of the
saints as miracle plays. But in England both types came to
be called miracle plays.

These simple one-act plays began in the chancel of the
church with only the priests as actors. But by the time they
had developed into cycles, that is, by the eleventh or twelfth
century, they had been taken over by laymen and were

acted by the craft guilds. Each guild sponsored the play that called most upon its peculiar skill. Thus, the Masons' Guild presented *The Creation of the World* play, the Shipwrights' Guild, the play of *Noah and the Ark*, etc. This change from priests to laymen as actors and producers was paralleled by a further change in the place where the plays were performed. They moved from the chancel to the nave of the church and then to a great outdoor platform built in the doorway of the cathedrals. At one end of this platform was a representation of the flaming jaws of hell; at the other end, the pearly gates of heaven. At the conclusion of the cycle the bad characters went into the flaming jaws, often chased there by Satan and his devils; the good characters went to heaven, led by some angel of the Lord. It was all very naïve, but it made a profound impression upon the huge crowds that came. Rich and poor, prince and thrall, old grandfather and young girl, stood for hours watching these stories unfold before their eyes. They were more than stories. They were the dramatized spiritual history of the human race as they understood it.

As an offshoot from the mystery and miracle plays, rather than as a development of them, came the moralities. These, too, were one-act plays, dramatizing not history but sermons. The characters were virtues and vices instead of human beings. *Everyman* is the best example extant. These morality plays make dull reading today, but in the twelfth and thirteenth centuries they were probably more interesting than the dry homilies of the priests.

The mystery, miracle, and morality plays in medieval England never achieved either the artistic form or the spiritual depth of the Greek tragedies. Perhaps the lack of the competitive element was responsible. Whatever the cause, the fact remains that the plays attained neither literary nor dramatic excellence. In time someone thought up the idea of putting wheels under the platform which served as a stage and rolling it out into the market place. Ultimately, it came to rest in the courtyards of the inns, where it became the predecessor of the English theatre. The character of the plays underwent a corresponding change. The farther the platform moved from the church the farther the plays moved from a sense of mission to the human spirit. Folk characters took the place of biblical ones. Comedy supplanted tragedy. Pontius Pilate and Judas Iscariot finally degenerated into *Punch and Judy*.[4] The innkeepers got control of the plays and produced them for revenue only. Finally, the Reformation swept them away.

Nevertheless, in the three centuries during which the mystery and miracle plays were under church auspices, they made a lasting contribution. They taught the people to think of life not simply in terms of the here and now, but of eternity. They kindled imaginations to see far beyond the horizons of local provinces. They touched human hearts with the immortal drama of the life and defeat and triumph of Christ. They lifted men's minds above pettiness and set them to contemplating the grandeurs of the lives of the prophets and heroes and saints of Hebrew and Christian history. Thus, though they contributed little to the technique of drama, they made England a nation of actors accustomed to presenting great themes and heroic struggles. They prepared the way for Shakespeare.

[4] There are, of course, various other explanations of the origin of *Punch and Judy*. Whether or not this one is historically accurate, it is at least a figurative description of the decline of tragic drama to the status of a puppet show.

The third great period in which religion and the one-act play have worked together to develop the inner life of men is the period which began about 1900 in America. No one can say just where and when it started. But any prescient soul, half a century ago, could have predicted that when religion began to put less stress on creed and more on understanding, less on sectarianism and more on social ethics, drama would come back into the church. That is exactly what has happened. Tentatively, at first, religious educators began experimenting with pious pageants and simple Bible stories. Unlike their predecessors in Greece and medieval England, they began with children rather than with adults. This is probably one reason why the productions at first were so amateurish, even puerile. In fact, the quality of most of these early one-act religious plays in America and England was so low that an argument for the indestructibility of the church might be made from the fact that it survived them.

In spite of poor dramaturgy these plays had a spark of life in them. That spark kindled the imaginations of young people who were starved for something creative to do. They had already become drama-conscious as a result of the movies and the teaching of "dramatics" in hundreds of high schools and colleges. Here was an outlet for their creative energies. They and their more alert teachers seized upon it and within a few years, throughout the North and East and far West in America and among the more progressive churches in England, drama groups began to form.

One might wish that the story from here on could be one of steady progress toward a type of religious drama comparable to that of the ancient Greeks. But the facts are otherwise. The propagandists for church agencies saw in these eager dramatic groups a means of promoting their own various causes. Thereupon, a flood of so-called religious plays, pageants, dialogues and what not began to pour out from mission boards, church-extension societies, budget-raising committees and a score of similar organizations. Commercial play publishers added to this flood a stream of "cheap and easy" plays written in off moments by well-meaning but sentimental persons who wanted to "help the cause," but who had never taken it seriously enough to discipline their own talents by a study of the basic principles of dramatic structure. Here and there an occasional good play appeared, but by and large the bulk of the output of one-act religious plays of the period from 1910 to 1925 was sentimental trash.

To the lasting credit of many of the dramatic groups in the churches, they refused to produce this stuff. They demanded better plays—plays that had reality in characterization, honesty in treatment, and skill in construction. This demand became so strong that in 1924 the Federal Council of Churches appointed a committee to survey the available religious plays and select a few that could be recommended. The writer of this chapter happened to be chairman of that committee. We read scores, even hundreds, of so-called dramas and finally chose about ten that we thought worthy of being bound in a single volume. Among these were Kenneth Sawyer Goodman's *Dust of the Road*; Percy MacKaye's *The Pilgrim and the Book*; Phillips E. Osgood's *A Sinner Beloved*; and Mary P. Hamlin's *The Rock*. These plays were welcomed by the more serious groups in the churches and provided models for better playwriting. About the same time many church organizations sought to raise the standard of play production in churches by introducing courses in that subject in their summer schools and conferences. Two theological seminaries established chairs in Religious Literature and Drama, and other seminaries also undertook advanced work in the field.

Meanwhile, in England, a similar development was taking place. A Religious Drama Council was formed with Laurence Housman (known on Broadway as the author of *Victoria Regina*) at its head. Mr. Housman's charming *Little Plays of St. Francis* and *Bethlehem* were among the first English contributions to better plays for churches. John Masefield followed with his *The Coming of Christ* and *Easter*.

Thus far the content of these plays, both in England and America, had been largely biblical or dealing with the lives of saints. But if religion means anything it means it for today, as well as for two thousand years ago. It must speak to the present or die. The struggle between good and evil, between the Golden Rule and the Rule of Gold, between the Law of Love and the "jungle law of fang and claw," is just as fierce now as ever. Therefore, it was inevitable that the plays in the churches should become more and more modern in their content; should visualize present battles as well as ancient ones. Laurence Housman, addressing the Religious Drama Council of England, put the matter thus:

If you are to have live drama, it must touch modern problems and conditions, even somewhat controversially perhaps. If the churches are to be alive they must show fight. . . . The question is: How can you set up live drama which will also be religious drama?

The real problem you are up against is a moral, a spiritual, problem. Is Christ still the Great Adventurer or is he only a reminiscence? Is to be Christian still the greatest social problem of today, or is it only a tradition? Are you going to put into your religious drama only those versions of Christianity which fit into our social system, which Caesar accepts and can make use of; or are you prepared to give Caesar the lie and to give institutional Christianity the lie when they bear false witness against what Christianity should stand for? On your answer to these questions depends whether or not you can have live drama in your churches.

If you mean to have live drama you must have the courage of your convictions and be ready to do the unfamiliar and unexpected thing. Put to yourselves this as a test: You are willing to have in your churches a mystery play, or something similar, from past ages; but are you equally willing to have a modern play, not merely a goody-goody play of pious, blameless characters, but a play of social conflict, like *Strife*, or a play exposing legal cruelty, like *Justice*, by Galsworthy? I do not mean necessarily those plays in particular, but plays generally as socially alive to our own times. . . .

If you ask me how to come by religious drama, take anything in the present social system you believe to be wrong and unchristian, tackle it ruthlessly and uncompromisingly, as you think it ought to be tackled. Show it up, make it as modern as you like, as controversial as you like; and if you have the dramatic gift and if your solution is a Christian solution, you have religious drama. You ask me for subjects? War, capital punishment, the soul-destroying system of our prisons, sweated labor, prostitution, the hardness of heart of the self-righteous, the color problem—out of all these you can get religious drama.

Just so! But to do this without going off into propaganda on the one hand or into preaching on the other is no easy matter. To present such subjects honestly, keeping characterization real and solutions convincing, is the difficult task of the modern playwright whether he works on Broadway or in Piccadilly or in the church. An increasing number of dramatists, both in England and in America, are attempting it. Witness *Pawns, Confessional* and *The Finger of God* by Percival Wilde, *Neighbors* by Zona Gale, *Tidings of Joy* by Elizabeth McFadden, *Monsignor's Hour* by Emmet Lavery, *The Deathless World* by J. M. S. Tompkins, *Prize Money* by Louis Wilson, *Twentieth Century Lullaby* by Cedric Mount, and the present writer's *Bread* and *The Great Choice*. These plays deal with such themes as war, unemployment, nationalism, the farm problem, and the struggle for roses as well as for bread.

In this transition from biblical and ecclesiastical plays to modern plays of social ethics and of spiritual power a new definition of religious drama has evolved. We have come to see that it is not the material of a play that makes it religious or secular but the *effect upon an audience*. A play may draw all its characters from the Bible, as in the story of *Jephthah's Daughter*, and yet send an audience away with no deeper understanding of its own struggles and no impulse toward righteousness or helpfulness or brotherhood. On the other hand, a play may take its characters from the slums or a battlefield or a farm and deal with them in such a way that the audience goes away exalted in spirit, with enlarged sympathies, a greater sense of fellowship, a new understanding of the spiritual forces of human life. When it does that it is a religious drama.

At first such plays were presented on week nights amid the same surroundings as plays whose only purpose was entertainment. They opened "cold" without any preliminary effort to establish a mood in the minds of the audience. But the more we have come to see the essential nature of the religious play as distinct from the entertainment play, the more we have come to see the necessity of giving it a religious setting. So, today, most religious dramas are presented on Sunday evenings, sometimes in the main auditorium of the church, more often in the parish hall.[5] They are set in a service of worship, with a prelude of organ music, hymns, prayers, and responses calculated to lift the minds of the audience, unite them, and prepare them for a serious contemplation of a great theme. The drama takes the place of the sermon as the climax of a religious service. If well done it is more effective than the usual sermon.

Thus, from a small beginning as a device for teaching Bible stories to young people the one-act play in the church has evolved into a medium for ministering to the spirits of men through a great art. It has withstood the opposition of those who felt that anything dramatic was of the devil. It has survived misuse by propagandists and promoters. In thousands, perhaps tens of thousands, of churches it is now being used to develop the creative and imaginative life of the players and the congregations. Through the one-act play, drama groups are seeking to portray the social and the spiritual struggles of modern life in vivid terms of characters in action.

These groups have not yet attained the skill of professionals. They suffer from lack of adequate equipment and

[5] A recent survey of 451 typical churches with a membership of 200 or more disclosed these facts: 411, or 91% of the 451, were using one-act plays. They had produced a total of 1,518 of them during the preceding year, or an average of 3.7 plays per church. Adults had produced 37%, young people 25%, mixed groups 21%, children 17%. Nearly half of the plays had been presented in the Christmas season and a third of them at Easter.

of intelligent criticism. Nevertheless, they are gradually developing discrimination in their selection of plays. They are acquiring better equipment. The quality of their productions, though in no way comparable to that of the ancient Greek religious dramas, is steadily improving.

The modern religious dramatist has a theme greater than the Greeks had. He has characters to portray whose stature dwarfs the pagan and the medieval heroes. He has titanic social conflicts to interpret—conflicts on the outcome of which the very life of civilization depends. If, through the one-act play, he can interpret these conflicts with insight and understanding and portray these characters honestly and convincingly, he will make an enduring contribution to dramatic art, lifting it to the place of dignity and power it held in the days of Aeschylus, Sophocles, and Euripides. More important yet, he will minister to the souls of a confused and troubled generation.

THE USE OF POETRY IN THE ONE-ACT PLAY

ALFRED KREYMBORG was born in New York in 1883. Aside from writing poetry and plays, Mr. Kreymborg has had two outstanding loves: music and chess. He has been affiliated with many artistic ventures, being one of the organizers of the famous Provincetown Theatre, editor of numerous magazines, the most successful being *Broom* and *Others*.

Mr. Kreymborg has always been interested in experimental dramatic art. His Poem-Mimes, as they were first called, or Puppet Plays, were first produced at the Provincetown Theatre and later by hundreds of Little Theatres and dramatic clubs all over the world.

With Van Wyck Brooks, Lewis Mumford, and Paul Rosenfeld, Alfred Kreymborg initiated that notable miscellany of American literature, known as *The American Caravan*, which first published the work of many writers who are now famous.

Mr. Kreymborg's best-known plays are *Manikin and Minikin*, *Lima Beans*, *Plays for Merry Andrews*, and *Commencement* (a full-length play). His poetry has been published widely in books and magazines.

THE USE OF POETRY
IN THE ONE-ACT PLAY

by Alfred Kreymborg

DURING the past year or two, renewed pleas have been made in behalf of poetic drama, and the speeches have an air of confidence lacking in former appeals. In the earlier years of the century, the appeals were defensive and drew a pessimistic line between the great classic eras when poets ruled the stage and our own time with its glorification of show business. The old apologist was reasonable. He spoke well and wrote well, but he had few or no poetic plays to illustrate his demand for a new theatre. Now and then such a play made the boards, from the days of William Vaughn Moody to the Provincetown Players. In the first instance, showmen and audience preferred Moody's pot-boiler, *The Great Divide,* to his poetic drama, while the Provincetown group owed most of its success to realistic thrillers in realistic prose. The average play in verse lacked reality. It was written by specialists for specialists, high-brows for high-brows, poets for esoteric audiences. In the days of the Greeks and their descendants, the poet be-longed to the race and developed familiar racial themes on the broadest scale, his speech raised, not in some ivory tower, but out of the fields and language of the people.

And this man, through many centuries, was a man of the theatre: *the* man, in fact. He directed and acted in his own plays and was even their entrepreneur. Thus it was from Aeschylus to Euripides, from Shakespeare to Molière, and with men approaching our time, Strindberg, Wedekind, Yeats.

Today the average author has been driven off the boards and his play, if accepted, is put on with a view of expressing the producer and his hirelings and behind these, the box office. All we ask of the show is that the show succeed and outrun its rivals. Nor is there a single Broadway group, however progressive at birth, which doesn't succumb to business in time. This charming hydra has three heads now: the stage, the screen, the radio, each with its wholesale appeal to the classic moron. Here and there the vicious circle is broken by a good play, a good film, a good skit, and all three draw a good audience. Then the circle tightens and grows more powerful, and once more farce, gangster, and wisecrack sweep the land. There is nothing more dismal and wasteful than American business and the destruction or perversion into which the arts are driven. And yet

On very little praise
and still less money
the poet persists
and the bee makes honey.

Why does the fellow persist? First of all, he can live no other way. Secondly, he knows humanity. He knows that humanity will follow the artist in the long run and that the artist survives evil and temporal things. And thirdly, since he has to exist, he knows that art pays. Though he doesn't earn a sou, his conscience is clear and

richer than any deposit in a mundane bank. He also knows
that as far as money is concerned, great works of art are
priceless, and the older they grow the younger they are in
the minds of succeeding generations. It is impossible to
compute the cash value of the Parthenon, the Venus of
Milo, the Taj Mahal, or the cathedral of Chartres. Or
of such epics as *The Iliad*, *The Divine Comedy*, and *Paradise Lost*. The greatest of dramatists is also the most popular and Stratford an empire. These are mere facts and "the
fact is the sweetest dream that labor knows." A man with
an eye to figures applied to cash values recently computed
that the works of Van Gogh, who sold nothing at all while
he lived, are now worth forty-eight millions. It wasn't very
long ago that Vincent shot himself and said to his brother:
"Misery has no end." He was certainly referring to the
flesh, not to the spirit. Or to the people who adore him
now.

Call the people what you will, they aren't morons for-
ever. Appeal to their cheapest instincts and get rich quick
there, they'll still escape you in time. Banish the poet as
Plato did; run him out of town like Dante; run him into
jail like Villon; see that he starve like Whitman; see that
his grave is unknown like Mozart's. Pile on the torments
of indifference and let stupidity rule your hour: what is
Greece if it isn't Homer; Italy if it isn't Dante; Austria
if it isn't Mozart; France if it isn't Villon; America if it
isn't Whitman? And what is England or the whole world,
real or theatrical, if it isn't Shakespeare?

To come down to modern cases and to our own land,
the note of poetic revival has risen in the short or one-act
play, and we owe this movement first to the Provincetown
Players, then to the Little Theatres of the land, and finally

to the poetic conquest of Britain by an enigmatic American, T. S. Eliot. The Provincetown group had the virtue of bringing the Greeks to a barn on Macdougal Street. They wrote and produced their own plays; the plays were short and dealt with life. This is as far as an old member dares to carry comparison. For their devotion to the untried, their resistance of commercial temptation, their horrendous labors for what they believed in, the group deserves lasting praise. And it developed Eugene O'Neill, not to mention a number of lesser lights. The Players succumbed to Broadway when O'Neill's destiny carried him there and the country gained what the group lost. But the short play, as germane to the American temper as the sprint, the lyric, the short story, found welcome in the Washington Square Players, forerunners of the Theatre Guild, and in the many amateur theatres dotting the nation. As long as these groups encouraged the native playwright and sought their material in native soil, the movement prospered. But when it succumbed to Broadway by reproducing seasonal hits, the movement lost its indigenous soul. Happily, some of the groups carried on the original vein and became self-supporting without too much compromise. They were joined by experimental university groups like the ones at Harvard and Yale, Cornell, Smith, and Iowa. But we heard less and less of purely poetic drama, notwithstanding the fact that our prewar poets, rising at the most unexpected time in the most unexpected places, led an American renascence which affected all our cultural energies. The influence of Robinson and Frost, Lindsay and Sandburg, Masters and the Imagists, and finally the Waste Land Eliot, penetrated everywhere and developed our arts, outside the theatre. I'm afraid the poets themselves are to blame, rather than producer and public, for the so-called neglect of the theatre. Maxwell Anderson, surely no great poet or dramatist, sold the poetic drama to Broadway and made quite a fortune for all concerned. But his plays do not touch, either in poetry or drama, the best of Eugene O'Neill. And O'Neill wrote in prose, not in verse.

For twenty-odd years, ever since the Provincetown days, I've harangued my fellows in an effort to lure them into the theatre: even to a window or a doorstep. But they feel more at home in themselves and their neighborly books; and so far as drama is concerned, in their dramatic lyrics or narratives. They have reason for skepticism: the argument is against Broadway—or was before Max Anderson. Revivals of Shakespeare, some in modern mufti, should have convinced the skeptic that great poetic drama has a place in the box-office world, providing it is stirring enough. It was always the province of the poet to surpass himself, to reach out toward the utmost horizons of consciousness and communication; and the ideal theatre takes in both. We are always arguing about the age: the age is ready for this, the age isn't ready for that. But this is sheer nonsense or an evasion of major problems.

Every age is great enough to command our best powers, and not just one power perfectly achieved and repeated, until it becomes a rubber stamp. The age we are entering now, and God knows what hells worse than Satan's, is possibly the greatest ever, the most tragic and difficult. Is it blind, tortured, divided, wretched, insane, half-dead and hopeless? Is there nothing for a man to grasp and an artist to reduce to paper? Even so, this and nothing less is the artist's job. If some glib soul maintain, with history behind him, that our best work comes at the end of an era, with peace and perspective behind us, are we to run from the present scene and dream of old lands or new where the artist is more at home? Since when has he had time for slippers and an easy chair? Books are born of the greatest travail even in times of bucolic serenity. Thus it is with the theatre, toughest of all the literary arts. Though there's no theatre that even approaches the ideal, we have to work in advance, like inventors of old. With one hand Dante created *The Divine Comedy* and with the other the Italian language. And Bach created the musical alphabet alongside the musical universe. Nothing is made to order for the poet. He may have models to work on and carry on certain traditions, but the noblest of all are the demons who recreate the world again. We had such a fellow in Whitman. Thanks to Emerson. Thanks to Carlyle. Thanks to the Germans. And wherever they go back to. We've carried on Walt and added to him. No one man does it all. And this is theatre too.

Meanwhile, what have we done in the theatre, real or ideal, to revive our faith in the poet or to waste our speech on an essay? I have to return to Tom Eliot, and to disciples of his who are disciples no longer. This involves examination of a certain vice and virtue to which all races are prone and ours most of all: individuality. And this involves in turn those dear old twins: self-expression and communication. Eliot was a Yankee individualist who rebelled against those immediate forebears in whom self-expression ran riot and almost ceased to communicate. A brilliant scholar, he set himself the deliberate task of analyzing a lost world and recreating a classic past. In his impassioned labors, tempered with the dispassionate, he brought about a neoclassicism in esthetics and religion without losing sight of his own world, the postwar era of despair and disillusionment. Nor did he lose sight of the common man: he let the vernacular elbow the grandiloquent. One fine day the report arrived from overseas that Canterbury Cathedral, looking for a poet to celebrate the death of Thomas à Becket, had turned to Thomas Stearns Eliot. Then we heard that the play, *Murder in the Cathedral*, was to open in London at a poets' theatre directed by Ashley Dukes.

In the course of events, this play came to America via Yale and the Federal Theatre, just off Broadway. Thither the people went at a fifty-five-cent top and in the hundreds and thousands. I'll never forget that audience, and I mean this in several ways. First of all, I'd sat out front ever since my New York boyhood and had never expected to find this. Secondly, I was a member of the Federal Theatre, intensely aware of its egregious problems, and had never expected to find this. Thirdly, the plot and characters of the play couched in exalted language—faith blended with satire and skepticism—these I had expected of Eliot, but not a responsive audience. And the play was short: it said what it had to say and sang what it had to sing and then, curtain. Further, the production came out of the economic depression. Broadway producers had closed their shops to experiment, and the unemployed put it on, the relief people. This gave a man food for some hopeful thinking and action. I went to work on the Federal Theatre. Here was our place and our future. This theatre was playing to the millions and playing at popular prices. And Americans paid the price, all on a level—twenty-two million so far. So I started the Poetic Theatre assigned to me as supervisor and laid out a breathless plan. But I reckoned without my superiors: only one play saw the lights, W. H. Auden's *The Dance of Death*. The title sounds rather symbolical.

I wish I had time for the infinite ramifications of the Federal Theatre, but time, they say, marches on. And, in a world as messy as ours, one has to dwell on constructive or hopeful things—especially in an argument. *The Dance of Death* introduced several new values. Here was a savage satire on the British Empire by the most brilliant young hand in Britain; here was a madcap affair which employed American vaudeville and jazz as though they'd been invented elsewhere; and here was a denunciation of decadence that made the Adelphi rock and sounded like a youthful Swift in modern arms. Auden, like Eliot, was not yet a man of the theatre, but, in collaboration with Christopher Isherwood, his dramaturgy is growing up. Other members of Auden's generation—first inspired by Eliot, but no longer his disciples—have entered the theatre: Stephen Spender, C. Day Lewis, and Louis MacNeice. The Tories have dubbed them dreadful names: leftists, radicals, Marxists. If we know what patriotism is we may safely assume it's the Tories, not the young Britons, who are unpatriotic. And these young Britons, caught up in growing favor, have mastered the microphone. Their plays, along with the Becket tragedy, are being broadcast over the air. And the air brings us back to America.

In a year rather poor in theatre and more and more lacking in experiment, a dramatic event of the first order struck the whole country in the course of a mere half hour. Since Americans are always a surprise, even to Americans, where did this event take place: on the stage, on the screen? No, where it was least expected: on the air in a national hookup. I refer to Archibald MacLeish's *The Fall of the City* as produced by the Columbia Workshop under young Irving Reis. Not long before, another young man, Orson Welles, had put on MacLeish's one-act study of the bank crash, *Panic*—but the entrance fee was $5.50 per head. Mr. Welles was here again, playing the Announcer, and at seven P.M. of a Sunday, just after some good old wisecrack tuned off, young Welles, young Burgess Meredith, and a company of two hundred actors, playing in an armory, began their conquest of air and theatre. What we listened to and what we actually *saw* was a poem dramatically rendered. The high-brows among us, who had always run from radio plays, discovered that radio is capable of infinite things, that radio is a great medium appealing directly to the imagination. The theatre of the mind was completely alive to what transpired over space. One was absolutely undisturbed. New York disappeared.

In the profoundly moving story, symbolical of dictatorship in any time or place, one was conscious of a deliberate mind calculating the effects of each line. The Announcer was used as an impassioned commentator, not alone on the actions of the characters and mob, but on the scene itself. One never lost sight of the great city square, of the hot sky dotted with hawks, of the surrounding mountains and of towns already burning in the footsteps of the Conqueror. In the midst of one's private emotions, the mind was respected and appealed to; the mind was open and alert; the mind could reflect on the tragic movement of the heart. There was nothing personal in the process; everything was objective. Words were picked out in space and projected over a microphone: a symphonic drama, precise and subtle, beautifully timed. And a thing in which characters played upon a mob and the mob upon the auditor. For I was a member of the mob and trembled for myself among them. And trembled for my brothers among them; trembled for civilization. As the mob turned to each old leader (minister, priest, general) and sought the old liberties there, I turned with them, made aware, however, of a growing premonition that the mob would turn to someone else, that one by one the old leaders would fall and unconsciously prepare for the oncoming dictator: a man in the image of the mob, created and minted by them. When the dread silence came and the mob lay prostrate on the square, one lay prostrate with them. One was not surprised that the Conqueror came in iron armor, with a visor on his head. And that no one dared raise his own head when the monster raised its arm. Nor was one amazed that when a hand raised the visor and all of us waited for the opening speech, no speech sounded. There was no head inside the visor, no body inside the armor. No one saw the image he had created, but worshiped it even so. A sudden fanfare blared and the curtain descended. And one had heard not the tale of one city, one land, but of all cities and lands that have lain under an iron heel or may lie there again. Everything had been timed to perfection: the half hour was over.

Enthusiasts among us were certain Eldorado had come at last. But we reckoned without the entrepreneur. Other short plays were put on, actually based on social material, and then less and less. Tripe and the tawdry returned to their former estate, and commercial chicanery ruled the air as of yore. Worse than this, the Puritans and Tories among us, whose wives are always discovering that the kiddies are in danger of hearing too much for their little pants and petticoats, tugged at official sleeves and the officials nodded. If anyone did any thinking over the air, the common man might follow, and this would never do. And so the air, for the most part, like the film, for the most part, appeals once more to the twelve-year-old mind, and business is at home again.

Now what is this common man we are always addressing and trying to coerce and capture or enslave? There are two ways of eying the fellow. We may eye him with an eye to fortune or with an eye to culture and art. The first course, in the field of letters, led to such giants as George Horace Lorimer, the glue manufacturer who rose to the ownership of the *Saturday Evening Post*. When someone asked Mr. Lorimer for the secret of his success, the great man replied: "I was always an ordinary man." In the realms of theater, screen, and microphone, similar replies would doubtless emerge from the hearts of our princes there. These men are undoubtedly of the people and know to a certain degree what the people want. If we care for the people at all, we have no right to quarrel with their taste, direct or perverted. There are other leaders who are of the people, and *by* and *for* as well. There was a tall, grave figure who addressed the nation at Gettysburg and who described government as of the people, for the people, by the people. And there was a man who wrote *Leaves of Grass* who had much the same notion and still appeals to the common man. It's more than a democratic principle. It applies to the ages, and its impulse was recognized by the revolutionary Shelley when he closed his *Defence of Poetry* with the magic line: "Poets are the unacknowledged legislators of the world." By poets he meant the creative spirit. It was this kinship, leadership, and response the Greeks enjoyed. They were fairly good business men too. Their plays had long runs and are running still. And in more than the language common to Athens.

Our failure as poetic dramatists lies in too great a divorce from our people. We're too easily annoyed with the soft success of the fakers among us and of those whose vast popularity is based on an honest approach to the market. The various types of escapism employed by artists at odds with their environment may be found in the language employed. Even in the plays I've been raving about, much of the speech is disdainful or precious and clings more to clouds than to earth. And yet these plays had an audience flatteringly large in proportion to audiences of a dismal yesteryear. We have universal problems these days in every turn of the news and newspapers. Events no longer affect one people, one nation, but all people and nations, America among them. We belong to the world as never before, tragically, comically, or tragi-comically. The man with the concentrated powers of vision, speech, and communication has powers far beyond those which lay in the circle surrounding the Greeks, the Romans, the Renaissance. His job is infinitely more complex and difficult, infinitely more uncertain. And he hasn't the faith of his fathers: that has to be hewn with the rest of the new world. But somehow or other, he has a certain substantial essence which, for want of a better word, we call Opportunity. You'll find it in every business house: it fills us with nausea. Nonetheless, it knocks at the door of the artist, along with his fellows. It is no longer a question of who will put on our plays and where. The question is simply who will write them. They'll get on somehow if they're great enough, and people will attend. An audience can also be great. Or we shouldn't have had what we had in the past.

In between the Greeks and our own time, many leading playwrights, whether poets or prosemen, have set themselves to the concentrated forms of the one-act play. The forms are as varied as the themes and tempers of their creators and backgrounds. Further, a man doesn't have to write in verse in order to achieve a poetic work. No plays are more truly poetic than the prose plays of Maeterlinck, of Synge, and of our own Conkle, Green, and Basshe. Poetry, after all, is a heightening of human consciousness, and there are many pages in novels which are closer to poetry than the blank verse dramas of Stephen Phillips. So are the essays of Van Wyck Brooks. A play like *Riders to the Sea*, lasting but twenty minutes, is a poetic reflection of an entire race caught in the tides of the tragic sea. And yet the play is as quiet as a stone and as simple as human bread. Its peasants are universal, though their speech has an Irish tang and inflection. Poetry is speech with an inevitable tone and rhythm. *Riders to the Sea* and other great lyric plays could not have been written in any other form. Synge was happy in the Aran Islands and the Islands in Synge. And on the strength of a few short plays his name and people are world-wide.

The poet of the people today is another John Synge confronted with international themes. There are so many themes and so many races involved that the author, whether he knows it or not, addresses the entire human race. He has no time for private ills or privacy unless those ills reflect something larger than himself and the lonely ego. It is possible that the world at large was never so lonely as now, and never so lost and out of love. His love song then—or what he's in love with—must go out among the streets and spheres, lonely on high or on earth, and show how human they are, however distorted in their relations. He may be a realist who shows things as they are, or the new romanticist who shows things as they ought to be. Either poet, realist or prophet, will bring about human relations the world is in need of. There's no art as communal as the theatre in setting forth every shade and variation of human activity. The swift short forms are always inclusive enough. They were good enough for the ancients and ought to suit our dizzy age.

PART III   HISTORICAL SURVEY

WHERE DOES THE ONE-ACT PLAY BELONG?

BARRETT H. CLARK received his schooling in several outstanding colleges and universities. At various times he has been an instructor and special staff lecturer at Chautauqua Institution, Bryn Mawr College, and Columbia University.

He became affiliated with the theatre in 1912 when he acted as assistant stage-manager and actor with Mrs. Fiske. Since that time he has been engaged in writing and editing articles and books dealing with the drama.

Mr. Clark's activities have been numerous, and a list of them would cover more than a page. But some of his outstanding accomplishments as an author are *The Continental Drama of To-day; The British and American Drama of To-day* (these two books were rewritten and brought up to date in a single volume, *A Study of the Modern Drama*); *Contemporary French Dramatists; European Theories of the Drama; Eugene O'Neill, the Man and His Plays; An Hour of American Drama.*

He has written editorial prefaces to plays by Paul Green, E. P. Conkle, Lynn Riggs, Virgil Geddes, Martin Flavin, Albert Bein, and Samson Raphaelson.

From 1918 to 1935 Mr. Clark was associated with Samuel French.

At present he is Executive Director of the Dramatists Play Service of New York.

WHERE DOES THE ONE-ACT PLAY BELONG?

by Barrett H. Clark

I AM afraid I have never altogether made up my mind about the one-act play. I mean as to just where it belongs, either in the theatre or in the vast hierarchy of art; not that it needs to be put into a category of its own, or defined or classified as we define or classify orations and odes; but it would be convenient to be able to say that the one-acter performs this function or that, that it is limited by such and such boundaries, and that its aim is to supplement the full-length play in such and such fashion. The thing seems, however, oftener than not, to be a stepchild, an exercise, a shadowy waif of the legitimate theatre written *in vacuo*, without a definite objective; a promise or preparation for something else that is rarely even hinted at.

In other countries it has here and there been evolved into a distinctive thing, a form existing independently for its own sake, like the *Grand Guignol* thriller or farce, or as a curtain raiser. In France, England, Germany, and Spain, for example, at various times during the past fifty years, the one-acter has been used to entertain the early comers before the chief play began. In Spain and Germany, as well as in France, whole bills were made up of short plays, very much as we now offer continuous showings of weekly newsreels; and occasionally a revue, probably an outgrowth of the cabaret or night-club entertainment, would include several "shorts" as integral parts of the program.

The most famous of all the short-play theatres was the *Grand Guignol* of Paris. For a generation and more this institution offered bills of six plays each, three thrillers and three farces or comedies. Almost without exception these were designed to produce quick and striking effects; they were a series of dramatic cocktails, clever, sophisticated, risqué.

The *Grand Guignol* created a demand both in France and elsewhere for the type of play which it required of its authors, and so ably produced.

In the United States, since 1910, several attempts have been made to transplant the *Grand Guignol* idea, but the public was not interested. It was not that we had no use for short plays, we just did not want them served alone; we refused to dine on hors d'œuvres. We had, nonetheless, and for some thirty or forty years, patronized the dramatic sketch as a feature in vaudeville. In earlier days the farce or "afterpiece" (shorter than the main play, but often of two or three acts, and occasionally one act) had been widely used, and then after the middle of the nineteenth century dropped; but when some sixty years ago vaudeville became "refined" we used a modified type of "afterpiece," the one-act sketch. This reached the height of its development and popularity about the time of the beginning of the World War. One of the classic sketches that played throughout the English-speaking world was the famous thriller of Austin Strong, *The Drums of Oude*. In the great days of vaudeville the one-act play was an almost invariable feature of every bill.

When at last vaudeville was superseded by the pictures, the demand for short plays for use in the professional theater practically ceased. Nevertheless, on occasion an actor demanded a sketch for some special use, either as a curtain raiser or for a starring tour in vaudeville, where it still existed, and some of the finest examples of the form were written to order, such as *Little Italy*, *The Valiant*, and *The Little Father of the Wilderness*.

Some years before the established playwrights had given up writing for the vaudeville market the experimental, "Art," or "Little" Theatre had begun to flourish, and because short plays were easier to write and produce than long, the nonprofessional playwright made tentative efforts to express himself and his world. Nearly forty years ago Evelyn Greenleaf Sutherland and Percy Mac-Kaye first wrote and published one-act plays in which we recognize a desire to express ideas and depict scenes and characters far different from those that had been the stock in trade of vaudeville; but it was not until about 1910 that the one-act play, as distinct from the vaudeville sketch, came into its own. The so-called Little Theatre offered a chance to the nonprofessional writer to see his "experimental" plays acted. The "one-act" playwright, a new figure, flourished widely between 1914 and 1925. Percy Mac-Kaye, Susan Glaspell, and Eugene O'Neill had, it is true, written long plays, but these writers were for years better known as the authors of such famous "shorts" as *Gettysburg*, *Suppressed Desires*, and *'Ile*; others, like Percival Wilde and Alfred Kreymborg, excelled as writers of one-acters. In the hands of these writers, and such play-wrights as Philip Moeller, Alice Gerstenberg, Colin Clements, Mary Aldis and at least a hundred others, the short play became a widely popular theatre form, and as the Little Theatre developed, it depended almost entirely upon that for its chief fare.

For the past fifteen years, however, one-acters have been turned out in ever-increasing quantities, and this in spite of the absence of what I may call a "natural" market such as existed in vaudeville or for a time in the Little Theatres. Of course, some market does exist, or short plays would not be written to any extent except as exercises. The dramatic departments of most colleges and universities, the producing classes in most high schools, women's clubs, and the almost innumerable odds and ends of "dramatic clubs," do indeed use one-act plays. Neither the Little Theatres nor the important college and university theatres use one-acters except for "studio" or private showings, yet our educational institutions go on encouraging young men and women to write them.

On the other hand, there is some evidence that the one-act play has a place in the modern theatre, that a persistent demand for it exists. There is first the very large "amateur" market in churches and schools, a demand that is satisfied by the publication annually of several hundred new plays, most of them intrinsically worthless; there is the radio, which on rare occasions challenges a writer to use to the fullest extent its technical possibilities; there is the professional revue (the modern counterpart of vaudeville), the motion picture, and the Labor or Left Wing Theatre, which on special occasions calls for a *Waiting for Lefty*

(Clifford Odets), a *Hymn to the Rising Sun* (Paul Green), a *Private Hicks* (Albert Maltz).

The more interesting and important and economically attractive the medium for which the play is required, the better the product. It should be clear that Archibald MacLeish would not have written *The Fall of the City* but for the chance that was given him to send his dramatic poetry over the air to hundreds of thousands of listeners; and the same thing is true of Maxwell Anderson's *Feast of the Ortolans*. Neither of these poets has anything to say in the black-out form, and it is hardly likely that any play from their hands would interest the Grangers.

Likewise Clifford Odets was moved to say his say to audiences gathered at Sunday night meetings because he felt sure that they were ready to listen to him; and Paul Green took time off from writing long plays to sing his *Hymn to the Rising Sun*, knowing that that devastating play would find the public it was intended for.

The revue sketch, or black-out, may have its counterpart in theatrical history—surely the ancients must have had something of the sort—but at its contemporary best it is a highly specialized, original, and effective form. Though shorter than the shortest *Grand Guignol* farces and comedies, it somewhat resembles these, inasmuch as it is an episode or joke told briefly for the sake of the "point." Marc Connelly's *The Travellers* and George S. Kaufman's *The Still Alarm*, though somewhat longer than most, are first-rate examples of the form.

We live in a world that is governed by considerations of interest, largely economic interest; and allowing for a few exceptions and granting the existence always of mixed motives, we should realize that the law of supply and demand is the law of our civilization. The one-act play, like the full-length play—*and* the sonnet *and* the automobile—flourishes at its best when and where the paying public is ready to patronize it.

Whether or not the one-act form can be used for the expression of ideas or the revelation of a character or group of characters, and used in some way peculiar to itself only —apart from the full-length play—is a matter for argument. At its very best it surely can offer, within its narrow limits, a kind of miniature drama which might, if forced into the longer form, prove too slight for full-length work; its originally sharp outlines might be blurred, over-emphasized, or probably lost. The exquisite point in *The Valiant* seems to be the sort of point that belongs only at the end of a half-hour play; the drama of a lifetime that is so ably presented in the fifteen minutes of E. P. Conkle's *Minnie Field* could scarcely have been so admirably set forth in any other medium; and O'Neill's *'Ile* and *Moon of the Caribbees* are beyond any doubt complete within their necessarily restricted limits. The same thing can be said of other undoubted masterpieces: Paul Green's *Hot Iron;* Lady Gregory's *Rising of the Moon;* and two or three plays each of Sir James Barrie, Percival Wilde, J. M. Synge, Harold Brighouse, Alfred Kreymborg, Austin Strong, and Susan Glaspell.

At this time, and in our country, the one-act play seems to be in need of a home and a legitimate reason for existence; in short, a market. It is not quite enough to claim that it is an exercise, unless we know for what the exercise is intended. Surely it is not a very useful exercise for the young writer who aims at the full-length form: I don't think that any young playwright, even after having written a trunkful of shorts, is any better equipped to write a three-act play than if he had written only one, and there is some danger that too constant application to the short form may even make the other more difficult to master.

And it is not enough to go on filling up anthologies with new plays in the hope that some particular use may be found for them.

If the one-act play is to flourish and mean anything at all, we must find a place for it—outside the study, the workshop, the magazine, and the textbook—a place either in the professional theatre or the nonprofessional, where some considerable part of the paying public will go because they want to go, in order to witness and be moved by work of a particular form and character, essentially different from the long play because of some inherent and necessary inner compulsion.

If the one-act play has a future in our country, I believe it will be in the special Labor groups, or among the experiments now tentatively begun by the dramatic poets; in the revues and over the radio and in a one-act theatre. Meantime our exercises in playwriting courses and in the schools and colleges will have fully justified themselves, if these possible markets are actually going to become as important as I believe they will.

THE ONE-ACT PLAY IN THE UNITED STATES

GLENN HUGHES was born in Nebraska in 1894. In 1912 he entered Stanford University, from which he graduated in 1916. In 1919 he was granted a fellowship at the University of Washington, Seattle, and in 1920 was given his M.A. degree in English. At the same time he was admitted to the faculty of that institution and immediately began the development of a curriculum in dramatic arts.

In 1928-29 Mr. Hughes spent a year in Europe as a Guggenheim Fellow, making a study of the Imagist movement in poetry. During the academic year 1929-30, he served as Professor of English at Scripps College, Claremont, California. In the autumn of that year he returned to the University of Washington as Professor of English and Director of the Division of Drama, a position he still holds. Since 1930, when he effected a complete reorganization of the curriculum, staff, and activities of the Division of Drama, he has developed one of the largest college drama departments in America, with a theatrical library of nearly twelve thousand volumes, two public theatres operating every week of the year, and a thorough five-year course of study.

In addition to his activities as a teacher and executive, Mr. Hughes has written a standard textbook, *The Story of the Theatre*, has edited several volumes of plays, has collaborated on dramatic translations from the French and Japanese, has contributed critical articles to magazines, and has published thirteen full-length and twenty-four one-act plays.

THE ONE-ACT PLAY IN THE
UNITED STATES

by Glenn Hughes

THE history of the one-act play in the United States is in effect a history of the decline of the professional theatre and the rise of the amateur, and the present vitality and importance of the short play indicates clearly the strength and scope of the amateur movement. For in this country the short play has never been taken seriously by the professional theatre. In the nineteenth century and during the first decade of the twentieth, one-act plays were employed only as curtain raisers and, in some instances, as afterpieces, for audiences which expected long programs and for whom even a five-act Shakespearian tragedy was insufficient return for the price of admission.

The curtain raiser and the afterpiece both inclined toward the farcical for the simple and good reason that the curtain raiser had the responsibility of putting the audience in a pleasant mood and the afterpiece was intended to send them home happy. Short plays of strong dramatic quality, most of them melodramatic, were composed chiefly for use in variety shows, where they served as starring vehicles for well-known actors. Then came changes in theatregoers' habits. Legitimate theatres trimmed their programs to the length of a single three-act play; vaudeville and revue gave way to films and radio. Professional performances of short plays are nowadays extremely rare.

But if the short play was unimportant in the professional theatre of the nineteenth century, it was even less important in the amateur theatre. Professional curtain raisers and dramatic vaudeville sketches did at least earn credit and financial return for the author, whereas short plays written for the amateur market seldom earned either. Amateur groups of that period were neither as numerous, as businesslike, nor as active as they are today. Colleges and secondary schools had not taken up the drama as an educational project, community theatres were unknown, and home-talent performances were sporadic, sociable affairs devoted to the presentation of operettas, minstrel shows, rural character sketches, specialty dance numbers, and, where the group possessed literary interests, famous plays of the past—Shakespeare, Goldsmith, Sheridan, and the like. If a short play was required there was always a professional curtain raiser available—usually one by J. M. Morton, the prolific British author of *Box and Cox*.

As in the case of full-length plays, the American stage before 1900 depended for its short plays chiefly upon Europe. There were, however, several American authors who composed in the one-act form—Bronson Howard, for example, whose *Old Love Letters* was produced in 1878. This is the only one-act play he contributed to our theatre, but it is of some significance because Bronson Howard was the most distinguished native playwright of his period and is frequently referred to as the father of the American drama.

During the same decade Edward Harrigan, of the famous comedy team of Harrigan and Hart, composed a large number of one-act pieces for his variety shows—approximately seventy-five of them between the years 1870 and 1879. These hastily written, low-comedy sketches are not, of course, in the same tradition as the literary one-act, but they belong in our general survey, and they are important as precursors of our modern revue sketches.

The professional playwright of the nineteenth century who contributed the greatest number of one-act plays to the professional legitimate theatre was Augustus Thomas. Beginning with *Editha's Burglar* in 1883, Thomas produced twelve short plays by 1898, all of which were performed on the professional stage and several of them with distinct success. He injected into these pieces the same skill at characterization and plot which marked his full-length productions, and although they have not survived as specimens of literature, they nevertheless were creditable dramatic compositions and helped to establish the American one-act play in our theatre.

Contemporary with Thomas was Clyde Fitch, whose artistic and financial success as a professional playwright set a new standard in the American theatre. And although Fitch did not make extensive use of the one-act form, he did compose three short plays, all of which were successfully produced. First, and best, was *Frédérick Lemaître* (1890); the others were *Betty's Finish* (1890) and *The Harvest* (1893).

Of that period, however, the American author who rendered the greatest service to the one-act play was William Dean Howells. Howells was not primarily a playwright. He was a magazine editor, essayist, novelist, *and* playwright. Although he composed several full-length plays (chief among them being *The American Claimant,* done in collaboration with Mark Twain), the bulk of his dramatic writing was in the shorter form. This predilection is explained partly by the fact that one-act plays are suitable for magazine publication, and Howells found that his readers enjoyed them immensely. It is therefore understandable that between 1876 (the publication date of *The Parlor Car*) and 1916 (*The Night before Christmas* and *Self-Sacrifice*) he composed twenty-five short plays, including such well-remembered favorites as *The Mouse Trap, Five O'Clock Tea, A Likely Story, The Albany Depot, Evening Dress, The Smoking Car,* and *The Garroters.*

It was Howells who introduced the literary note into the American one-act play. Written particularly for cultivated readers of *The Atlantic Monthly* and *Harper's Magazine,* his plays possessed a grace of expression and a refined humor which set them apart from the rough-and-ready pieces written directly for the theatre. And yet they were not by any means impractical when transferred to the stage. Several of them became favorites on the amateur stage. Two of them, *The Garroters* and *The Mouse Trap,* were played professionally in London, where they attracted considerable attention, and were hailed by critics (one of whom was George Bernard Shaw) as a welcome change from the typical curtain raisers of J. M. Morton and other British *farceurs.*

At least two other eminent literary men of the period were impelled to try the one-act form—both, no doubt, influenced by Howells. These were Brander Matthews and John Kendrick Bangs. Matthews, professor of dramatic literature, critic, and historian, was, like Howells, only occasionally a playwright, but alongside his half-dozen full-length plays are to be found four one-act pieces: *This Picture and That* (1887), *In the Vestibule Limited* (1892), *The Decision of the Court* (1893) and *Too Much Smith* (1902). Bangs was one of the most popular humorists of the period and was the author of many successful stories and sketches. He also served as editor of several magazines, one of which was *Harper's Weekly*. Like Howells, he wrote literary farces suitable for publication but at the same time suitable for the stage, and between 1896 and 1909 ten of these were published, the most popular being *The Bicyclers* and *A Proposal under Difficulties*.

We may therefore think of the period from 1870 to 1900 as the era during which the American one-act play was created and established. The next decade (the first of this century) did not witness any great development of the form, although several new playwrights contributed to it. One reason for the lack of notable development was the passing of the curtain raiser from standard usage. The use of short plays as vaudeville acts was the only effective stimulus toward their creation.

Typical of professional playwrights who wrote short plays for the theatre of that decade was William Gillette, revered actor and author of *Sherlock Holmes, Secret Service*, and other famous melodramas. Gillette wrote five short plays, all of which were performed professionally: *The Painful Predicament of Sherlock Holmes* (1905), *The Red Owl* (1907), *Ticey* (1908), *The Robber* (1909), and *Among Thieves* (1909). Another writer, though only secondarily a dramatist, of this period was Richard Harding Davis. He composed six short plays, the best-known of which is *Miss Civilization* (1906), a melodramatic comedy which illustrates very well indeed its author's emphasis on human interest and story value. Rachel Crothers, a highly successful playwright today, had her first professional production in 1902 with a one-act play, *The Rector*, but moved quickly on to full-length productions, pausing in 1909 for two short plays, *Katy Did* and *Mrs. Molly*, which were published in *The Smart Set*. A considerable number of competent playwrights rose to fame in the American theatre between 1900 and 1910 (George Broadhurst, George M. Cohan, James Forbes, Charles Klein, William Vaughn Moody, Edwin Milton Royle, Edward Sheldon, Winchell Smith, Eugene Walter) but one searches the records of their work in vain for one-act plays. The form was neither popular nor important.

The year 1911 marks the change. In that year and in the years immediately following, events transpired which brought the one-act play into extraordinary prominence.

In that year the Irish Players from the Abbey Theatre of Dublin brought their plays on tour to America, and with the captivating short pieces of Synge, Yeats, and Lady Gregory they fired a great many Americans with the desire to establish artistic repertory companies and to create folk plays of American life. The Drama League of America (which had been organized in 1910 at Evanston, Illinois, as a development of women's club activities) took on immediate life and began to establish chapters throughout the country, many of them dedicated to the writing and acting of plays. The Wisconsin Players were founded (1911) at Madison, with Thomas H. Dickinson of the University of Wisconsin as guiding spirit; Mrs. Lyman W. Gale founded the Toy Theatre in Boston (1912); Maurice Browne and Ellen Van Volkenburg founded the Chicago Little Theatre

(1912); Professor George Pierce Baker of Harvard University established his famous 47 Workshop Theatre (1912); in short, the Little Theatre movement was launched. And with it, inevitably, toward a place in the sun, rode the one-act play.

Some of the specific results of these pioneer organizations were as follows:

The Drama League of America took over the publication of *The Drama*, a quarterly magazine (founded in 1911) and through it promoted literary drama, both foreign and native. Considerable emphasis was laid on the one-act play, and both translations and original plays were regularly published. In 1919 the magazine was changed to a monthly, and from that date until its suspension in 1931 it was customary to publish at least one short play in each issue. Many of these plays, chosen with a view to their amateur usefulness, found their way into the repertoire of producing groups throughout the country. In addition to its publishing activities the Drama League promoted lectures, exhibits, and national conferences, all designed to further the amateur theatre movement. Eventually the work of this pioneer organization was taken over by other agencies, chiefly educational, but its influence during two decades was considerable, and the development of the one-act play owes a great deal to its sponsorship.

The Wisconsin Players, with one producing group at Madison and another at Milwaukee, stimulated the creation of many excellent short plays, several of which were published under the title *Wisconsin Plays*, the first volume appearing in 1914 and the second in 1918. The first volume was distinguished by the inclusion of Zona Gale's *The Neighbors*, which immediately became and still is a stand-by of amateur groups—one of the most popular short plays in the English language.

The work of the Chicago Little Theatre is well-known to all students of the modern American theatre. For five years after its founding it continued under the inspiring direction of Maurice Browne and Ellen Van Volkenburg, emphasizing the short play and particularly the poetic short play. Much of its repertoire was drawn from English and Irish sources, for Mr. Browne, an Englishman, had come straight from the Little Theatres of Great Britain; but native playwrights were encouraged, and it was in this theatre that Alice Brown's immensely success-ful comedy, *Joint Owners in Spain*, had its première. After their Chicago venture Mr. Browne moved westward to Seattle, where at the Cornish Theatre he continued his career as a Little Theatre enthusiast, consistently promot-ing the artistic short play.

The story of Professor Baker's 47 Workshop Theatre is also an oft-told tale. But in chronicling the development of the short play in this country it is necessary that we re-mind ourselves of the part Professor Baker played in that development. Not only was his course, from its establish-ment in 1912 until his retirement in 1933 .(though it was moved from Harvard to Yale in 1925) the most effective play laboratory in the country, but it was also the progeni-tor of many other college courses with similar aims. In ad-dition, therefore, to the hundreds of short plays written directly for Professor Baker by the many students who flocked to him from all corners of the United States, we must add the thousands which have been written for other college instructors, most of whom would not be offering such courses had it not been for the example set at Harvard.

Four volumes of one-act plays were published under the title *Plays of the 47 Workshop* (1918, 1920, 1922, 1925) and two volumes under the title *Harvard Dramatic Club Plays* (1918, 1919). They included such favorites as *The Florist Shop* by Winifred Hawkridge; *Three Pills in a Bottle* by Rachel Field; *Two Crooks and a Lady* by Eugene Pillot; and *The Good Men Do* by Hubert Osborne. To read a list of Baker students in playwriting is almost to read a list of successful contemporary playwrights. Some of them did not tarry long in the field of the one-act play; others, such as Eugene O'Neill, served a considerable apprenticeship.

Among the colleges which followed Harvard in the creation of dramatic laboratories and which have promoted the writing of short plays as well as long, are: the Carnegie Institute of Technology at Pittsburgh, whose laboratory theatre was founded in 1914 under the direction of Thomas Wood Stevens, himself the author of several excellent one-act plays; the University of North Dakota, where the Dakota Playmakers were organized in 1914 by Professor Frederick H. Koch, a group which was among the first to strive consciously toward an American folk drama; Cornell University, where Professor A. M. Drummond has for many years directed the writing and production of interesting short plays, ten of which have been published under the title *Cornell University Plays;* the University of North Carolina, where since 1918 the Carolina Playmakers, under the direction of Professor Koch, have earned an international reputation as creators and interpreters of folk drama, with four volumes of plays in print and a Pulitzer Prize winner, Paul Green, as a notable member; Yale University, with a curriculum formed by Professor Baker in 1925 and carried on since his retirement by Professor Allardyce Nicoll, assisted by Walter Prichard Eaton and others, with a theatre devoted to the production of original plays and with two volumes of *Yale One-Act Plays* in print; the University of Washington at Seattle, where the present writer has offered a course in playwriting since 1920, and where three volumes of short plays have been published under the title *University of Washington Plays;* the University of Iowa; Northwestern University; the University of Utah; and dozens of other institutions of which detailed mention is here impossible.

Connected with the university dramatic movement but inspired also from other sources was the creation in 1914 and 1915 of two experimental theatres whose history provides the most exciting chapter in the narrative of the American one-act play. These theatres came into being as a result of the organization of two producing groups, the Washington Square Players and the Provincetown Players.

The Washington Square Players, whose first production was made during the autumn of 1914 on an improvised stage in the rear portion of a store in Washington Square, New York City, with Robert Edmond Jones as designer, dedicated itself to the performance of European and American short plays. Its activities attracted writers as well as actors, and presently it moved into the Bandbox Theatre, where for two seasons it continued its original policy. In 1919 its leading spirits formed the now famous and powerful Theatre Guild. Among other plays on its early programs are found *The Clod* by Lewis Beach; *The Last*

Straw by Bosworth Crocker; *Helena's Husband* by Philip Moeller; *The Shepherd in the Distance* by Holland Hudson; *Overtones* by Alice Gerstenberg; and *Another Way Out* by Lawrence Langner. These names and these titles suggest the dramatic talent which the group embraced. The fact that the playwrights of the Washington Square Players so quickly forswore the short play for the long, the informal production for the pretentious, indicates merely how swiftly their abilities were recognized. This group offers but one of many examples of a general rule in the American theatre: namely, that the Little Theatre is but a steppingstone to the large theatre—the short play but a preliminary to the long. In certain parts of Europe this rule does not obtain, but in America it regrettably does.

The Provincetown Players were a tougher breed. Organized informally at Provincetown, Massachusetts, during the summer of 1915, where they gave their first performance in a disused fishhouse at the end of a wharf, they adopted as their ideal the presentation of original American plays, particularly short plays. They emphasized the element of originality, and they clung during their corporate existence to the concept of the experimental. After two summers in Provincetown they opened a playhouse in the Greenwich Village quarter of New York City (first in a remodeled dwelling, later in more ample quarters) where they gave regular performances until December, 1929, when they succumbed to the financial crash. During the fifteen seasons of their existence they stimulated the creation of an extremely large number of good one-act plays. Many of these plays were published and became popular with amateur groups throughout the country; some of them are contemporary classics. For example, these authors

and these titles: Eugene O'Neill: *Bound East for Cardiff,
'Ile, Before Breakfast, The Long Voyage Home, In the
Zone, Where the Cross Is Made, The Moon of the Caribbees;* Floyd Dell: *Sweet and Twenty, King Arthur's
Socks;* Edna St. Vincent Millay: *Aria da Capo, Two Slatterns and a King;* Alfred Kreymborg: *Lima Beans, Manikin and Minikin;* Susan Glaspell: *Trifles;* Susan Glaspell
and George Cram Cook: *Suppressed Desires, Tickless
Time;* and a host of less famous titles by Harry Kemp,
Djuna Barnes, Michael Gold, Neith Boyce, Theodore
Dreiser, John Reed, Wilbur Daniel Steele, Hutchins Hap-
good, Rita Wellman, Bosworth Crocker, Lewis Beach,
and Lawrence Langner.

O'Neill was, of course, the great discovery of the Provincetown group, and a considerable portion of their fame
is due to his subsequent fame. But even without O'Neill
the group would have more than justified its existence.
Not only did it enrich our dramatic literature by the creation of a score of short dramatic masterpieces, but it also
furnished us with the best proof to date that a theatre
can operate in America with short plays as its principal
offering.

Had there been more theatres like the Provincetown,
with a firm faith in the artistic validity of the one-act play,
more playwrights of talent would have essayed this form.
But the Provincetown was in a class by itself, and most professional playwrights saw no good reason for writing short
plays for mushroom theatres with amateurish standards.
There were, however, two notable exceptions: George
Middleton and Percival Wilde. Both these writers adopted
a serious professional attitude toward the short play.
George Middleton, an excellent craftsman, was a real pio-

neer in the Little Theatre movement and brought forth
his first volume of short plays in 1911 (*Embers and Other
One-Act Plays*). This was followed by other collections in
1913, 1915, and 1920. But shortly after the appearance of
the 1920 volume he grew discouraged with the prospect
and abandoned short plays for long. Percival Wilde, on
the other hand, with his first collection of one-acters published in 1915 (*Dawn and Other One-Act Plays*) has continued for more than twenty years to supply the Little
Theatres of America with effective short plays. Nine volumes of these have been published, and many of the individual plays have appeared in anthologies. Wilde is probably the most successful as well as the most consistent
American writer in this field. When Margaret Mayorga
edited in 1937 a revised edition of her anthology, *Representative One-Act Plays by American Authors*, and included Wilde's play, *Pawns*, the author wrote to her as follows: "It may interest you to know that your 1919 anthology was the first volume of the kind in which I was included. Your new one will be the fiftieth."

Wilde's work could not have been included in an earlier
anthology of one-act plays because Miss Mayorga's 1919
collection was the first in the field. An astonishing fact to
many of us. And all the more astonishing when we consider how many similar collections are now available. As a
matter of curiosity the present writer paused long enough
to count the anthologies of short plays on the shelves of
the Division of Drama Library at the University of Washington, and found one hundred and two. This collection is
not complete, but it represents most of the anthologies published in English since 1919. Not many of the volumes are
restricted to American plays, but the majority of them con-

tain American plays. And these volumes are of course distinct from the collected one-act plays of individual authors, which are fairly numerous.

If we examine the product of professional American playwrights during the past twenty-five years we find, as we have indicated before, that many of them have written no short plays and that nearly all the others have employed this form infrequently. A quick survey of the records gives us, however, the following one-act plays:

George Ade: *The Mayor and the Manicure* and three other titles; Zoë Akins: *The Magical City* and *Such a Charming Young Man;* E. P. Conkle: *Minnie Fields, Sparkin', 'Lection,* and a dozen more titles; William C. de Mille: *Food,* and *In 1999;* Beulah Marie Dix: *Allison's Lad, Across the Border,* and ten other titles; Martin Flavin: *Brains* and five other titles; Kenneth Sawyer Goodman: *Dust of the Road* and a dozen more titles, in addition to *Ryland* and *Holbein in Blackfriars* written in collaboration with Thomas Wood Stevens and *The Wonder Hat* and *The Hero of Santa Maria* written in collaboration with Ben Hecht; Rupert Hughes: *The Ambush* and *On the Razor Edge;* George S. Kaufman: *The Still Alarm* and *If Men Played Cards As Women Do;* George Kelly: *Finders-Keepers* and four other titles; Clare Kummer: *So's Your Old Antique* and five other titles; Elizabeth McFadden: *Why the Chimes Rang* and five other titles; Percy MacKaye: *Napoleon Crossing the Rockies, Sam Average,* and ten other titles; Kenyon Nicholson: *Bedside Manners, Meet the Missus, The Marriage of Little Eva,* and sixteen other titles; Clifford Odets: *Waiting for Lefty* and *Till the Day I Die;* Elmer Rice: *The Passing of Chow-Chow* and *A Diadem of Snow;* Lynn Riggs: *Reck-*

less and *Knives from Syria;* Austin Strong: *The Drums of Oude* and (with Lloyd Osbourne) *Little Father of the Wilderness;* Booth Tarkington: *Beauty and the Jacobin, The Ghost Story,* and six other titles; Dan Totheroh: *A Tune of a Tune* and ten other titles.

The above list excludes, of course, those professional playwrights whose work has been mentioned earlier in this chapter, such as Eugene O'Neill, Paul Green, and others who were connected with early Little Theatre or university groups.

During this same quarter century there have been many American writers who, though not professional playwrights, have nevertheless contributed effectively to our one-act play literature. A comprehensive list of such writers would extend beyond our present limitations of space, and we must therefore content ourselves with a mention of but a few. Some of them are novelists, others are teachers, publishers, and what not. They are all familiar names in the one-act field:

Colin Clements: *Pierrot in Paris* and twenty-six other titles, as well as *All on a Summer's Day* and sixteen other titles written in collaboration with Florence Ryerson; Sada Cowan: *Pomp, Sintram of Skaggerak,* and eight other titles; Theodore Dreiser: *Laughing Gas* and six other titles; John Farrar: *The Wedding Rehearsal* and three other titles, in addition to a collection of plays for children; Oscar W. Firkins: *Two Passengers for Chelsea* and twenty other titles; Carl Glick: *The Fourth Mrs. Phillips* and six other titles; Doris Halman: *Will o' the Wisp* and eleven other titles; Phoebe Hoffman: *Martha's Mourning* and ten other titles; Babette Hughes: *One Egg, Mrs. Harper's Bazaar,* and fifteen other titles; Charles O'Brien

Kennedy: *And There Was Light* and ten other titles; Constance D'Arcy Mackay: *The Beau of Bath* and twenty-five other titles; Mary Macmillan: *A Fan and Two Candlesticks* and twenty-five other titles; Jeannette Marks: *The Merry Merry Cuckoo* and six other titles; Christopher Morley: *Thursday Evening* and eight other titles; David Pinski: *A Dollar* and eighteen other titles; J. W. Rogers, Jr.: *Judge Lynch* and seven other titles; Ridgely Torrence: *The Rider of Dreams* and three other titles; Stuart Walker: *Six Who Pass While the Lentils Boil* and eight other titles; Stark Young: *The Twilight Saint* and six other titles.

The number of one-act plays now being written in the United States is enormous. The number published annually is about two hundred. And because most of the published plays are by nonprofessional playwrights, the standard of originality and workmanship is not very high. The basic reason for the low standard, however, is, as has been indicated above, that there is scarcely any professional use made of one-act plays in this country. The Little Theatre either dies or becomes a large theatre; community and college theatres start with the short play but graduate quickly to the full-length. The only consistent consumers of short plays are the high schools and social or professional clubs. It is obvious, therefore, that when a one-act play is destined to be used by the least skilled amateur groups, no rigid standard of excellence will be maintained by the playwrights. The huge number of such groups creates a considerable market, but that market is served with quantity rather than quality. Even the possibility of large royalties does not tempt the typical professional playwright to compose one-act plays for high school use. One might suppose that a potential thousand performances at five or ten dollars for each performance would tempt a good many of our Broadway craftsmen—particularly in these days of a shrunken Broadway. But either through oversight or choice the professionals ignore the short play.

Occasionally an American returned from Europe dreams of a professional one-act theatre in New York or Los Angeles, but either his dream dies a-borning or else it is shattered by the indifferent public. In Paris there is a tradition for this type of theatre; in this country there is not. And it required the dazzling virtuosity of Noel Coward to sell a bill of one-act plays to Broadway. At the moment there is considerable talk of the commercial possibilities of the form, but it seems unlikely that many writers or producers will actually attempt to follow in Mr. Coward's footsteps. Meanwhile it is interesting to hear reasonably well-educated persons imply that Noel Coward invented the one-act play.

. . . .

The American one-act play, like the American long play, represents a steady striving toward individuality and native character. It seems to most of us that considerable progress in this direction has been achieved. And yet it is difficult to define the American quality, particularly in the matter of style. For a great many years critics have accused our playwrights of being slaves to foreign models. Occasionally they have hailed someone as a liberator, and have rejoiced in the literary independence which they perceived on the horizon. But even in these instances it has been possible to discern in the author's work distinct influences of European literature. The American playwright who has called forth the greatest burst of patriotic enthusiasm is

Eugene O'Neill, and yet O'Neill leans heavily on Strindberg and on the Greeks. What is more, it is possible to contend that O'Neill's psychology does not conform to the typical American psychology. His subject matter is usually American, his bluntness may be called American, but like most playwrights, he is compounded of European inheritances and influences.

More than any other country, the United States is a mixture of racial stocks and cultural traditions. It has achieved some unity of thought and feeling but scarcely enough to bring forth a great body of characteristic literature. Our life is tremendously diversified, with the consequence that those of our playwrights who have yearned toward a truthful expression of American life have been forced into regionalism. Paul Green has interpreted the whites and blacks of North Carolina; Lynn Riggs has captured the lusty life of Oklahoma; Clifford Odets has excelled in depicting certain characters and aspects of existence in New York City; E. P. Conkle has drawn his themes from Nebraska town and farm. The work of each of these playwrights (as well as the work of many others) may be called, and truthfully, American, yet such a term is too general—it must be qualified by the regional designation. And their strong regionalism—that quality which gives them strength and reality—interferes with their general popularity.

There are one-act plays by Americans which seem to possess a general American quality and which achieve popularity in all sections of the country, but these are apt to be considered superficial. Such plays attempt to exhibit national rather than local psychology and to present characters which are the embodiment of this psychology: the harassed but good-natured business-man, the energetic, culture-seeking clubwoman, the spoiled and thoughtless but still admirable young son, the recklessly independent but fundamentally lovable girl—in other words, types of Americans that are to be found in all regions of the country and represent a kind of composite of Americanism. Booth Tarkington, Christopher Morley, Zona Gale, and many other writers have created effective plays from this material. Optimism, courage, honesty, and unpretentiousness are the human qualities involved, and it is these qualities which most Americans like to believe are the national characteristics. Short plays by O'Neill and Green are widely read and studied, but plays by Tarkington and Morley are widely performed. The former group, because of their probing power, are admired as literature; the latter are enjoyed as theatrical entertainment.

Although American one-act plays written before 1911 were few and limited as to types, since 1911 they have run the gamut of style and content. The rise of the Little Theatres, inspired by European examples, brought every kind of one-act play before American audiences. The Irish folk play, the Strindbergian psychological melodrama, the Maeterlinckian mystical fantasy, the French shocker as well as the French drawing-room farce, the Russian peasant farce, the Viennese comedy of sophistication, the whimsical English comedy, these and other types of play were given their American hearing. All of them were imitated— few of them were approved. Gradually it became apparent that although there are audiences in this country for every sort of play, there are not very large audiences for many sorts. Generally speaking, American audiences do not enjoy poetic fantasy, gruesome melodrama, or cynical comedy. They admire poetic tragedy, they will accept ingenious farce, but they enjoy realistic comedy. One hesitates to set down these generalizations because it is obvious that there are so many exceptions, but the present writer's observations over a period of twenty-odd years lead him to the above conclusions. And it seems no disparagement of the American people to accept these conclusions. They may not indicate a superior artistic perception, but they do point to a healthy mental condition.

It is a far cry from the gentility of William Dean Howells to the raciness of George S. Kaufman, but in the plays of each we have examples of American humor. The tempo and the idiom have changed, the healthy good-naturedness has not. But whereas Howells stood almost alone as a writer of short farces and comedies, Kaufman is but one of many, in kind if not in quality.

In recent years there has been a tendency to praise that play which is based on what appears to be a "significant" theme and to cry down the play which professes only to entertain or which has to do with unchanging aspects of human nature. This tendency has led at times to an admiration for propaganda at the expense of other values; for timeliness at the expense of eternal verity. This is a tendency which has been felt in periods other than our own, and one which occurs with inevitable frequency. It affects the short play as well as the long, and it has resulted lately in the composition of many pieces dealing with the conflict between capital and labor, with war, and with racial conflict.

America has written its share of "significant" short plays, and while some of them have combined art with enthusiasm, a great many have been content to appeal to prejudice rather than to reason or artistic sensibility. Generally speaking, plays of the latter category have found their audiences among those sections of the public which were already in sympathy with the propaganda of the play.

Plays on controversial themes, whether short plays or long, professional or amateur, seldom achieve wide popularity in this country, but short plays do so even less frequently than long plays, for the reason that the production of short plays is chiefly in the hands of groups associated with the public schools, of church groups, or of social and literary societies. Such auspices are inclined toward conservatism or at least toward an avoidance of inflammatory material. The propaganda play is, in consequence, left in the hands of the propagandists.

The inclination of American audiences to resent propaganda in the theatre is irritating to those whose special interests lead them to employ the theatre as a propagandist agency, but it is a strongly rooted tradition among us to enjoy ourselves rather than disturb ourselves in the theatre. To the average American a play is fun, not worry; it is a "show," not a political or social or religious document. And although from a radical point of view this attitude is objectionably smug, lethargic, and cowardly, it is from a conservative point of view eminently defensible. To the conservative the theatre represents not so much an escape from life as an escape from the irritating aspects of life. It represents harmony and tolerant good nature. It is, from this standpoint, an essentially democratic institution, serving all the people and acting as a common denominator. This fact must be borne in mind when one attempts to evaluate the many one-act plays which lack distinction but which nevertheless enjoy an extraordinary popularity.

THE ONE-ACT PLAY IN ENGLAND

JOHN BOURNE is editor of the highly successful English publication *Amateur Theatre and Playwrights' Journal*, which is considered the official organ of the Little Theatre movement in Great Britain. He has edited over ten collections of one-act plays and has adjudicated all over Great Britain on over five thousand dramatic societies most of which have presented one-act plays. Mr. Bourne is the author of seven one-act plays, one of which had a better run in the festivals during the last seven years than any other play.

THE ONE-ACT PLAY IN ENGLAND

by John Bourne

SINCE the development of the one-act play in Great Britain is inseparably bound up with the growth of the amateur drama movement in postwar years, it is necessary to begin by considering how that movement stands today. It is impossible, in an activity so essentially anarchic, to illustrate its energy by the statistical method. Guesses as to the extent of its hold vary according to the temperament and practical knowledge of the authority of the moment. Some short time ago, for instance, there appeared in one national newspaper the information that "probably 100,000 persons in this country today get a good deal of fun out of the amateur theatre," while, on the same day, a more enthusiastic contemporary declared to its million and a half readers that "the amateur dramatic cast in this country is about 1,000,000 players strong."

Whatever the number of people in some way or another actively engaged in amateur drama, there are certain reliable methods of estimating the amazing growth of the movement in postwar years. It is not disputed that there must be between twenty and thirty thousand amateur societies in this country. It is also certain that the majority give part of their attention each year to the production of one-act plays. For instance, during 1937-38, at least three hundred new one-act plays were printed—most of them in separate acting editions—entirely for the amateur market. Entries in the annual national festival of one-act plays organized by the British Drama League and a similar festival for Scotland run by the Scottish Community Drama Association together numbered about a thousand. Entries in various locally organized one-act play festivals must have numbered at least as many. Collections of one-act plays still seem to be a profitable enterprise for the publishers who care to take their pickings in an apparently inexhaustible market. On the surface, the one-act play is in an extremely healthy condition. There exists a blessed state of steady demand and plenteous supply: a state, I might add, which is a fruitful text for after-dinner speakers and similar optimists who are always with us in the boom years when there seems no reason why the boom should not be everlasting. For the one-act play *is* booming in this country. And if I give it as my opinion that the peak of the boom has already passed and that (as is the nature of booms) it is due for a decline, it is not because I am antagonistic to the one-act play. On the contrary, as one who has played a small part in the birth and development of the postwar amateur movement—which is also the story of the re-development of the short play—I know that (as Mr. Ivor Brown recently put it) "the present and future of the one-act play is with the amateurs." But I confess to a feeling that the place of the one-act play in the amateur movement of this country is insecure; that it is in danger of being considered merely as a technical exercise; that present attitudes to it tend to turn it into nothing but a chrysallis-stage struggle towards the greater glory of producing three-act plays released from the professional theatre.

The professional theatre in England has never concerned itself seriously with the short play, and one looks in vain for a revival of professional interest in it. A year or two ago, it is true, Noel Coward presented nine one-act plays for a brilliant season in this country. But what attracted at the box office was not the audacity of presenting three forty-minute plays instead of one play of three forty-minute acts, but the glamour of the season's bright particular stars—Gertrude Lawrence and Noel Coward. Apart from this one fugitive appearance, an even more fleeting glimpse of a Thornton Wilder short play as curtain raiser to a recent revival of Shaw's *Candida*, and the occasional presentation of short plays by a very few provincial managers (notably Mr. William Armstrong, of the Liverpool Playhouse), the professional theatre has remained as oblivious as ever to the appeal of the one-act play. All the tremendous activity of the past fifteen years among amateur players has failed to convince the professionals that the one-act play has claim to equal consideration with the three-act play. I do not imply that the professional managers are right to ignore it. I state the fact, and shall draw a conclusion from it later. It is true, however, that English audiences in the professional and amateur theatre prefer a long play to a triple bill.

I have stated that the professionals never concerned themselves seriously with the one-act play. But a brief word on the use they have made of it is necessary, since from these somewhat arid roots the postwar amateur movement has sprung.

No need, I think, in a brief essay to recapitulate the

history of the short play from the earliest moralities, interludes, and farces of medieval times. If I refer to the
Pyramus and Thisbe interlude in *A Midsummer Night's
Dream* ("Is there no play to ease the anguish of a tortur-
ing hour?" said Theseus, thereupon establishing the status
of the short play from that day almost to this) or to the
appearance of the Players in *Hamlet* it is enough to indicate that the short play has a respectably ancient, if somewhat misty, ancestry. As an interlude it persists throughout theatrical history: something to ease an idle half-hour,
a relaxation taken in the middle of the gargantuan enter-
tainments that our forefathers expected when they took
their seats in the gallery.

Close enough to our own time, about the days when
Sir Henry Irving was making his first appearances in
London, these hardy playgoers could sit through an hors
d'œuvres of a solo or two, pass on refreshed to a short
play (generally full of body and rank of bouquet), settle
down to the main item of the evening, a full-length play,
and top off the banquet with a lavish ballet. A moneyed
middle class then becomes more stabilized. Its necessary
social habits are made conventions. It looks for entertainment only when the essential business of making money
and feeding itself has been accomplished—and the theatre
adapts itself to changing conditions. By the end of the
nineteenth century the infinite variety of a night at the
theatre has given way to a program consisting of a short
play and the main piece of the evening. The "curtain
raiser" has made its appearance. No nonsense is talked
about art or problems of technique. For the benefit of
those playgoers who want full value for their money, a
short play is provided as appetizer for the longer dish of

the evening. Those who wish to eat their dinners in comfort know that they may wander into a theatre whose business has already started without missing anything of great consequence. "Curtain raiser." The very name is eloquent of an attitude of toleration and contempt. And for the professional, that attitude largely remains.

Nonetheless, famous playwrights did on occasion turn their hands to the short play as curtain raiser. Pick up a bundle of current newspaper cuttings, and it is more than likely that you will find record of a performance of Barrie's *The Twelve Pound Look*, Shaw's *How He Lied to Her Husband*, or Pinero's *Playgoers*. These, and others like them, survive because they are examples of technical excellence in the one-act play form. For the most part, the curtain raisers of this period were plays of situation. What happens when the servants are invited into the drawing room; the dire fate that awaits burglars who hide in safes; the perils run by ardent gentlemen who make love to other men's wives in the other men's studies—and so forth. The plays were not intended to do more than give the house its preliminary warming-up; therefore, a strong plot was all that was needed, and no problem of one-act play construction was tackled other than that of exposing, developing, and completing a situation within the space of some thirty or forty minutes. In the hands of the best of these playwrights, of course, the curtain raiser became technically perfect. On the postwar playwrights who turned to writing plays for the amateur market, these short pieces had an influence of the first importance. They survived, be it added, until before the war —then disappeared from the professional stage.

But there is also another strong link between the modern writer of one-act plays and the nineteenth century theatre. This is to be traced through that peculiarly English institution, the Music Hall.

Here we are much closer to the crude "humours" of the medieval players: and I should hazard an opinion that whereas the late-Victorian curtain raiser has largely determined the technique of today, it is the music-hall sketch which has most influenced the spirit of the short play. This is not a conclusion that the arty and crafty take kindly to, but the fact remains that for one experimental or expressionistic effort staged in this country today, twenty broad farces or comedies are given.

In the prewar music hall there was always place for the short sketch. (There still is, for that matter, though present-day fashions are all for the anemic bit of dialogue leading up to what is euphemistically described as a "snap ending.") Sometimes it was the strong play of situation— I instance here the famous W. W. Jacobs piece *The Monkey's Paw*—but more often it was a mere framework for a display of individual virtuosity in the arts of throwing custard pies, of falling down ladders, of impersonating the fruity idiosyncrasies of Cockney charladies, or of relating the trials and tribulations that beset the man who has a mother-in-law. (England's oldest joke—and still good for a laugh. We are a conservative nation.) The best of these plays, too, survive—such as *A Sister to Assist 'Er* —and they survive because they are, in a crude form, interested in the quirks and oddities of character. In the music hall the devotee paid his money to see a display of personality. He wanted his personalities thrown at him in the broadest and most unsubtle colors. Therefore, the sketch was built around the characteristics of the individual star, and plot was of secondary importance.

The classification of these two sources are somewhat rough and ready. But the main implication is true: that the postwar playwrights had at their hands the right material for development. The curtain raiser had achieved much in overcoming the technical problems of the short play; the music-hall sketch was continuing to present the characteristic "humours," which are much the same in modern English slapstick as they were when Snug the joiner made a mess of his appearance as the Lion. A reference might also be added to the successful introduction in this country in the early 1920's of *Grand Guignol*, which had valuable technical lessons to teach.

In addition, there were scattered attempts to use the short play form for more than merely ephemeral purposes. There was some recognition that the one-act play was as capable of serious literary treatment as the short story—notably among the Irish playwrights encouraged by that remarkable woman, Lady Gregory. Four famous one-act plays by Irish writers will suffice to demonstrate the vitality of their work: Lady Gregory's *The Rising of the Moon*, W. B. Yeats's *Deirdre*, Lord Dunsany's *The Golden Doom*, and, of course, Synge's *Riders to the Sea*. Of the last mentioned, it is sufficient to say that no one-act play has yet been written to equal it for technical brilliance and universality of its tragedy and that its influence on postwar playwrights has been incalculable—if only because it showed them what could be achieved within the limits of the short play by a writer of genius.

It is essential, when examining the extremely rapid growth of interest in the one-act play among amateur players, to remember that it was the sudden postwar creation of numerous amateur societies clamoring for short pieces on which to try their skill that produced the one-act playwrights. There was no "school" of playwrights who set out to show the world that the one-act play was worthy of more dignified treatment than it had received hitherto. There arose no master of the one-act play form who inspired others to follow his example or forced amateur companies to present his work. The distinction is worth emphasizing, for it means that the majority of the one-act plays that have been written during the past ten years are so much flapdoodle turned out to meet a current need. The situation bears some similarity to that caused when incautious speculators get wind of a rumor that barren land is about to produce oil. The sharks and financial thimbleriggers step in, companies are floated, the sharks step out—and what might have proved with careful nursing to be a profitable business for all concerned is left barren before real work is begun.

It would assuredly be wrong to apply this parallel to the achievements of the amateur movement in this country as a whole. Not all the one-act playwrights are opportunists, nor is all their work meretricious. But the fact that the majority of playwrights have been brought out on the crest of a rising tide of demand for their wares—and not because they *must* write one-act plays or perish—is one of the reasons why, after ten to fifteen years of activity, one feels a sense of insecurity about the future.

I do not think anyone will dispute 1926 as the most important date in the history of the revival of the one-act play. In that year, the British Drama League held its first experimental festival of one-act plays.

The Drama League has a lengthy list of charter aims and objectives; but essentially it is an association composed of individual co-operators in amateur drama and affiliated amateur dramatic groups. It provides a central organization for a considerable number of amateur societies throughout the country, conducts drama schools, runs a drama library, and so forth. Its most important—at least, most publicized—activity, however, is the organization of a competitive festival run on knockout lines between affiliated groups which enter one or more one-act plays each year. The plays are seen by adjudicators, who decide, on the basis of a marking system, which are the best productions in their areas; send their selections forward to a second round in the competition which is reviewed by another set of adjudicators, who, in turn, send a selection forward to a final round held annually in a London theatre.

In the first year (1926) seven societies took part in this competition—always, by the way, named (or misnamed) a festival. The idea caught on. There were plenty of societies who were either presenting one-act plays after a fashion or who were willing to produce them with the slightest encouragement. In 1927 a hundred and fifty groups entered the competition; in 1930 the entrants numbered four hundred; by 1932 the number had reached six hundred; and the peak entry so far recorded was that of 1936 when seven hundred and forty-seven groups entered.

Boom years indeed! For the success of the British Drama League's festival inspired others to do likewise. In Scotland, a similar organization, the Scottish Community Drama Association, developed its annual knockout festival. This, begun in 1927, experienced a similarly swift rise in popularity and now attracts about three hundred and fifty entries. Indeed, the annual drama festival in Scotland is said to attract as much discussion among its fans and followers as do the chances of the football teams playing their league matches throughout the winter.

Nor is this the end. One-act play festivals are variously organized with the support of town councils who consider it profitable to advertise the excellencies of their airs and waters besides giving crowded audiences a week of one-act plays and a dash of excitement inspired by the question: Who is going to win? Local drama associations (formed voluntarily by groups of societies all over the country for mutual self-help) run their own drama weeks of one-act plays. Some festivals—running from two to nine nights—are simply got up by local residents interested in nothing but encouraging drama in their town or district. The Women's Institutes hold their own festivals, so do various rural County Committees. There are single societies who, with large membership lists capable of providing anything up to twelve casts for one-act plays, run their own annual drama festivals and invite an adjudicator to decide which team has done best. Even professional managements in the provinces have begun to organize local one-act play festivals for amateur groups. The venture is financially profitable (festivals draw the crowds)—and the event is not without significance in view of the professional actor's traditional dislike of "amateurs."

The result of this manifold festival activity (there are as yet comparatively few competitive festivals devoted to three-act plays) has therefore been to create a wide and steady demand for new one-act plays. I have already mentioned that in 1937 at least three hundred new ones were added to the large number published during the past ten years. It can therefore be definitely stated that, without the rise of the festival movement, the one-act play as we know it would not exist today. The festivals have been almost the only begetter of its new-found prosperity. This does not mean, of course, that one-act plays are performed only at festivals. There are many societies, unable to handle full-scale productions, who are in the habit of presenting triple bills. There are as many who vary the presentation of three-act plays with occasional programs of one-act plays. There is a considerable number among which the practice of presenting a curtain raiser to a three-act play has become part of theatrical routine. And among the many Women's Institute drama groups in Britain, the one-act play has proved a godsend. Handicapped by reason of small stage space, casting difficulties, and lack of rehearsal time, Women's Institutes everywhere have been released by the flood of new one-act plays from having to confine their theatrical activities to such things as the Trial Scene from *The Merchant of Venice,* an extract or two from *Twelfth Night,* and a few monologues and brief sketches that have grown bleached with the passage of time.

But in these cases, the opportunity to choose at large among a variety of one-act plays is primarily due to the festival movement. The drama festival therefore, playing as it does the highly important part of midwife to the nascent one-act play, deserves to have its credentials for the job examined. And it is here that thoughtful critics in this country begin to have their doubts.

I have already mentioned that it was the festivals that brought forth the dramatists. Now in the ideal state, the process would have been reversed. That is, a vigorous one-act drama should have come first, and a festival movement developed out of it because amateurs everywhere were already producing one-act plays. It is useless to propound the impossible. But the proposition should make clear an important point: namely, that the majority of dramatists now using the one-act play as a means of expression would just as readily turn their hands to three-act, two-act, or five-minute plays if the festivals suddenly decided to concentrate on any one particular form as from tomorrow. These playwrights write one-act plays because it is immediately profitable for them to do so, and while this makes for no restraint upon individual genius (many great artistic masterpieces in painting, music, and literature were done under compulsion and to satisfy a particular client or market), there is considerable danger in the fact that most of the output is opportunist and without any valid artistic justification.

But the more serious dangers arise from the organization of the festivals themselves. Where there is competition, there also are bound to be rules and regulations. If there is a race for a prize, it will not attract a mass of entries unless provision is made to ensure some uniformity of conditions among the competitors.

Therefore, if the playwright wishes to receive a modest return for the labor of his creation, he must in this country look to it that his play acts for no more than forty minutes. Why? Because it is a general rule in festival work that any play which runs over the forty minutes is disqualified instantly. Equally, he should see that it plays for at least twenty minutes; for if it plays for only fifteen, no competing team will present it; it would be again disqualified. He may not write a duologue, for such plays are barred from competitive festivals. He would be well advised, indeed, to include at least five or six characters if his play is to be popular; for entrant teams know very well that the adjudicator is instructed to be more sympathetic to a team with a large cast than he is to a group which puts forward three or four players only—regardless of the artistic merits of the play. Moreover, if he really wants a good return for the effort of creation, the playwright will rack his wretched brains for a plot that will include as many women as possible. If he can manage to make the entire cast one for women only, his success is assured. For good amateur women players are available in plenty; the men are much harder to find.

With all these points in mind, the playwright must next consider his setting. He has perhaps conceived of a drama set upon an alpine glacier. In the moment of his inspiration he cries: "That setting, and none other!" But a moment's reflection proves to him that his probable purchasers will refuse his play at once if he makes use of the alpine glacier —because the festivals (necessarily short of time) allow only ten minutes to each team in which to set the stage and (wishing to allow uniform conditions of entry for everyone) demand that all teams play in a curtain fit-up. Therefore, the playwright will be advised to forgo anything that complicates stage-setting problems, and he will probably set his play in the everlasting "drawing room of Mrs. So-and-So" and vary this procedure, when he is bored, by shifting his drama back into the kitchen.

Above all, he will avoid if he can any change of scene during his play. Even one curtain or one black-out is suspect, since it not only implies the danger of overrunning the time limit but puts a strain upon scene-shifters and/or the man in charge of the switchboard. Curtain up and curtain down: that is the general rule for the author of one-act plays who desires success. The episodic short play (so full of possibilities) has hardly been touched in England for this reason.

But the most serious limitation of all has still to be discussed. I refer to the marking system.

I may as well confess here and now that I have probably done more adjudicating in drama festivals than any other man in this country. Furthermore, I am the author of one of the marking systems which is widely in use among the so-called independent (as opposed to the nationally organized) festivals. I deplore the marking system on several grounds—chief of which is that it is impossible to assess the comparative merits of theatrical productions on a basis of so many marks for this and so many for that. On the other hand, given the festival system and the purpose for which it was first framed, I can make no valid objection to it.

When the festivals began on a large scale in this country, technical achievement among amateur players was at an extremely low level. Acting, production, stage management, make-up, lighting—all were, in the main, of a poor standard. It was therefore necessary first of all to raise the technical standards of the numerous amateur companies in the country. To this end the marking system was framed.

Here is one system (my own), which is much the same as those generally in use.

	Marks
Acting	45
Production	30
Stage presentation	10
Dramatic merit of play	10
Enterprise	5

It is immediately obvious that no less than eighty-five percent of the adjudicator's marks are awarded purely for technical achievement; that five percent are given for enterprise, whether it be for choice of play or for some bold stroke of imaginative interpretation or staging; and that *only ten percent* go for the excellence of the chosen play.

I shall not enter into a discussion of the marking system, which is a particularly thorny subject and one most fruitful of argument. But I should point out that it has achieved much of what it set out to do. The technical standards of amateur production have made tremendous strides under its guidance during the last decade. Moreover, it has still much work to do, as any adjudicator with painful experience among the immature societies can prove. A marking system does not perfect the technique of an almost entirely untried drama within the space of ten years.

But from the point of view of those whose first interest is in the plays that amateur societies are performing and not in the way they stage them, the marking system is gravely overweighted in favor of technique. Ten marks out of a hundred for the dramatic merit of the chosen play is so small a proportion that it does little positively to encourage new authors, nor does it offer much encouragement to societies to look for the best. Naturally enough,

the better the play the better should be the performance.
But, with the emphasis on technique, authors are in the
main content to write pieces which are virtually little more
than good test pieces that will give a team the best possible technical exercise. The author watches changing
fashions, changing tastes. He obeys every rule and regu-
lation that I have noted, with scrupulous care. He tries to
write the sort of piece which will hit the widest market—
which will appeal as much to Women's Institutes as to the
more advanced societies. He takes care not to set over-
difficult problems for producer, scene-designer, or players.
He remembers the marking system—and writes accordingly. Small wonder that many of the plays written annually are of negligible artistic quality, show no advance
whatsoever either in technique or in content on Pinero's
Playgoers, and have about as much expectation of life as
a May fly. Small wonder, too (to revert to a point I raised
earlier), that the professional theatre has yet to be persuaded to take the one-act play seriously. What have the
amateurs to show them that they have not already got?
The blunt answer is: Little or nothing.

So much for the general situation as it exists in Britain
today. And now for a few of the one-act playwrights of
note to whom the new amateur movement has given a
wider opportunity. Harold Brighouse is one of the playwrights who was writing one-act plays before amateur
acting became the universal activity it now is. Amateurs,
I fear, are inclined to regard him as a "difficult" author.
Difficult or no, he is the most consistent and most reward-
ing of the one-act playwrights who is content to use a
familiar technique and to enrich it with a discussion of
modern problems. If I quote a play like *The Boy: What*

Will He Become? it is not because it is anything like his best play, but because the title expresses admirably the quiet, nonviolent methods of its author. Brighouse excels at dialogue which provokes disturbing echoes, which rarely makes direct statement, but which hints, as it were obliquely, at the emotional currents stirred in each of his characters by the social or ethical problem he is discussing.

Sydney Box, among the most prolific of English one-act playwrights, has also been one of the most successful in recent years. He can with equal facility produce a straightforward play built to suit the Women's Institutes and a piece so obscure that it sets the adjudicator guessing! His work is always of extremely efficient craftsmanship: he is the least "untidy" of playwrights. His most important work has undoubtedly been with the experimental play. He has, for example, compressed within thirty-five minutes of playing time the story of the rise and fall of a financier (*Self-Made Man*), has given us in *Waiter* a fine example of simultaneous presentation of direct action and "thought action," and has made a highly interesting experiment in symbolism with his play about dual personality, *The Tree*. More than any other one-act playwright in this country, Box has pointed the way for future exploration of the technical possibilities of the one-act form.

Another playwright of significance is that sturdy individualist, F. Sladen-Smith. Like all individualists, he has paradoxically had considerable influence among the younger writers. Sladen-Smith is lucky in that he possesses, or rather is in control of, his own theatre group. Most of his short plays have been written for the Unknown Theatre, Manchester, and are blessedly free from the influence of current tastes elsewhere. His style is unmistakable: situations fantastic, dialogue polished and witty, ideas improbably audacious. It is typical of this author that he excels in light but telling satire of the more heavy-handed dramas of mighty situation. For he is (and has proclaimed the fact in his only novel) an unrepentant escapist. His plays spin fancies in a happy vacuum—brilliant bubbles of witty dialectic floating in a clear air. He just doesn't like his fellow-men, and cares less for their continuously clumsy though well-meaning efforts to straighten things out.

The playwright whose work has, in the past few years, been more performed than that of any other is Philip Johnson. For at least three years he has far outdistanced his rivals when a count is taken of the authors represented in the national festival. All forms appear to come alike to this author: comedy, tragedy, fantasy, and bold experiment. But he is at his best in straightforward comedy— particularly of northern types. His characterization is always clear cut, his style fluent, and his technique assured— a brilliant craftsman who has never given us a botched piece of work.

In Scotland two names stand out, and in complete contrast to one another—Gordon Bottomley and Joe Corrie. Bottomley is actually an Englishman, and lives in the north of England; but since he is President of the Scottish Community Drama Association and has made much use of the old Gaelic legends of Scotland in his verse plays, Scotland can rightly claim him as her own. He is the foremost poet dramatist in this country today and the verse drama's best propagandist. His plays are of most careful craftsmanship, and the verse of a fine musical quality which is written to be spoken: indeed, only in performance is the true quality of Bottomley's work apparent.

Corrie, on the other hand, is a dramatist of his day and age. Once a miner, his roots are firm in his own class, and he knows all its problems. Much of his work is open to criticism on technical grounds: he is weakest in dealing with passages of sentiment and does not always succeed in masking his own voice by those of his characters. But, as the only working-class playwright of note in Britain, he represents what is still an untapped source of strength for the future. For the fact is that the postwar amateur movement in this country is almost entirely middle class in origin and outlook. Working-class sentiment has, as yet, remained unvoiced. Or, if voiced at all, it has been done through the medium of sympathetic middle-class writers who know of working-class conditions only at second hand.

In Wales, few authors of note have emerged in recent years. (I speak, of course, of Welsh playwrights writing in English. Of plays in the Welsh language I know nothing.) I am inclined to rank Ronald Elwy Mitchell (now resident in America) as the best of them. Mitchell is only now beginning to receive the recognition that is his due. His one-act plays of Welsh life break no new ground technically, but do present an extraordinarily virile picture of his fellow-countrymen. He has a deep understanding of the Welsh character, creates individuals who linger in the memory, and satirizes the follies and vices of his race unmercifully! J. O. Francis, author of *The Bakehouse, Birds of a Feather,* and *The Poacher* is kinder. He knows how to touch up the humors of Welsh life so that, although we relish the inconsistencies, we enjoy the characters.

Had I the space, many other playwrights should be mentioned—particularly those who have only recently come to notice and have yet to prove themselves. It is always more exciting to try and spot the future winners than to make a note on established reputations. And the mention of six authors only gives by no manner of means a true indication of the widespread activity of short-play authorship in a country where every other amateur actor is said to have at least one unpublished manuscript in his desk. This activity still persists—even if it is beginning to show signs of slackening.

In my view, the boom years of indiscriminate one-act play acting and writing have passed. It is being realized that the festivals alone supply no real incentive for the writing of one-act plays of merit. Critics begin to feel that a festival system which is based almost entirely upon a desire to raise the standard of technique in acting and production can do little to bring out new writers with new methods and a fresh point of view, that, on the contrary, it stultifies genuine creation. We are, in fact, at a period when decisions will have to be taken by those who control the national festivals with regard to their duties to authors. If they do not, then the job of carrying the development of the one-act play a step further will be taken out of their hands.

And there are signs that this job may be undertaken. During the past year (1937-38) there has sprung into being an avowedly propagandist theatre movement which insists upon calling itself by the unwieldy title of The Left Book Club Theatre Guild. It was born out of a remarkable workers' theatre in London, the Unity Theatre, which suddenly made a reputation for itself by giving the first production in this country of Odets' *Waiting for Lefty*. Within the space of twelve months a nation-wide workers' theatre movement has been created, and in January, 1938, no less than three hundred groups, most of which had never undertaken theatrical productions before, were affiliated to the Guild.

I care not two hoots for the political slant of this or any other drama movement. But I do care deeply for the fact that here, for the first time, the working classes are being drawn in to the amateur movement and are being encouraged to create one-act plays of their own. They are not limited by festival rules—indeed, they are limited by nothing as yet but their comparative ignorance of the theatre! So far, little creative work has been achieved. *Waiting for Lefty* is the inevitable choice of the moment, and there exist only half a dozen or so native products that are worth more than a minute or two of consideration. But potentially the movement is strong. In its hands the festival movement has placed the one-act play, admitted that its own inspiration is, for the moment, exhausted, and has marked the assignment "ripe for development." Whether these three hundred groups are capable of tackling the job I cannot say. But I do state with confidence that this is their opportunity. If they fail to take it, and if the national festivals fail to recognize that they are working a vein that is perilously near exhaustion, then the one-act play created by the amateur drama movement in this country will fizzle out—an episode in theatrical history which promised much and achieved little.

THE ONE-ACT PLAY IN THE REVOLUTION-
ARY THEATRE

JOHN W. GASSNER is considered one of the most advanced American drama critics living today. He combines sociologic with esthetic criticism, and since this approach is rare in theatrical criticism and since he was associated with the militant magazine *New Theatre* as its only permanent dramatic critic, he has been sometimes referred to as a "left-wing" writer. Richard Watts, Jr., dramatic critic of the New York *Herald Tribune*, described Mr. Gassner as "the best left-wing dramatic critic in America." "As a matter of fact," Mr. Watts went on to say, "there is no reason for placing such a limit to my admiration for him, since Mr. Gassner is, in truth, one of the ablest dramatic critics in the country, without respect to social and political adherence." Mr. Gassner prefers to regard himself simply as a practising dramatic critic who has no political affiliations but entertains a healthy respect for the social forces which manifest themselves in so social an institution as the theatre.

With Burns Mantle, Mr. Gassner edited *A Treasury of the Theatre*, published in 1935. He is an instructor in the English department of Hunter College and head of the Playreading Department of the Theatre Guild. He was associated last summer with the Bread Loaf Writers Conference of Middlebury College, and has lectured widely on the theatre. He is at present reviewing the drama for *The Forum, The One Act Play Magazine*, and other publications, and is a member of the New York Drama Critics Circle.

THE ONE-ACT PLAY IN THE
REVOLUTIONARY THEATRE

by John W. Gassner

PASCAL once wrote, "I have no time for a short letter. Therefore I am writing you a long one." When the theatre does not take time to deal with essential matters and to deal with them cogently, it is content to ramble, hoping that the sum of its irrelevancies will somehow assume relevance, that many things poorly said will become one thing well said. It is then that some alert idealists, generally young and rebellious, take time to write a short letter. A one-act theatre comes into existence, ready to excise the hypertrophic tissues of the established full-length theatre. Although not all new movements begin with shorter forms—witness the birth of European realism—the Irish renaissance, the Little Theatre movement in America, and left-wing insurgency in the thirties favored the one-acter.

The history of the revolutionary theatre had many points in common with the earlier movements. It returned to the "people," it expressed the leaven of new forces in the social and political sphere, it broke with commercialism, and it attracted a new generation of theatre folk. Like the earlier movements, it produced a large body of half-realized drama and an impressive number of short master-pieces.

Again, moreover, the shorter form was not dictated solely by esthetic considerations. It is more economical to produce a one-acter than a full-length play, and new movements are notoriously short of cash. Their proponents are also short of time. They earn their living by means of some concession to Mammon, and what leisure they have is sometimes divided between art and politics or some form of social activity. The young men of the thirties earned their living as best they could in offices and factories, acted in professional companies, or wrote for the radio. Their rehearsals or wrestlings with the muse would have to give precedence also to party meetings, protest meetings, pick-etings, and other so-called "dress rehearsals" for revo-lution.

Many of the playwrights were impatient with extended and arduous writing. Art struck them as an anachronism in a world cracking in the joints and falling to pieces, a bourgeois luxury, and a sign of decadence. The theatre they held to be a weapon in the class struggle, in the war against poverty, unemployment, and class and racial op-pression. What they wanted to say had to be said simply and directly, had to be addressed to agricultural and in-dustrial workers who had rarely been inside a theatre. Subtleties of characterization and development did not seem to matter when larger issues were at stake, nor would such refinements avail much in galvanizing an audience into indignation or inculcating the principles of mass action. Many of the playwrights were, moreover, unprepared to cope with larger forms, even if they had been inclined to favor them. Their apprenticeship to the theatre had been of short duration, they were young, and some of them were primarily sociologists rather than natural-born artists.

If their selection of the shorter forms was partly dictated by the deficiencies of their talent and the limitations of their audiences, there is a difference between the halting steps of childhood and doddering old age. Childhood is a promise and a capacity for growth, and the new movement began to grow in talent, as well as in numbers. Moreover, even its inadequacies possessed a certain attractiveness, just as childhood has a charm all its own. The crude early efforts of the playwrights may have been negligible as drama, the early productions may have fallen short of the fine art of theatre, but their enthusiasm and vigor were attractive by comparison with the tired sophistication of many Broadway cream puffs. They were also indirectly useful to the theatre as a whole. A new audience was being won for the theatre, an audience that had been hitherto regaled solely by the films. This became evident when the Theatre Union began to muster a working-class audience to its support; when the principle of a low-priced theatre culminated in the Federal Theatre; when amateur organizations sponsored by the New Theatre League began to recruit an audience in the hinterland after the "road" had collapsed as a result of the depression and of competition with the motion pictures.

New writing talent was developed in the political theatre ushered in by the one-act movement—one need only list the names of Clifford Odets, Irwin Shaw, Albert Bein, Victor Wolfson, Marc Blitzstein, Paul Peters, George Sklar, Albert Maltz, and Michael Blankfort, who made their mark in the professional theatre. Older writers like Paul Green, Claire and Paul Sifton, John Howard Lawson, and John Wexley found a new place in the theatre. Not merely did they find a new theatre hospitable to their outlook, but they could only feel encouraged by the work of the novices who were exciting audiences. Other playwrights must have been brushed with the wings of the new spirit: Elmer Rice turned from profitable ventures in the general theatre to the field of social drama in which he had won his spurs; Sidney Kingsley turned to vigorous playwriting with *Dead End;* Maxwell Anderson's *Both Your Houses* and *Winterset* bowed to the time spirit which was being so insistently promoted by the young apostles; *Idiot's Delight* was a new departure for the author of *Reunion in Vienna.*

New, important producing units were either born of the movement (the Theatre Union and the Actors Repertory Company) or affected by it, as in the case of the Group Theatre and the Mercury Theatre, not to speak of the Federal Theatre and its inclination toward social drama. New dramatic forms were either created or disseminated by the ferment—the "Living Newspaper" form, the epic theatre and its variants, and the mass recitation. Even the musical revue was subjected to the new influence —in the Theatre Guild's *Parade* and Labor Stage's widely heralded *Pins and Needles.* It is incontestable that, with all its errors and blanks, the revolutionary one-act movement wrote a significant chapter in American theatre history. In fact, it is still writing it, though it seems to have passed its peak in the season of 1936-37.

II

The Worker and the Theatre

In the gilded twenties, when the Little Theatre movement ripened into the progressive professional theatre, a purely working-class theatre was almost unthinkable. A benevolent capitalism was the order of the day; organized labor, dazzled by high wages, tended to identify its interests with the capitalistic economy; and the progressives of the theatre were far more concerned with the dangers of mechanization and the vulgarities of successful business, popularly known as Babbittism, than in class conflicts. Moreover, the struggles and problems of the working class were incorporated somewhat in the so-called middle-class theatre. O'Neill described the homelessness of the proletariat in his seapieces and symbolized its rebellion in *The Hairy Ape*. Elmer Rice dramatized the mechanization of the worker in *The Adding Machine* and the life of the slums in *Street Scene*. Imported dramas like Toller's *Masses and Man*, Kaiser's *From Morn to Midnight* and Werfel's *Goat Song* variously represented the worker's insurgency. Associated causes, such as peace and the rights of the Negro people, were expressed in *What Price Glory, In Abraham's Bosom, All God's Chillun*, and other plays. None of the above-mentioned plays would have satisfied the demands of the revolutionary theatre of the thirties, but they went as far as most professional playwrights could go and sometimes further than their audiences would follow them.

Efforts to create a workers' theatre that would toe the class line and avoid the mixed sympathies of the more established playwrights were sporadic. Foreign language groups arose from time to time, but their work was not always clearly defined, and the linguistic barrier was too great to be overcome. A Workers Drama League, founded in 1926, had no language problems but lasted only two years. It provided a leaven, however, for the one considerable radical theatre of the twenties. In 1927, a group which called itself the New Playwrights Theatre, prevailed upon the unfailingly generous Otto Kahn to grant it a subsidy of one hundred thousand dollars. It enlisted the services of the insurgent writers John Dos Passos, John Howard Lawson, Francis Faragoh, Paul Sifton, Emjo Basshe, and Michael Gold. Though some of the plays seemed foggy enough in execution, a number of them confronted working-class problems more single-heartedly than had been hitherto the case. Lawson's *The International* dramatized aspects of American imperialism; *The Belt* by Sifton described the struggle against the Taylor system and Fordism; Upton Sinclair's *Singing Jailbirds* dealt with the framing of a labor organizer, a subject perhaps inspired by the Mooney-Billings case. In spite of its peregrinations from Greenwich Village to Broadway the New Playwrights' group remained a small patch of revolutionary theatre without a mass basis and failed to make an impression on the country as a whole. It was not even, strictly speaking, a workers' theatre; it was *for* the workers but was hardly *of* them. After three seasons the New Playwrights Theatre called it a day.

Consequently the workers' theatre of the thirties started almost from scratch. Fired it must have been by the New Playwrights' effort and by the early experiences of the Little Theatre movement, which had proved that it was possible to begin on a small scale and reach new audiences with a minimum of expense. The experiences of foreign language groups and of the workers' theatre groups in Germany also contributed an impetus. The immediate inspiration of the movement, however, came from conditions outside of the theatre.

The movement arose as a response to the terrifying conditions of the depression. The stock-market crash left about thirteen million people unemployed, the wages of those fortunate enough to remain employed were slashed mercilessly, labor unions were helpless in the grip of economic circumstance, unemployment relief was still in the apple-selling stage; and everywhere, including the circles of the rich, there was talk of the imminent collapse of the social order. Banker and worker alike expected a death struggle for domination. And abroad there was Soviet Russia making giant strides, a visible symbol of what could be accomplished by successful revolution. "Theatre is a weapon in the class struggle," the motto of the John Reed Group Theatre of Philadelphia, expressed the objectives of the new movement, which took as its twofold aim the spreading of the communist gospel and the agitation for specific palliatives, which could be, and were as a matter of fact, slowly adopted by the American people without commitment to revolution.

Two theatre groups, working at first independently, became the spearhead of the movement—the Prolet-Buehne, a German-speaking unit, and the Workers Laboratory Theatre of New York. The former, founded in 1925 and strongly influenced by the workers' theatre movement in Germany, adopted a militant policy. By the fall of 1930, under the vigorous leadership of John Bonn and Anne Howe, Prolet-Buehne was appearing at a variety of mass meetings, on improvised stages, with few props, and inexpensive facilities. Its plays, stylized, rhythmical, and adapted to chanting, called "agit-prop" because their object was agitation and propaganda, frankly dispensed with characterization and developed situations. To the student of dramatic literature they are worthless. Whatever artistic merit they could claim lay entirely in production. Prolet-Buehne depended on a theatre of slogans, denunciation, and caricature, held together by rhythmic movement and songlike expression. Its characters were broad types, easily distinguished and symbolic; thus, the capitalist wore a top hat and the worker an open shirt, the employer was a mealy-mouthed oppressor, the employee a downtrodden worm until he turned. The subjects ranged from the speed-up in industry to the Scottsboro case. In its typing, stylization, and popular style, agit-prop was almost a species of *commedia dell'arte,* which has never been judged by literary standards. This drama also marked a return to folk theatre, in which the common people voice their resentments by satirizing their masters and parasites. The frontal satire of agit-prop spared no one, not even socialists and labor leaders, who were accused of misleading the working class.

This style was adopted and extended by the English-speaking organization that paralleled the work of the Prolet-Buehne, the Workers Laboratory Theatre, founded in 1929. Its members were possessed of all the enthusiasm of youth, but they had little use for collegiate high jinks. Many of their actors and writers had grown up in poverty and had worked in factories. Few of them had gained practical experience in the theatre; their ablest director,

Alfred Saxe, a fiery and gifted young man, had only a year of acting to his credit.

By 1931 the group was actively engaged in propaganda, appearing at mass meetings in New York and elsewhere. Its first production, in the winter of 1930-31, a skit entitled *Unemployed*, had for its lesson the necessity of organizing the unemployed to demand humane treatment and work when this could be managed. The group participated in political campaigns. Its contribution to the 1932 election was a skit, *The Sell-Out*, attacking ameliorative liberalism and socialism because it deflected the struggle for a collectivist society. An auctioneer selling "Civil Librolax" offered the workers "A cure for unemployment, A cure for corns and bunions," and assured them that "Our laxatives are gentle, mild. . . . They do not pinch, they do not gripe." Another political burlesque, *The Great Show*, had for its characters a Worker, a Speaker, a Capitalist, and a political charlatan named "Chameleon," described with *double entendre* as "a reptile possessing the power of changing its color."

Resolved to spread its type of drama over the country, the Workers Laboratory Theatre encouraged the creation of similar units elsewhere, until even Canada had its agit-prop. Los Angeles had its "Rebel Players," Chicago its "Blue Blouses" and Brahmin Boston its "Solidarity Players." Contacts with these and other groups were maintained largely by means of a new publication, *Workers Theatre*, which grew from two hundred mimeographed copies in April, 1931, to one thousand printed ones by the beginning of the next year. In April, 1932, the movement had grown to proportions that warranted the holding of a national festival and conference, the so-called Workers

Theatre Spartakiade and Conference, in New York City. Ben Blake, the left theatre's first chronicler,[1] notes with some pride that this was "the very spring when for the first time since its initiation in 1923 the National Little Theatre Conference Tournament annually staged by Walter Hartwig was unable to take place." The conference made it evident that the theatre had given birth to a lusty infant inclined to strangle serpents in its cradle and bent upon keeping the neighborhood awake with its howling. Its Dramatic Bureau, which had been created in the middle of 1931, now had twenty-three short plays in its repertory. A central organization, the League of Workers Theatre, abbreviated in New Deal fashion as the LOWT, was established, and *Workers Theatre* magazine was adopted as its official organ.

The Conference was a landmark in more than an organizational sense. The agit-prop groups surrendered much of their brash certainty and self-assurance, and a commendable capacity for self-criticism became apparent. Hitherto they had scorned the professional stage as a fen of stagnant waters and an abomination in the sight of the deified proletariat. They had behaved as if there had been no theatre before them, as if everything "bourgeois" was simply waiting for the harvester Death. Some respect for the continuity of culture, a principle recognized by Marx and Engels, even if forgotten by their more or less recent converts, became apparent. A healthy concern with theatre technique became manifest, training schools were established, and appeals for assistance were sent to the professional theatre and the Little Theatres. Attracted by the

[1] Ben Blake, *The Awakening of the American Theatre*, New York, Tomorrow Publishers, 1935.

sincerity and enthusiasm of the new groups and by an opportunity to exercise talents lying fallow in the depressed theatre, professionals soon responded in increasing numbers. Their effect upon the movement was eminently salutary, and the movement amply discharged its indebtedness by providing them with a new stimulus.

At first, direct agitation was not greatly abated, and it is a matter of record that it was never wholly abandoned. The first signs of growth were felt in the efficiency of the new productions. As late as November, 1934, the Workers Laboratory Theatre, whose most active members lived for a time in a collectively run apartment, reaffirmed the ideals of its inception, by establishing a "shock troupe" prepared to perform at a moment's notice wherever agitational drama was urgently needed. Collectively, the shock troupe created a topical *montage, Newsboy,* which was vibrantly directed by Alfred Saxe. Technically, *Newsboy* was a unique fusion of suggestions from *Merry-Go-Round* and the Jooss Ballet that would interest the student of esthetic forms without respect to political sympathies. But the form was primed for agitational effectiveness. Later, when it was temporarily included in the Theatre Guild's *Parade* in Boston, it was still sufficiently point-blank to shock the Governor of Massachusetts out of his seat with the query, "Do you remember Sacco and Vanzetti?" A powerful *montage, Free Thaelman,* which made an impression on students of the theatre, agitated for the release of the German leader then languishing in a concentration camp. For elementary agitation, the group also established a puppet department devoted to such topical titles as *Mr. Morgan's Nightmare* and *N.R.A. and Blue Eagle,* in which the President was made to say: "If the workers are striking, we'll give them the *bird*," and Punch, the Worker, declared:

> My stomach often rubs my spine
> And now it's started shrinking.
> And though my head is made of wood
> I've lately started thinking.

III

The New Theatre Movement

The natural processes of growth and the influx of professional people nevertheless operated increasingly against the agit-prop drama. The principle of "a theatre greater than the labor movement but drawing its inspiration from the latter and continuing the new social outlook on a broader scale," to which the movement had committed itself, was beginning to be realized both organizationally and artistically. In response to this trend, *Workers Theatre* magazine changed its name to *New Theatre* in September, 1933. The magazine ushered in the new policy by distributing a questionnaire on the social relations of the theatre among prominent playwrights, producers, and craftsmen. Among the many to respond to *New Theatre's* appeal were Paul Green, Philip Barry, Sidney Howard, Sherwood Anderson, and Hallie Flanagan. In September, 1934, the magazine, which acquired an exceptionally gifted editor in Herbert Kline, of Davenport, Iowa, announced flatly that "the day of the cliché and mechanical statement has gone by for the workers' theatre." Another factor in the broadening realism of a movement that had begun by specializing in dramatized poems, expressionistic satires, and mass recitations (of which Alfred Kreymborg's *America, America* remains the finest example) was the

success of the Theatre Union in full-length social drama of
the type of *Stevedore* and *Black Pit*. This institutional
radical theatre, which owed its inception to the spadework
of the League of Workers Theatres, repaid its debt by setting the one-act movement an example in rounded characterization and dramatic development.

In response to the new trend, which would have been
regarded earlier as perniciously compromising, the League
of Workers Theatres changed its name in January, 1935,
to the New Theatre League, with Mark Marvin, another
immigrant from Iowa, as its executive secretary. Eligibility
to membership was construed along the broad lines of opposition to war, fascism, and censorship—a policy that left
the door wide open to writers, actors, and directors who
would have otherwise remained aloof. (The precise for-
mulation of the program was: "For a mass development
of the American theatre to its highest artistic and social
level; for a theatre dedicated to the struggle against war,
fascism, and censorship.") Almost at once New Theatre
affiliates sprang up in approximately one hundred and
fifty communities. Little Theatre groups became increasingly hospitable to New Theatre plays; and the "road,"
which had been largely lost to the professional theatre,
showed recovered vitality. The repertory department became an active play bureau and play publisher, stimulating production throughout the country; and the New
Theatre School, which attracted a vigorous student body
and an advanced faculty, became a major institution of its
kind. *New Theatre*, which became increasingly hospitable
to writers of different shades of opinion without sacrificing
its social critique, grew rapidly in circulation, which
at one time reached the high-water mark of twenty-three

thousand. Soon recognized as the most vital publication in the theatre even by those who still found many of its policies unacceptable, it gave impetus to the composition of distinguished one-acters. Its annual contests, given in conjunction with the New Theatre League and other organizations, netted numerous playlets of variable quality, and made such notable discoveries as *Waiting for Lefty* and *Bury the Dead*. Under these auspices, "New Theatre Nights" became a regular feature, attended by large audiences and respected by the press. It was at one of these special performances, in January, 1935, that the prize-winning play, Clifford Odets' *Waiting for Lefty* received its first production. Another New Theatre Night unveiled Irwin Shaw's *Bury the Dead*, written for another annual contest. A third evening saw the production of Paul Green's *Hymn to the Rising Sun*, considered one of the short masterpieces of the American theatre and subsequently revived by the Federal Theatre. Albert Maltz's *Private Hicks*, though a less distinguished work, achieved another respectable success. In each instance, moreover, production in New York was followed by performances throughout the country.

The Workers Laboratory Theatre veered to realism in Peter Martin's *Daughter*, a dramatization of a short story by Erskine Caldwell, in January, 1935, and in Michael Blankfort's *The Crime*, in the spring of 1936. Changing its name to The Theatre of Action the group also turned to full-length drama in *The Young Go First*, a collaboration by three young writers which represented conditions in the C.C.C. camps. But the honor of shaking down the ripened fruit of the revolutionary one-act movement was reserved for groups that had started less militantly—the

Group Theatre and the "Let Freedom Ring" Company, later known as the Actors Repertory. Both were professional units, drilled in the technique of realism, though not impervious to the influence of agit-prop. It is significant, too, that both companies had been producing full-length plays before turning to one-acters, a reversal of tradition.

The Group Theatre, which had begun as an affiliate of the venerable Theatre Guild, was an actors' company that had been a collective since 1930, after germinating in the minds of its leading spirits, Harold Clurman, Cheryl Crawford, and Lee Strasberg. From an ideal of collective acting it was a short step to a more or less collectivist social ideal. The group, according to Clurman, would eschew doing merely "amusing things." In 1931 he wrote to the Directors of the Theatre Guild:

We are passionately devoted to the theatre because only through it can we most successfully say the things we have to say. We believe that men cannot live without giving themselves completely to some force outside themselves and that this must have a concrete object and form which can absorb the activities of men in their daily lives. The generations before us seemed to have been strenuously individualistic without believing very steadily in any particular good for their individuals. We, on the contrary, feel that the individualism of self-assertion which made of the ego the sole and final reality of life is self-destructive, and we believe that the individual can realize himself only by seeking his spiritual kindred and by making of their common aspirations and problems the object of his active devotion. We believe that the individual can achieve his fullest stature only through the identification of his own good with the good of his group, a group which he himself must help to create.

The Group's productions strove to realize these ideals, both in technique and choice of plays.

In the fall of 1931, while still functioning under the Guild's directorate, the group had given a memorable production of Paul Green's *The House of Connelly*, a sensitive study of decayed Southern aristocracy. Its next production, the Siftons' *1931*, also owned by the parent organization, proved to be the first full-length study of the actual effects of the depression. After a brief excursion into romanticism with Maxwell Anderson's *Night over Taos*, the first independent venture, this organization returned to the social theatre with John Howard Lawson's *Success Story* in the fall of 1932. *Big Night*, which followed it, was only mildly satirical and died a-borning, but the socially insignificant *Men in White*, produced in association with Broadway managers, proved a bonanza and won the Pulitzer Prize. With its next two plays, Lawson's *Gentlewoman* and Melvin Levy's *Gold Eagle Guy*, the Group returned to social drama but in a muddled and inconclusive manner which bespoke neither commercial nor artistic success. The Group was stumped. It possessed a play, *Awake and Sing*, by a member of the company, but seemed disinclined to risk it after two failures.

It was at this point that *New Theatre* came to the rescue. It had offered a prize for the best one-act play, and Clifford Odets, locking himself in a hotel room, set his nose to the grindstone. After three days he completed *Waiting for Lefty*, a playlet revolving around a recent taxi strike, which won first prize. Members of the Group Theatre accepted the magazine's invitation to perform the play at a special showing as a kind of extra-curriculum performance. The opening night at the old Civic Repertory Theatre, then occupied by the Theatre Union, proved memorable. The audience wept and refused to leave the theatre. The enthusiastic reception became the making of the most promising playwright to be discovered in years. The Group resolved to give the play a professional run, and to fill out the evening at the Longacre the wildly acclaimed young author prepared another short play, *Till the Day I Die,* less enthusiastically received but regarded by such authorities as Richard Watts, Jr., and Percival Wilde as the most distinguished of his shorter pieces. Convinced that it had a full-fledged playwright in its ranks, the Group looked again at *Awake and Sing* and produced his first full-length drama with uncommon success. Thus the New Theatre movement had given birth to a new and important playwright.

The two short plays, which opened on March 25, 1935, enjoyed an excellent press and a respectable run; with the exception of George O'Neil's *American Dream,* which was presented by the Theatre Guild as a single play, Odets' one-acters were the first in a decade to be successful in the professional theatre. But the history of *Waiting for Lefty* went far beyond the limelight of Broadway, which was as the folk-minded New Theatre movement would have it. Six months after its première, this one-acter was being played from coast to coast in twenty cities by twenty different companies. Eventually, more than a hundred cities saw the play. Even conservative England played host to it in London, Durham, Newcastle, and other places. The Unity Players who produced it in New Haven won the much-coveted George Pierce Baker cup at the Yale Dramatic Tournament and gained the right to present the piece throughout the state in spite of opposition from the police department and sundry irate elements. Numerous efforts to suppress *Waiting for Lefty* made the one-acter a *cause célèbre,* and the New Theatre League soon had a censorship fight on its hands, which it fought to a successful conclusion with the aid of divers liberal and theatre-loving friends. Not all of its enemies, however, were in the ranks of capital. Some of the most indignant protests came from labor itself—more precisely, from its conservative leadership which was angered by the charge of racketeering within unions. Thus *Labor Chronicle,* organ of Joseph P. Ryan, old-line leader of the Longshoremen's Union, complained that the play held "legitimate unionism up to obloquy."

The Group's other ventures in the one-act field were less overwhelmingly successful. *Till the Day I Die,* which dealt with foreign fascism, was less calculated to attract American audiences, although in point of distance its productions outranked *Waiting for Lefty* when the play was given in Perth, West Australia. *Dmitroff,* an early play, written by two other members of the Group, Elia Kazan and Art Smith, and the latter's *The Tide Rises,* a picture of the San Francisco water-front strike, won attention on a smaller scale.

Less eminent in full-length production, but the Group's peer in the one-act field, proved the "Let Freedom Ring" Company, originally assembled by Albert Bein for the production of his full-length drama of the Southern mills, *Let Freedom Ring.* Ultimately organized along collective lines, and keenly alive to the struggles of the day, this company contributed its services to a number of New Theatre Nights. After giving two short pieces at the first Night, in November, 1935, the company was allowed to present the prize play of the year, *Private Hicks,* on January 11, 1936. This playlet proved eminently successful in its numerous productions throughout the country, perhaps largely because it voiced labor's opposition to the use of militia in strike areas.

It was not long before the company's impressive showing attracted new players, as well as plays that were to excel *Private Hicks.* In their next appearance on a New Theatre Night, also in January, 1936, they unfolded Paul Green's *Hymn to the Rising Sun,* an exposure of the Southern chain-gang system, which had been first published in *New Theatre.* With Charles Dingle in the role of the sadomasochistic chain-gang boss and an effective cast of prisoners and guards, the playlet made a profound impression upon audiences and critics. Supplementing it, the company revived the same author's satire on evangelism, *Unto Such Glory,* a folk piece that was invested with new relevance by the players, among whom the excellent actor Will Geer was most impressive.

Paul Green did not of course need to be "discovered." At most it can be assumed that the New Theatre movement gave him renewed impetus and an audience which his earlier dramas had barely scratched. Irwin Shaw's antiwar drama *Bury the Dead* was, however, a real discovery, and the honor of presenting it for the first time under New Theatre League auspices devolved upon the group, which soon constituted itself as a collective known as the Actors Repertory Company. When this long-acter was chosen prize winner of a New Theatre contest, Irwin Shaw, who had seen the actors at work, selected them to perform his play. It was instantly acclaimed at the 46th Street Theatre, and the press was so favorable that a commercial manager, Alex Yokel, whose current success was a far cry from the social drama, undertook to finance it for a Broadway run. Directed by Worthington Miner, it opened in May, 1936, at the Ethel Barrymore Theatre, with a curtain raiser collectively composed by the actors. Although *Bury the Dead* did not prove a bonanza to its angel, it had a respectable run and was a success of esteem having few equals in the contemporary theatre. And again, as in the case of Odets' one-acter, the triumph of the play can only be measured by its dispersion over the country. A most colorful moment in its history occurred in Hollywood at a preview arranged to stimulate interest in its forthcoming production by the Contemporary Theatre of Los Angeles. The occasion took the form of a public reading by Fredric March and Florence Eldridge. Among other notables who participated were James Cagney, Francis Lederer, Donald Ogden Stewart, and Arthur Kober; and Lewis Milestone, the film director, who was subsequently to take Odets under his wing in pictures, telegraphed the audience, "Let there be more of these plays for the sake of humanity."

When *Bury the Dead* closed in New York, the Actors Repertory Company returned to full-length production with a high-minded drama of unemployment rehabilitation, E. P. Conkle's *Two Hundred Were Chosen*, but it was unable to match its previous triumph. The group, however, continued to have faith in the one-act form. It was prepared to present another New Theatre winner, Marc Blitzstein's music drama *The Cradle Will Rock*, when it was prevented by the financial failure of its full-length play. It remained for the Mercury Theatre, an offshoot of the Federal Theatre and an organization not uninfluenced by the New Theatre movement, to salvage *The Cradle Will Rock* from the Federal Theatre's scrap heap, to which it had been relegated in the summer of 1937. The Actors Repertory Company is still interested in one-acters; recently it contributed an enchanting musical skit, *A Town and Country Jig,* which should commend itself to many groups.

The early work of the Prolet-Buehne and the Workers Laboratory Theatre and the later accomplishments of the Group Theatre and the "Let Freedom Ring" Company comprise the most colorful aspects of the movement. But by no means do they exhaust it. Thus The Theatre Collective of New York produced numerous social playlets and launched another able, if less widely recognized, writer, Philip Stevenson. The Collective made an impressive showing with his satire on lukewarm liberalism during the American Revolution, *You Can't Change Human Nature.* One of the directors of the Collective, Brett Warren, subsequently made his mark with an admirable production of the Federal Theatre's "Living Newspaper," *Power.* It is in fact impossible to record the work of groups like the Collective individually. At the peak, the New Theatre movement could boast of more than three hundred affiliated groups throughout the country.

To their activities, moreover, must be added the work of independent organizations like The Vassar Experimental Theatre under Hallie Flanagan, soon to become national director of the Federal Theatre Project, which produced a militant farm drama, *Can You Hear Their Voices,* by Mrs. Flanagan and her student Margaret Clifford as early as 1931. (This play and W. H. Auden's *Dance of Death,* produced first at Vassar, are classified as full-length plays. Actually, they are long one-acters, as a glance at their structure would reveal.) Independent, but allied in spirit, were also the Brookfield Players, who held forth in a converted tobacco barn on the Pittsfield Post Road near Danbury and presented the work of Virgil Geddes. Though his plays were listed by their author as full-length dramas forming a tetralogy, *From the Life of George Emery Blum,* they were individually long one-acters in structure. The Rebel Arts Group of New York, another independent unit of Socialist inspiration, offered a number of short plays, the most recent and impressive being Michael Blankfort's drama of the Spanish civil war, *The Brave and the Blind,* given in the spring of 1937. Noteworthy, too, was the annual tour of the Brookwood Labor College Players, who at one time covered as many as one hundred and fifty cities with short labor plays and mass recitations given mostly in union halls under union auspices. "Economics without tears, and history with footlights instead of notes," the motto of this the leading labor college in the country, was scrupulously adhered to, although its writing talent was meager. For the record it must also be noted that the Theatre Guild's trilogy of one-acters, George O'Neil's *American Dream,* consisting of episodes in the American struggle for freedom, had much in common with the revolutionary one-act movement, as did the better skits of its musical revue *Parade,* to which many a Theatre Unionite contributed.

Finally, there is a phase of the movement to which this historian cannot do justice. Its active proponents can paint a vivid picture of participation in vital industrial conflicts. When relief workers in Madison, Wisconsin, took possession of a courthouse, it was a theatrical unit that kept up their morale. *Private Hicks* was based on the Auto-Lite strike, during which a number of strikers were killed by the militia in Toledo, Ohio; it was not surprising, therefore, that this playlet should have been presented wherever its protest seemed called for. From the General Motors strike a number of embattled actors still retain souvenirs—blackjacks with which the strikers are said to have armed themselves for defense against hired thugs. Actors played to rubber strikers in Akron during freezing weather. The Mass Action Theatre played to the steel strikers' picket line the day after the "Memorial Day Massacre" in Chicago. When the civil war broke out in Spain there was no dearth of actors who went to the front to fight or to entertain the fighters, some, like John Lenthier, to lay down their lives in the struggle against their arch-enemy, fascism. Units of the one-act movement not only expressed the ardors of the industrial conflicts that were to culminate in the birth of the C.I.O., but participated in them. Whether this activity enhanced or detracted from the quality of the plays and performances is of course a debatable subject. Perhaps we may reach a suitable compromise by suggesting that the movement would have had to forgo its inspiration if it had maintained a high-minded neutrality.

IV

The Recession

In 1936 the New Theatre movement entered a period of recession, as well as of transition. As a result of the decline, as well as of a necessary cleansing of the stables and concentration of the work, it has shrunk considerably in size and activity. Among a variety of causes perhaps the prime one was the development of a subsidized Federal Theatre offering many of the movement's workers a livelihood, however meager, and also an opportunity to carry their ideals into an institution that bore the seeds of a full-grown national people's theatre. The assimilation of their objectives, to some extent, in the Federal project and, to a slighter degree, in the general theatre did away with the uniqueness of their stage for audiences that might have otherwise supported it. A temporary lifting of the heavier clouds of the depression in 1936 disposed an increasing number of regular playgoers in favor of light entertainment. The suspension of *New Theatre* magazine (which became *New Theatre and Film* for the two last issues) deprived the movement of a valuable organ in the spring of 1937. Debts resulting from the bankruptcy of its commercial distributor undermined this publication at a time when the need for its influence was greater than ever, leaving *Theatre Workshop*, a technical, nonpolitical quarterly, as the sole publication of the New Theatre League. Support from sympathetic sources also declined; perhaps chiefly because other causes, like Spanish loyalism, were regarded as more immediate.

Intrinsic weaknesses also contributed to the recession. Although the movement afforded opportunities for young and talented directors, its collective ideals did not suffice to encourage the emergence of a directorial personality or magnetic *régisseur* sufficiently potent to create a solidly grounded one-act theatre. Theoretical hair splitting has always been the bane of a semipolitical movement; if the Irish theatre once suffered from such disadvantages, the New Theatre League's energies were even more decidedly depleted by them. Moreover, the emphasis upon economic struggles tended to produce monotony of treatment. It is perhaps not so curious that the libido should be able to endure countless regurgitation in the theatre while the repetition of social problems in unsublimated form should try the patience of audiences. Playgoers bring a variety of resistances to anything that does not titillate them. "Escapism," a much overworked charge, may be more inherent in the theatre than the movement could realize. It failed to sublimate much of its depressing and strident material. That there is an essential difference between escape and isolation is something the theatre of social purpose has yet to learn and apply. The weaknesses of this type of theatre were inherent in its strength, and once the physical energies and novelty of the movement suffered depletion, its shortcomings became apparent even to sympathizers.

At the same time, the recession is hardly an adequate reason for a funeral oration. It is difficult to believe that a theatre so rooted in contemporary realities can end in the morgue so long as those realities continue to exist. In fact, there is much evidence of continued activity and of some very respectable achievement since the 1935-36 peak. Pre-eminent is Marc Blitzstein's music drama *The Cradle Will Rock*, another New Theatre League prize winner, which had a checkered history in the Federal Theatre until it was given special performances by the Mercury Theatre beginning on December 12, 1937, and set for a regular run by the commercial producer Sam H. Grisman on January 4, 1938. This long one-acter was promptly hailed as a major *tour de force* and considered the equal of practically anything discovered by the New Theatre League. The first half of 1937 also saw productions of Michael Blankfort's *The Brave and the Blind*, a moving drama of civil war in Spain, by the Rebels Arts Group and by the Current Theatre of New York. Another impressive event was the appearance of William Kozlenko's indictment of unscrupulous utility corporations, *This Earth Is Ours*, produced by a New Theatre League group in February, 1937, to much acclaim, cited as one of the best one-act plays of 1937, and included in four general anthologies of short plays. Productions of this piece took place in Chicago, Pittsburgh, New Haven, Boston, London, Prague, and Melbourne. The nonpartisan *One Act Play Magazine*, founded by Kozlenko in May, 1937, has continued to reveal a number of respectable one-acters of social purpose, such as Percival Wilde's *Blood of the Martyrs*, a dramatization of Stephen Vincent Benét's anti-fascist short story, which should rank as one of the most gripping of contemporary one-acters, and Philip Stevenson's *Transit*, a dramatization of Albert Maltz's novelette *Season of Celebration*, which is even more deserving. Most recently, the New Theatre League revealed a touching and colorful short sit-down play, Ben Bengal's *Plant in the Sun*, and the Actors Repertory Company produced the earlier mentioned satirical skit, *A Town and Country Jig*, which should go to the top of its class.

Perhaps most significant is the progress that has recently been made in the broadcasting field, largely owing to the interest of Irving Reis, former director of the Columbia Broadcasting Company's Workshop. Marc Blitzstein's *I've Got the Tune*, a radio music drama, was an interesting accomplishment, and Archibald MacLeish's *The Fall of the City* was universally regarded as the most significant event in radio theatre. In *The Fall of the City*, broadcast on April 11, 1937, the New Theatre movement, which supported this poet's first appearance in the theatre in *Panic* and found him one of its most ardent champions, could prop rly take credit for a short American masterpiece.

It is evident, then, that the afore-mentioned recession has not been followed by anything describable as *rigor mortis*. At the peak it was possible for Sheldon Cheney, one of the fathers of the Little Theatre movement, to report that he "felt the surge of a new theatre life in the workers' theatres: that the leftist stage has afforded me, personally, the most poignant theatrical emotion born out of the clash of modern living that I have experienced." Turning to the older movement which he had sponsored, he mourned, perhaps a trifle exaggeratedly, "We were thinking of the theatre only on the esthetic side; thought to perfect it as a form of art expression . . . , not recognizing that there must be significant life-content—the play, and this in turn vibrating to the deepest life-consciousness of the audience." [2] As late as December, 1936, Archibald MacLeish could write: "No man who has had the experience of presenting plays first before Broadway audiences and thereafter before such audiences as the radical theatres would ever of his own choice return to the Broadway audience." The picture changed in 1937, but by then the movement had already sown its seeds in the American theatre, ensuring the continuance of short drama of social purpose. Since, moreover, the New Theatre League is still active and may be galvanized into even greater activity by

[2] Sheldon Cheney, "The Art Theatre—Twenty Years After," *The New Caravan*, W. W. Norton, 1936, pp. 426-445.

the events of the immediate future, it is highly probable that the present survey will have to be extended and even modified.

v

Sociology and Playwriting

Ultimately, of course, the movement will have to be judged by the plays it leaves to posterity, as productions are too elusive to withstand the erosion of time and memory. Although it is impossible to consider all or even a large portion of the plays, the chronicler must give some brief consideration to the body of dramatic literature available to us. Misrepresentations and misunderstandings have, however, abounded in all considerations of this drama. Friends, as well as enemies, have laid down a smoke screen which must be dissipated before a just evaluation is possible.

The plays have frequently been referred to as brutally realistic. A blanket charge of unmitigated propaganda has also been their lot. They have also been referred to as an absolutely new phenomenon in the theatre. Like most generalizations, these are at best only partially true. The margin of error comes, in part, from the fact that art rarely toes the mark of a prescribed formula. Art has its own momentum, and the personality of the writer is highly individual even when it owes much to the general environment. The playwrights were individuals differing in temperament, politics, and social background. Not all of them were revolutionaries, and, strictly speaking, not many of them emanated from the working class. Even those who did could not always claim a patent of proletarian royalty, for nearly every artist in a variously stratified society embraces in his imagination, education, and taste the other classes. As a matter of fact, many of the playwrights were charter members of the middle class who may or may not have been temporarily in bad standing, though perhaps no more so than most artists from time immemorial. Man, being a mammal, is an umbilical-minded animal—which is perhaps all to the good, since art owes its depth and scope to the fact that it possesses a multifarious root system. Nevertheless, few of the playwrights could avoid acceptance of the principle of class conflict and of revolutionary philosophy.

Some of the plays were unmistakably revolutionary; others, like *Hymn to the Rising Sun,* were reformist. Still others were both. In describing them as a group, it is therefore perhaps nearer to the truth to call them "sociological" rather than "revolutionary" or even "left." They may be called "revolutionary" in a strict sense only in deference to their formative period. If they were revolutionary, in a wider sense, they were so because the abuses they described struck most of the leaders of the movement as remediable only by the inauguration of a new collective social order.

To say that the movement was unmitigatedly realistic is also an exaggeration. Omitting the early agit-prop forms, which were completely stylized and made scant use of realistic modes, we must still note that the expressionistic technique was apparent more or less in the flashbacks of *Waiting for Lefty* and in the warp and woof of *Bury the Dead. The Fall of the City* is altogether a feat of the imagination rather than of documentation and realistic development.

I would go further and claim considerable romanticism

for many of the formally realistic pieces. They romanticized the worker, who was frequently a Bayard in overalls, while his capitalistic antagonist could trace his descent from the mustachioed Mephistos of early American melodrama, if not from *Die Räuber*. Greatly in favor for a time were conversion endings; Michael Blankfort referred to such pieces, whose object was to "show a worker or intellectual swing from a conservative position . . . to a militant class-position by the final curtain," as "pendulum plays." [3] Apologists for "pendulum plays" liked their conclusiveness and found them realistically justified by the fact that many workers and intellectuals did undergo conversion. In practice, however, the conversion was frequently effected too rapidly and unconvincingly in a short play. It looked like wish fulfillment, and stood suspiciously close to romantic hero-worship. Conversion endings, in fact, often made the play puerile, although they sometimes infused better-written pieces like *Waiting for Lefty* and *Bury the Dead* with poetic fire.

A cynic might even say that the entire movement, often so all-fired proud of its tough-minded realistic outlook, was cut from the cloth of romanticism. And if one holds that faith in human nature, in the possibilities of changing mankind for the better, is a major delusion, the cynic would be undoubtedly right. Short of such a view, however, one must allow the movement its claim to a modified realism, a realism with a purpose, sometimes described as "socialist realism." This is in fact the only sense in which the revolutionary one-acters could be freely regarded as a new

[3] Michael Blankfort, "Facing the New Audience." *New Theatre*, November, 1934.

phenomenon in American playwriting, since realism was nothing new on our stage.

What was the nature of this new realism? On the one hand, it shrank from nothing sordid, horrible, and painful. The horrors of poverty, of industrial conflicts, or life in the chain gang were set down with resolute fidelity. Still, they were not set down with an eye to sensationalism or simply for the record. They were intended to inculcate a lesson, agitate for the elimination of abuses, and indict a social order that tolerated them. They were not recorded pessimistically, but in the belief that society could be transformed, that in fact it was already being changed. They were set down in hope rather than in despair, and their ultimate object, though sometimes honored only in the breach, was to exhilarate. They aimed at the catharsis that comes with recognizing an evil and endeavoring to remove it. In every event, they saw symbols of a vast struggle between the owning classes and the workers, between the servants of injustice and justice, between Ahriman and Ormuzd. Theirs was the drama of dynamic processes affecting society and its individuals.

Not only was such a viewpoint relatively new in the American theatre, but it frequently expressed itself in new forms—new at least on the American stage. The earliest form, agit-prop, was essentially an expression of conflict, in which the two sides were sharply and arbitrarily divided, the viewpoint was stated as baldly as possible, and the lesson was pressed home beyond all possibility of misunderstanding by means of caricature, insinuating rhythm, and broad acting, as well as verbally. The mass recitation, a secondary form, broke up a recitation into its dramatic components and underscored them by means of appropriate gesture and movement, using different voices for different characters or groups, in an effort to present a lesson as tellingly as possible.

When, later in its history, the movement turned to fully developed plays, these frequently retained agit-prop elements in solution. They were primed for a rousingly militant ending that frequently propelled the characters, as well as the audience, out of the immediate situation into the world of larger social conflicts. Thus the strike situation of *Waiting for Lefty* is only a springboard to a call for action on all fronts for the overthrow of the old order and the creation of the new. Thus the soldiers who come to life in *Bury the Dead* march out of the grave not merely because they have renounced imperialistic war but because they intend to set the world to rights—the world that cheated them as much back home as when it sent them to their death on the battlefield.

Technically, moreover, the plays tended to be inclusive and frequently even, as in the case of *Waiting for Lefty*, *The Tide Rises*, and *Bury the Dead*, kaleidoscopic. Although *Waiting for Lefty* deals primarily with the calling of a taxi strike, it is largely composed of vignettes describing an assortment of lives and a series of indictments of the social order in such varied fields as medicine, industrial chemistry, and the theatre. Although *Bury the Dead* has for its central situation the revolt of a group of soldiers against death it moves far afield in dramatizing their individual frustrations in society. *Till the Day I Die* alternates between scenes of the National Socialist terror and the underground movement in Germany. Despite extreme concentration, *Hymn to the Rising Sun* manages to bring Southern legislation within the compass of a chain-gang drama. *The Fall of the City* shifts its camera eye constantly in the effort to describe a mass drama. Even the less ambitious plays strove for scope and mass. The objectives of the movement expressed themselves technically in considerable extension of the one-act form. The one-acter became generally longer and more varied, favoring many scenes, the use of black-outs and flashbacks, and large casts. In this respect, the movement blazed new possibilities of expression in the short play.

VI

The Plays

A descriptive account of the hundreds of short plays written between 1930 and 1937 would make a formidable volume. Fortunately this is not necessary, not merely because many of them would be thrown out of court by any discriminating judge, but because so many of them fall into a few convenient classifications. Trade unionism occupied the foreground of a great many of them; the most notable perhaps were *Waiting for Lefty*, *The Tide Rises*, *Plant in the Sun*, *The Crime*, and *I Take My Stand*. Militarism and war were the subjects of *Bury the Dead*, *Private Hicks*, *The Trumpets of Wrath*, by Kozlenko, and a number of less distinguished pieces. Sharecroppers and the submerged farmer received attention in *His Jewels* (Bernice Kelly Harris), *This Earth Is Ours*, *Mighty Wind A'Blowing* (Alice Holdship Ware), *Daughter*, and *Can You Hear Their Voices*. Problems of the Negro race were treated by several of the aforementioned plays and by *Trouble with the Angels*. Poverty and city life found expression in Virgil Geddes' *In the Tradition*, A. B. Shiffrin's *Kids Learn Fast* and *Return at Sunset,* and Stevenson's *Transit.* Fascism was excoriated in *Till the Day I Die, The Fall of the City, The Brave and the Blind,* and *Blood of the Martyrs.* Sundry abuses filled other plays and served as secondary motifs in a number of the aforementioned one-acters.

A considerable percentage of the play crop was, as noted, rank and worthless, which is perhaps no great indictment of the movement when we consider the mortality rate on Broadway. Many of the playwrights were unskilled, and their philosophy of art was too sophomoric to promote good work. Gradually, however, some of them grew in power and their ranks were augmented by respectable and in a few instances superlative talents.

The gifts of satire and humor were underdeveloped in them at first, perhaps because few of the playwrights were disposed to find anything amusing in the world about them. But the blanket charge that the movement lacked humor is a rank libel. One of the first to disprove the indictment was Philip Stevenson, whose *God's in His Heaven* and the more fully rounded *What It Takes* satirized the complacencies of average Americans. The last-mentioned play, in particular, revealed a fine feeling for characterization and wry pathos. Another play of his, *You Can't Change Human Nature,* owed much of its power to its humorous treatment of fence-straddling elements in the American Revolution. Particularly apt seemed his parallels between 1776 and 1936, and especially pointed was the implication that the American fathers had been revolutionists. Later, in dramatizing Albert Maltz's novelette, Stevenson also uncovered a talent for stark realism rarely associated with a humorist; *Transit* is a profoundly moving transcription of life among society's outcasts that comes close to the spirit of Gorky's *The Lower Depths*.

Stevenson's comrade in arms was A. B. Shiffrin, who moved from a brutal exposure of slum life in *Kids Learn Fast*, a play in which a number of white children lynch a Negro boy in jest, to one of the most amusing comedies of the movement, *Return at Sunset*. How poverty grinds the faces of the poor into the dust is not a naturally entertaining subject. Shiffrin makes it both entertaining and moving in his rather diffuse one-acter by virtue of some keen observation of shanty-Jewish life, by the accumulation of tragi-comic errors which approach the fantastic. Pithy folk humor studs its family scene in which the paterfamilias loses his horse, the son gets a broken head for listening to a street-corner speaker, and the daughter leaves a position because her employer has made advances to her. A real jewel for a humorist is Wassermann, the boarder, who had a nervous stomach and was told to go to a farm. "So what happened? I got sick. I had to go back to the city again. I couldn't stand the fresh air." He tried to join the army, when his trade was eliminated, but he was rejected. "I wasn't healthy enough for them. To get killed in a war you first got to be healthy."

In time, too, there appeared considerable talent for musical comedy and the composition of satiric skits dear to our musical revues. One of the earliest examples was the collection of sketches by Paul Peters, George Sklar, Alan Baxter, Frank Gabrelson, and David Lesan in the Theatre Guild's ill-fated revue, *Parade*. Harold J. Rome, who composed most of the skits, lyrics, and music for the highly entertaining Labor Stage revue *Pins and Needles*, is an impressive craftsman in the musical comedy form.

A curious, mordant type of humor also makes itself felt in some of the work of Virgil Geddes, whose *Native Ground* is no criterion of the range of his talents. A macabre and savage humor pervades *In the Tradition,* which dramatizes the economic plight of an undertaker—almost unbearably for some tastes. A bizarre feeling for the tragi-comedy of human relationships in *I Have Seen Myself Before* underscores the same character's search for a job.

The undisputed master of them all in a satiric vein is, however, Marc Blitzstein, who uses the resources of both music and drama to send his points home. *I've Got the Tune,* his radio play, produces incisive and bitter effects with the device of propelling a composer who has the tune out into the world to look for the words; he finds them at last after surveying the social scene. *The Cradle Will Rock,* a rich satire on respectability and an excoriation of the professional men and artists who sell their souls to Mammon, proved a major event in the season of 1937-38. Blitzstein has a biting feeling for lines and music; he is a caricaturist who transmutes the clichés of the old agit-prop into artistry. In a more realistic genre he is equaled only by George O'Neil, whose third one-acter in *American Dream,* entitled *1933,* is a vigorous satire on the decadence of upper-class society. Though it ends tragically, with the suicide of the last of the Pengree dynasty, its force resides in its vitriolic treatment of social parasites and futilitarians.

Less abundant than humor is, as a matter of fact, imaginative drama, the relative absence of which is, however, characteristic of our entire theatre. Moreover, the movement did produce two of the rare imaginative works of the thirties, against which we can set only one example from the full-length nonpolitical stage—namely, Anderson's

High Tor. Irwin Shaw's *Bury the Dead* possesses pathos and indignation in its diatribe against war and frustration. But much of its uniqueness resides in its fantasy of dead soldiers coming to life, an idea used before in the Theatre Guild's *Miracle at Verdun* but expressed by Shaw more dynamically and with a spare economy which guards against operatic fireworks. MacLeish's *The Fall of the City* went even further in its claim upon the imagination with its use of mass effects and adaptation to the demands of the nonvisual medium of radio drama. That so distinguished a poet should have added the imaginative qualities of the most forceful verse written for the American theatre goes without saying. In comparison with MacLeish's poetry most of Maxwell Anderson's sounds epigonal, an echo from the past. The theme, within the small compass of a thirty-minute play, is epic.

> The city of masterless men
> Will take a master.

When the dictator before whom the populace bends in adoration and submission appears,

> The helmet is hollow!
> The metal is empty! The armor is empty! . . .
> The push of a stiff pole at the nipple would topple it.

But,

> . . . they don't see! They lie on the paving. They lie in
> Burnt spears: the ashes of arrows. They lie there.
> They don't see or they won't see. They are silent. . . .
> The city of masterless men has found a master!
> The city has fallen!
> The city has fallen!

Confronted with the uncanny power of imaginative drama, however, realism has no reason to turn away abashed when it is deeply and excitingly realized. The bulk of the plays were realistic, and although many of them were pedestrian, their militancy stood them in good stead, ensuring them excitement and vigor. The least successful plays were naturally those which lacked these attributes. Folk drama like Alice Holdship Ware's *Mighty Wind A'Blowing* and Bernice Kelly Harris's *His Jewels* is distinguished in dialogue and native characterization. In the first, the rapprochement between Negro and white sharecroppers is treated with verisimilitude and charm. *His Jewels* possesses an unusual central situation—the eviction of a sharecropper and his daughters from the church in which they have sought shelter—which lends itself to much pathos and irony. The Siftons' *Give All Thy Terrors to the Wind* is an admirably rounded drama of a ship disaster caused by the greed of the shipping interests. Michael Blankfort, one of the leaders of the Theatre Union, contributed a searching, if somewhat static, study of a vacillating but honest labor organizer in a flavorsome long one-acter, *The Crime*. His drama of the siege of the Alcazar or some similar fortress in the Spanish civil war, *The Brave and the Blind*, is likewise distinguished by its just appraisal of men and their motives. Although it is characteristic of Blankfort that his psychological insight and molding of character are not always equaled by his dramatic feeling, his work possesses rare persuasiveness. William Kozlenko, another exponent of the long one-act form, shows a stronger feeling for drama with very much the same talent for characterization in *This Earth Is Ours*. The persecution of an obdurate farmer by a power company which wants the right of way for its lines makes an affecting short play, one of the strongest in the movement's realistic repertory. Finally, there are the three acknowledged masterpieces *Waiting for Lefty*, *Till the Day I Die*, and *Hymn to the Rising Sun*.

The first mentioned remains the most exciting of the trio. A panoramic study of suffering and injustice in society, it draws its lines together in a terrific onslaught on the whole social fabric and fulfills Odets' requirement that "art must be about something. It must be hot and spiteful." Anybody, however, can be hot and spiteful. In *Waiting for Lefty* Odets revealed an uncanny sense of showmanship, which is not so easily encompassed. Three strike scenes, well placed at the beginning, center, and conclusion of the play, provide an exciting framework for flashbacks into the lives of the strike committee, each of which forms a brief history of a man driven to militant action by poverty, frustration, and injustices covering a wide range of abuses. Suspense is the keynote of the play from the moment it begins in the hall where a strike vote is being taken. It is resolved at the end when we learn that the leader of the militant faction has been murdered, presumably by the racketeer who runs the union for his own profit. Dialogue of rare vigor, sensitively attuned to living speech, flavors the drama and reflects its drive. The passions are involved in the struggle against the racketeer, who is imaginatively treated in successive scenes as an incarnation of predatory society. Pathos is distilled from several pictures of suffering and humiliation. Occasional lapses into sophomoric or cheap dialogue and some exaggerated stridency vitiate the little drama but do not destroy its total effect, which is pure theatre. Even those who disagree with its viewpoint must pay tribute to its power. If it did not leave one with reservations regarding the easy way in which it sees only one aspect of human experience, it could be unhesitatingly set down as a little masterpiece of the theatre.

This playwright's second short play, *Till the Day I Die*, uses a plummet that sinks deeper into human drama and contains an even more affecting theme, compounded of pity and terror, in the tale of a German revolutionist who asked his brother to kill him before he revealed the secrets of his party and betrayed his comrades under torture. It overreaches itself in its satirization of the fascist tormentors, suffers from some arbitrary theatricalism, and some of its details ring untrue. But for all its unevenness, *Till the Day I Die* compresses its ardors and endurances into something very close to a masterpiece. It is "hot and spiteful" in a finer sense than these words would indicate; it is heroic. In both plays Odets, who loves music passionately, is a symphonic artist, with a fine mastery of crescendo and decrescendo, of the development and weaving of themes, and of climactic force. They are youthful works, and their flaws could only become more conspicuous when their author turned to full-length drama. But without the *élan* of young manhood, which found inspiration in the revolutionary leaven of the movement, they could not have been written.

For maturity we must turn to the last of the trio of realistic masterpieces, Paul Green's *Hymn to the Rising Sun*. In anguish and irony there is perhaps no short play in the theatre's treasury to excel this masterly description of chain-gang horrors,—which take place on Independence Day! Dedicated to "Tom Thumb, the brave legislator who, in the confines of the little black bag, declaims of liberty," *Hymn to the Rising Sun* is a lambent protest against a long-standing blot on the American scutcheon. To wish to erase it, it is not necessary to accept the First, Third, or Fourth International, it is necessary only to be human. It is the distinction of the play that it abates nothing of its proper indignation and yet meets its audience on the lowest common denominator of humanity. This beautifully compressed and poignant work may serve as a fitting conclusion to the survey of a movement that began as partisan agitation and ended as art.[4]

[4] Most of the material in this chapter is based on information contained in *Workers Theatre, New Theatre,* and *New Theatre and Film.* Two pamphlets, *Audience Organization,* edited by Mark Marvin, and *Censored,* by Richard Pack and Mark Marvin, contain helpful information. Both are published by the New Theatre League, 132 West 43rd Street, New York City, the only office from which it is possible to secure literature bearing on this subject. For other aid, the author wishes to express his gratitude to: Emanuel Eisenberg, press representative of the Group Theatre, John O'Shaughnessy, of the Actors Repertory Company, Ben Irwin and Mark Marvin, of the New Theatre League.

BIBLIOGRAPHY

Below are listed the plays, both one-act and longer, which are named in this book and which have been published in book form, with the authors, and details of publication.

When the play has been published singly, the place of publication, the name of the publisher, and the date of publication are given immediately after the name of the play. If the play has also been printed in a collection or collections of plays by the same author, these details are given next. When the play has been printed in an anthology, such publication is indicated by a number which refers to the list of anthologies printed at the end of this bibliography.

Across the Border, by Dix. New York. Holt. 1915

Adding Machine, The, by Rice. New York. Doubleday. 1923
   Also in *Plays of Elmer Rice.* London. Gollanz. 1933
   Also in 20, 49

Albany Depot, The, by Howells. New York. Harper. 1892
   Also in *Minor Dramas.* Edinburgh. Douglas. 1907. Vol. 1

All God's Chillun Got Wings, by O'Neill. New York. Boni.
   1921. (Also London. Cape. 1937)
   Also in *Collected Plays.* New York. Boni. 1925-1926
   Also in *Complete Works.* New York. Boni. 1924. Vol. 2
   Also in *Nine Plays.* New York. Liveright. 1932

All on a Summer's Day, by Clements and Ryerson. New York.
   Appleton. 1926. (Also New York. French. 1934)
   Also in *All on a Summer's Day, and Six Other Short Plays.*
   New York. French. 1928
   Also in 84

Allison's Lad, by Dix
   In *Allison's Lad, and Other Martial Plays.* New York. Holt.
      1910
   Also in 27
Ambush, The, by Hughes. In 89
Among Thieves, by Gillette. In 56
Another Way Out, by Langner. In 87, 88
Antigone, by Sophocles. Toronto. Nelson. 1937
Aria da Capo, by Millay. New York. Harper. 1920
   Also in *Three Plays.* Harper. 1926
   Also in 5, 71, 88
Awake and Sing, by Odets. New York. Random House. 1935
   Also in *Three Plays.* New York. Random House. 1935.
      (London; Gollancz. Toronto; Macmillan)

Bakehouse, The, by Francis. Cardiff. Educational Publishing
      Co. 1914
Battle Hymn, by Blankfort and Gold. New York. French.
      1937
Beau of Bath, The, by Mackay. In 102
Beauty and the Jacobin, by Tarkington. In 13
Bedside Manners, by Nicholson and Behrman. New York.
      French. c. 1924
Before Breakfast, by O'Neill. New York. Shay. 1916
   Also with *The Great God Brown.* London. Cape
   Also in *Complete Works.* New York. Boni. 1924. Vol. 2
   Also in 85
Belt, The, by Sifton. New York. Macaulay. 1927
Bicyclers, The, by Bangs. In *Bicyclers, and Three Other
      Farces.* New York. Harper. 1896
Birds of a Feather, by Francis. Newtown, Wales. Welsh Out-
      look Press. 1927
   Also in 61
Black Pit, by Maltz. New York. Putnam, 1935
Blood of the Martyrs, by Wilde. New York. French. 1937

Both Your Houses, by Anderson. New York. French. 1933
and 1937
Also in 33
Bound East for Cardiff, by O'Neill
In *Collected Plays.* New York. Boni. 1925-1926. Vol. 5
In *Complete Works.* New York. Boni. 1924. Vol. 1
In *The Great God Brown, and Other Plays.* New York.
Boni. 1926
In *Moon of the Caribbees, and Six Other Plays of the Sea.*
New York. Boni. 1919
Also in 8, 71, 73
Box and Cox, by Morton. In 29
Brains, by Flavin. In *Brains, and Other One-Act Plays.* New
York. French. 1926
Brave and the Blind, The, by Blankfort. New York. French.
1937
Bread, by Eastman. In 8, 22, 68
Bury the Dead, by Shaw. New York. Random House. 1936

Clod, The, by Beach. New York. French. 1935
Also in 99
Coming of Christ and Easter, The, by Masefield. New York.
Macmillan. 1928
Confessional, by Wilde
In *Confessional, and Other American Plays.* New York.
Holt. 1916
In *Question of Morality, and Other Plays.* Boston. Little.
1922
Also in 22, 26, 62, 97
Crime, The, by Blankfort. New York. New Theatre League.
1936

Dance of Death, The, by Auden. London. Faber. 1936
Dead End, by Kingsley. New York. Random House. 1936.
(Toronto; Macmillan)

Deathless World, The, by Tompkins. In 22

Decision of the Court, The, by Matthews. New York. Harper. 1893

Deirdre, by Yeats. London. Bullen. 1907
 Also in *Collected Works.* London. Chapman. 1908. Vol. 2
 Also in *Collected Plays.* Toronto. Macmillan. 1935
 Also in *Plays for an Irish Theatre.* London, Bullen
 Also in *Plays in Prose and Verse, Written for an Irish Theatre.* London. Macmillan. 1922
 Also in *Poetical Works.* New York. Macmillan. 1916. Vol. 2

Diadem of Snow, A, by Rice. In 59

Dollar, A, by Pinski. New York. French. 1932
 Also in 31

Drums of Oude, The, by Strong
 In *The Drums of Oude, and Other One-Act Plays.* New York. Appleton. 1926

Dust of the Road, by Goodman. Chicago Stage Guild. c. 1912
 Also in 22, 26, 80

Emperor Jones, The, by O'Neill. Cincinnati. Kidd. 1921
 Students' Edition. New York. Appleton-Century. 1934.
 With *Anna Christie* and *The Hairy Ape.* Toronto. Macmillan. 1937
 Also in *Nine Plays.* New York. Liveright. 1932
 Also in *The Emperor Jones, Diff'rent, Straw.* New York. Boni. 1912
 Also in *Collected Plays.* New York. Boni. 1925-1926. Vol. 3
 Also in *Complete Works.* New York. Boni. 1924. Vol. 2
 Also in 5, 19, 32, 34, 46, 49, 76, 96, 100

Evening Dress, by Howells. New York. Harper. 1893
 Also in *Minor Dramas.* Edinburgh. Douglas. 1907

Everyman, by Lady Egerton. New York. Phillips. 1922

Examination, by Eastman. Boston. Baker. 1937

Fall of the City, The, by MacLeish. New York. Farrar. 1937

Fan, A, and Two Candlesticks, by Macmillan. Cincinnati. Kidd. c. 1922

Finders-Keepers, by Kelly. Cincinnati. Kidd. 1923
    Also in 52, 82, 86

Finger of God, The, by Wilde
    In *Dawn, etc.* New York. Holt. 1925
    In *One-Act Plays of Percival Wilde, First Series.* London. Harrap. 1933
    Also in 88

Florist Shop, The, by Hawkridge. In 69

Four Comedies from the Life of George Emery Blum, by Geddes. Brookfield, Conn. Brookfield Players. 1934

Fourth Mrs. Phillips, The, by Glick. In 58

From Morn to Midnight, by Kaiser. New York. Brentano's. c. 1922
    Also in 19, 48

Garroters, by Howells. New York. Harper. 1894
    Also in *Minor Dramas.* Edinburgh. Douglas. 1907. Vol. 1

Gentlewoman, by Lawson
    In *With a Reckless Preface. Two Plays.* New York. Farrar. 1934

Gettysburg, by MacKaye. New York. French. 1934
    Also in *Yankee Fantasies.* New York. Duffield. 1912
    Also in 12, 30

Ghost Story, The, by Tarkington. Cincinnati. Kidd. c. 1922
    Also in 52

Goat Song, by Werfel. Garden City, L. I. Doubleday. 1926

God's in His Heaven, by Stevenson. New York. Theatre Union. 1934. (Also London. Gollancz. 1936)

Gold Eagle Guy, by Levy. New York. Random House. 1935. (Also Toronto. Macmillan. 1935; New York. French. 1937)

Golden Doom, The, by Dunsany
  In *Five Plays.* London. Richards. 1914
  Also in 6, 43
Good Men Do, The, by Osborne. In 1
Great Choice, The, by Eastman. In 68
Great Divide, The, by Moody. New York. Macmillan. 1909.
    (Also New York. French. 1937)
  Also in *Poems and Plays.* Boston. Houghton. 1912
  Also in 17, 64

Hairy Ape, The, by O'Neill. London. Cape. 1937
  Also with *The Emperor Jones.* Toronto. Macmillan. 1937
  Also in *Collected Plays.* New York. Boní. 1925-1926.
    Vol. 3
  Also in *Complete Works.* New York. Boni. 1924. Vol. 2
  Also in *The Hairy Ape, and Other Plays.* New York. 1922
  Also in *Nine Plays.* New York. Liveright. 1932
  Also in 20
Helena's Husband, by Moeller
  In *Five Somewhat Historical Plays.* New York. Knopf.
    1918
  Also in 88, 99
Hero of Santa Maria, The, by Goodman and Hecht. New
    York. Shay. c. 1920
  Also in 75, 82, 86
High Tor, by Anderson. New York. Dodd. 1937
Holbein in Blackfriars, by Goodman and Stevens. Chicago
    Stage Guild. c. 1913
Hot Iron, The, by Green
  In *Lonesome Road.* New York. McBride. 1926
House of Connelly, The, by Green
  In *House of Connelly, and Other Plays.* New York. French.
    1931

BIBLIOGRAPHY

How He Lied to Her Husband, by Shaw
In *Complete Plays.* London. Constable. c. 1931
Also in *Man of Destiny, and How He Lied to Her Husband.*
New York. Brentano. 1907
Hymn to the Rising Sun, by Green. New York. French. 1936

I Have Seen Myself Before, by Geddes
In *Four Comedies from the Life of George Emery Blum.*
Brookfield, Conn. Brookfield Players. 1934
Idiot's Delight. New York. Scribner. 1936
If Men Played Cards as Women Do, by Kaufman. New York.
French. c. 1926
Ile, by O'Neill
In *Collected Plays.* New York. Boni. 1925-1926. Vol. 5
Also in *Complete Works.* New York. Boni. 1924. Vol. 2
Also in 7, 13, 26, 30, 62, 88
In Abraham's Bosom, by Green. London. Allen. 1929
Also in *Field God, and In Abraham's Bosom.* New York.
McBride. 1917
Also in *Lonesome Road; Six Plays for the Negro Theatre.*
New York. McBride. 1926
Also in 19, 32, 37
"In 1999," by De Mille. New York. French. c. 1914
In the Tradition, by Geddes
In *Four Comedies from the Life of George Emery Blum.*
Brookfield, Conn. Brookfield Players. 1934
In the Zone, by O'Neill
In *Collected Plays.* New York. Boni. 1925-1926. Vol. 5
Also in *Complete Works.* New York. Boni. 1924. Vol. 1
Also in *Moon of the Caribbees, and Six Other Plays of the
Sea.* New York. Boni. 1919
Also in 45
International, The, by Lawson. New York. Macaulay. 1928

Jephthah's Daughter, by Levinger. New York. French. c. 1921
Joint Owners in Spain, by Brown. Chicago Little Theatre.
　1914
　Also in 54
Journey's End, by Sherriff. New York. Brentano's. 1929
　Also in 4, 25, 38, 67
Judge Lynch, by Rogers. New York. French. c. 1924
　Also in 32, 55
Justice, by Galsworthy. New York. Scribner. 1910
　Also in *Plays, Series 2*. New York. Scribner. 1913
　Also in *Works* (Manaton Edition). London. Heinemann.
　1923
　Also in *Representative Plays*. New York. Scribner. c. 1924
　Also in *Plays*. New York. Scribner. 1928
　Also in 64, 101

Katy Did, by Crothers
　In *Smart Set*. 1927. No. 1
King Arthur's Socks, by Dell
　In *King Arthur's Socks, etc.* Provincetown Players, 2d
　　Series. New York. Shay. 1916
Knives from Syria, by Riggs. New York. French. c. 1928
　Also in 7, 57

Laughing Gas, by Dreiser
　In *Plays of the Natural and Supernatural*. New York. Lane.
　1916
'Lection, by Conkle
　In *Crick Bottom Plays*. New York. French. 1928
Let Freedom Ring, by Bein. New York. French. 1936
Likely Story, A, by Howells. New York. Harper. 1924
　Also in *Minor Dramas*. Edinburgh. Douglas. 1907. Vol. 1
Lima Beans, by Kreymborg. New York. French. 1925
　Also in *Plays for Poem-Mimes*. New York. The Other

Press. 1918. (Same as *Puppet Plays*. London. Secker. 1923)

Also in 45, 74

Little Father of the Wilderness, The, by Strong and Osbourne. New York. French. 1924

Also in *The Drums of Oude, and Other One-Act Plays.* New York. Appleton. 1926

Also in 11, 55

Little Italy, by Fry. New York. Russell. 1902

Long Voyage Home, The, by O'Neill

In *Collected Plays.* New York. Boni. 1925-1926

Also in *Complete Works.* New York. Boni. 1924. Vol. 1

Also in *The Great God Brown, and Other Plays.* New York. Boni. 1926

Also in *Moon of the Caribbees, and Six Other Plays of the Sea.* New York. Boni. 1919

Also in *Smart Set Anthology*

Lower Depths, The, by Gorky. New York. Duffield. 1912. (Also New York. Brentano's. 1922)

Also in 3, 18, 64, 78

Manikin and Minikin, by Kreymborg. New York. French. 1925

Also in *Plays for Poem-Mimes.* New York. The Other Press. 1918. (Same as *Puppet Plays*. London. Secker. 1923)

Also in 31, 85

Marching Song, by Lawson. New York. Dramatists Play Service. 1937

Marriage of Little Eva, The, by Nicholson

In *Garden Varieties.* New York. Appleton. 1924

Martha's Mourning, by Hoffman. Boston. Baker. 1923

Also in 45

Masses and Men, by Toller. London. Lane. 1936

Mayor and the Manicure, The, by Ade. New York. French.
  c. 1923
  Also in 55
Meet the Missus, by Nicholson. In 55
Men in White, by Kingsley. New York. Covici. c. 1933.
  (Also New York. French. 1935)
  Also in 40
Merry-Go-Round, by Becque
  In *Vultures,* etc. New York. Kennerley. 1913
Merry Merry Cuckoo, The, by Marks
  In *Three Welsh Plays.* Boston. Little. 1917
  Also in *Merry Merry Cuckoo, and Other Welsh Plays.* New
    York. Appleton. 1927
  Also in 12, 13, 45, 92
Mighty Wind A'Blowin', by Ware. New York. New Theatre
  League. 1936
Minnie Field, by Conkle
  In *Crick Bottom Plays.* New York. French. 1928
  Also in 2, 8
Miracle at Verdun, by Chlumberg. New York. Brentano's.
  1931
  Also in 4, 23
Miss Civilization, by Davis. New York. Scribner. 1905
  Also in *Farces.* New York. Scribner. 1906
Monkey's Paw, The, by Jacobs and Parker. New York.
  French. c. 1910
  Also in 42
Monsignor's Hour, by Lavery. New York. French. 1937
Moon of the Caribbees, by O'Neill. London. Cape. 1937
  Also in *Collected Plays.* New York. Boni. 1925-1926
  Also in *Complete Works.* New York. Boni. 1924. Vol. 1
  Also in *The Great God Brown, and Other Plays.* New
    York. Boni. 1926

Also in *Moon of the Caribbees, and Six Other Plays of the
Sea.* New York. Boni. 1919
Also in 83
Mouse Trap, The, by Howells
In *The Mouse Trap, and Other Farces.* New York. Harper.
1889
Also in *Minor Dramas.* Edinburgh. Douglas. 1907
Mrs. Harper's Bazaar, by Hughes. New York. Dramatists Play
Service. 1937

Napoleon Crossing the Rockies, by MacKaye. In 5, 57
Native Ground, by Geddes
In *Native Ground: A Cycle of Plays.* New York. French.
1932
Neighbors, by Gale. In 21, 22
Night Before Christmas, The, by Howells
In *Daughter of the Storage.* New York. Harper. 1916
Night over Taos, by Anderson. New York. French. 1932
1931, by the Siftons. New York. Farrar. c. 1932

Ol' Captain, by Baker. New York. French. 1937
Old Lady Shows Her Medals, The, by Barrie
In *Echoes of War.* London. Hodder. c. 1918
Also in *The Old Lady Shows Her Medals.* London. Hod-
der. 1921
Also in *Representative Plays.* New York. Scribner. c. 1926
Also in *Plays of J. M. Barrie, in One Volume.* New York.
Scribner. 1929
Old Love Letters, by Howard. London. French. 1897; also
1936
On the Razor Edge, by Hughes. New York. French. 1930
Also in 53
One Egg, by Hughes. In 52
Our Lean Years, by Stevenson. In 68

Overtones, by Gerstenberg. New York. French. c. 1929
  Also in 16, 99

Pair of Lunatics, A, by Walkes. Hardin. 1937
Panic, by MacLeish. Boston. Houghton. 1935
Parlor Car, The, by Howells. Boston. Houghton. 1924
  Also in *The Sleeping Car, and Other Farces.* Boston.
    Houghton. c. 1892
  Also in *Minor Dramas.* Edinburgh. Douglas. 1907
Passing of Chow-Chow, The, by Rice. New York. French.
    1933
  Also in 55
Pawns, by Wilde. New York. French. 1936
  Also in *Unseen Host, and Other War Plays.* Boston. Little.
    1917
  Also in *One-Act Plays of Percival Wilde.* London. Harrap.
    1933
Pierrot in Paris, by Clements. In 66
Pilgrim and the Book, The, by MacKaye. New York. Ameri-
    can Bible Society. c. 1920
Playgoers, by Pinero. London. Chiswick Press. 1913
Poacher, The, by Francis. Cardiff. Educational Publishing Co.
    1914
  Also in 44
Pomp, by Cowan
  In *Pomp, and Other Plays.* New York. Brentano's.
    c. 1920
Proposal Under Difficulties, A, by Bangs. New York. Harper.
    1913
  Also in *The Bicyclers, and Three Other Farces.* New York.
    Harper. 1896
Purple Door Knob, The, by Eaton. New York. French. 1936

Queen Victoria, by Eaton and Carb. New York. Dutton. 1922

Reckless, by Riggs. In 8, 58
Rector, by Crothers. New York. French. c. 1905
 Also in 55
Red Owl, The, by Gillette. In 55
Reunion in Vienna, by Sherwood. New York. Scribner. 1932
Rider of Dreams, The, by Torrence
 In *Granny Maumee, etc.* New York. Macmillan. 1917
 Also in 32, 92
Riders to the Sea, by Synge. Boston. Luce. 1911
 Also in *Works.* Dublin. Maunsel. 1910. Vol. 1
 Also in *Shadow of the Glen, and Riders to the Sea.* London.
  Mathews. 1910
 Also in *Four Plays.* Dublin. Maunsel. 1911
 Also in *Works.* Boston. Luce. 1912. Vol. 1
 Also in *Works.* Boston. Luce. 1913. Vol. 4
 Also in *Plays.* London. Allen. 1932
 Also in 6, 10, 12, 13, 17, 27, 30, 101, 103
Rising of the Moon, by Lady Gregory
 In *Seven Short Plays.* Dublin. Maunsel. 1910
 Also in 17, 42, 93, 102
Rock, The, by Hamlin. Boston. Pilgrim Press. c. 1921. (Also
 New York. French. 1935)
Ryland, by Goodman and Stevens. Chicago Stage Guild.
 c. 1912
 Also in 45

Sam Average, by MacKaye
 In *Yankee Fantasies.* New York. Duffield. 1912
 Also in 31, 45
Secret, The, by Alehin
 In *First Sin, and Other One-Act Plays.* Boston. Expression
  Co. c. 1927
Secret Service, by Gillette. New York. French. c. 1898
 Also in 64, 77

Self-Made Man, by Box. New York. French. 1937

Self-Sacrifice, by Howells

In *Daughter of the Storage, and Other Things in Prose and Verse.* New York. Harper. 1916

Shepherd in the Distance, The, by Hudson. Cincinnati. Kidd. c. 1921

Also in 88

Sherlock Holmes, by Gillette. New York. Doubleday. 1935

Shewing Up of Blanco Posnet, The, by Shaw. New York. Brentano's. 1909; New York. Dodd. 1937

Also in *The Doctor's Dilemma, and Other Plays.* New York. Brentano's. 1911

Also in *Complete Works.* London. Constable. c. 1931

Show-Off, The, by Kelly. Boston. Little. 1924

Also in 35, 49

Singing Jailbirds, by Sinclair. Pasadena. The Author. 1924

Sintrim of Skaggerak, by Cowan. New York. French. 1930

Also in *Pomp, and Other Plays.* New York. Brentano's. c. 1920

Also in 9, 45

Six Who Pass While the Lentils Boil, by Walker. Cincinnati. Kidd. c. 1921

Also in 45, 51, 70, 92

Smoking Car, The, by Howells

In *The Smoking Car, and Other Farces.* Boston. Houghton. c. 1892

Also in *Minor Dramas.* Edinburgh. Douglas. 1907. Vol. 2

So's Your Old Antique, by Kummer. New York. French. c. 1928

Also in 58

Sparkin', by Conkle

In *Crick Bottom Plays.* New York. French. 1928

Also in 58

Stevedore, by Peters and Sklar. New York. Covici. c. 1934;
   Cape. 1935
Still Alarm, by Kaufman. In 60
Street Scene, by Rice. New York. French. 1926; also 1937
   Also in 4, 38
Strife, by Galsworthy. New York. Scribner. 1920
   Also in *Plays*. New York. Putnam. 1909
   Also in *Works* (Manaton Edition). London. Heinemann.
     1923
   Also in *Representative Plays*. New York. Scribner. c. 1924
   Also in *Plays*. New York. Scribner. 1928
   Also in 17, 41, 103
Success Story, by Lawson. New York. Farrar. 1932
Such a Charming Young Man, by Akins. New York. French.
     1933
   Also in 55
Suppressed Desires, by Glaspell and Cook
   In *Plays by S. Glaspell*. Boston. Small. c. 1920
   Also in *Trifles, and Six Other Short Plays*. London. Benn.
     1926
   Also in 45, 73
Sweet and Twenty, by Dell. Cincinnati. Kidd. 1921
   Also in *King Arthur's Socks, etc.* Provincetown Players. 2d
    Series. New York. Shay. 1916
   Also in 82, 86

They Shall Not Die, by Wexley. New York. Knopf. 1934
   Also in 40
This Picture and That, by Matthews. New York. Harper.
     1894
Three Pills in a Bottle, by Field. New York. French. 1935
   Also in *Six Plays*. New York. Scribner. 1924
   Also in 2

Tickless Time, by Glaspell and Cook. Boston. Baker. 1925
Also in *Plays by S. Glaspell.* Boston. Small. c. 1920
Also in *Trifles, and Six Other Short Plays.* London. Benn.
1926
Also in 28, 82, 86
Tidings of Joy, by McFadden. New York. French. c. 1933
Till the Day I Die, by Odets
In *Three Plays.* New York. Random House. 1935. (Also
London; Gollancz, and Toronto; Macmillan)
With *Waiting for Lefty.* New York. Random House. 1935.
(Also Toronto; Macmillan)
Tinker, The, by Eastman. New York. Century. c. 1930
Also in 68
Tonight at 8.30, by Coward
In *Plays.* Garden City, L. I. Doubleday. 1936
Too Much Smith, by Matthews. Boston. Baker. 1902
Also in *Comedies for Amateur Acting* (under the title,
Heredity). New York. Appleton. 1880
Tree, The, by Box. New York. French. 1937
Trifles, by Glaspell. New York. Washington Square Players.
1916
Also in *Plays by S. Glaspell.* Boston. Small. c. 1920
Also in *Trifles, and Six Other Short Plays.* London. Benn.
1926
Also in 8, 62, 63, 88
Twelve Pound Look, The, by Barrie
In *Half Hours.* New York. Scribner. 1914
Also in *The Twelve Pound Look, and Other Plays.* London. Hodder. 1921
Also in *Representative Plays.* New York. Scribner. c. 1926
Also in *Plays of J. M. Barrie, in One Volume.* New York.
Scribner. 1929
Also in 31

Twentieth Century Lullaby, by Mount. New York. French. 1937

Twilight Saint, by Young. New York. French. c. 1925
  Also in *Addio, Madretta, and Other Plays*. New York. Sergel. 1912
  Also in 12, 13

Two Crooks and a Lady, by Pillot. In 1

Two Hundred Were Chosen, by Conkle. New York. French. 1937

Two Passengers for Chelsea, by Firkins
  In *Two Passengers for Chelsea, and Other Plays*. New York. Longmans. 1928

Two Slatterns and a King, by Millay. Cincinnati. Kidd. 1921
  Also in *Three Plays*. New York. Harper. 1926
  Also in 82, 86

Unto Such Glory, by Green
  In *In the Valley, and Other Carolina Plays*. New York. French. 1928
  Also in 57

Valiant, The, by Hall and Middlemass. In 22, 98

Waiting for Lefty, by Odets
  In *Three Plays*. New York. Random House. 1935. (Also London; Gollancz, and Toronto; Macmillan)
  With *Till the Day I Die*. New York. Random House. 1935. (Also Toronto; Macmillan)

Wedding Rehearsal, The, by Farrar. In 59

What Price Glory?, by Anderson
  In *Three American Plays*. New York. Harcourt. 1926
  Also in 4, 36

Where the Cross Is Made, by O'Neill
  In *Collected Plays,* New York. Boni. 1925-1926. Vol. 5
  Also in *Complete Works.* New York. Boni. 1924. Vol. 2
  Also in *The Great God Brown, and Other Plays.* New
    York. Boni. 1926
  Also in *Moon of the Caribbees, and Six Other Plays of the
    Sea.* New York. Boni. 1919
  Also in 10, 11, 97
White Dresses, by Green. New York. French. 1935
  Also in *Lonesome Road.* New York. McBride
  Also in 31, 32
Why the Chimes Rang, by McFadden. New York. French.
    c. 1915
  Also in *Why the Chimes Rang, and Other Plays.* New
    York. French. 1925
Will o' the Wisp, by Halman. In 45, 79
Winterset, by Anderson. Washington. Anderson House. 1935.
  (Also New York. Dramatists Play Service. 1937)
Wonder Hat, The, by Goodman. New York. Shay. c. 1920
  Also in *The Wonder Hat, and Three Other One-Act
    Plays.* New York. Appleton. 1925
  Also in 45
Workhouse Ward, by Lady Gregory
  In *Seven Short Plays.* Dublin. Maunsel. 1910
  Also in 10, 26, 50, 97

1. Baker, G. P., ed. *Plays of the 47 Workshop. Series 1.*
   New York. Brentano's. 1918
2. Baker, G. P., ed. *Yale One-Act Plays.* New York.
   French. 1930
3. Bates, A. *Drama.* London. Athenian Society. 1903
4. Chandler, F. W., and Cordell, R. A., eds. *Twentieth
   Century Plays.* New York. Nelson. 1934
5. Church, V. W., ed. *Curtain! A Book of Modern Plays.*
   New York. Harper. 1932

6. Clark, B. H., ed. *Representative One-Act Plays by British and American Authors*. Boston. Little. 1921

7. Clark, B. H., and Cook, T. R., eds. *One-Act Plays*. Boston. Heath. 1929

8. Clark, B. H., and Nicholson, K., eds. *American Scene*. New York. Appleton. 1930

9. Clements, C. C., ed. *Sea Plays*. Boston. Small. c. 1925

10. Coffman, G. R., ed. *Book of Modern Plays*. Chicago. Scott. c. 1925

11. Cohen, H. L., ed. *More One-Act Plays by Modern Authors*. New York. Harcourt. 1921

12. Cohen, H. L., ed. *One-Act Plays by Modern Authors*. New York. Harcourt. 1921

13. *Same;* 1934

14. Cohen, H. L., ed. *One-Act Plays for Stage and Study*. New York. French. 1924

15. *Comediettas and Farces*. New York. Harper. 1886

16. Dickinson, A. D., ed. *Drama*. Garden City, L. I. Doubleday. 1924

17. Dickinson, T. H., ed. *Chief Contemporary Dramatists*. Boston. Houghton. c. 1915

18. Dickinson, T. H., ed. *Chief Contemporary Dramatists. Series 2*. Boston. Houghton. c. 1921

19. Dickinson, T. H., ed. *Chief Contemporary Dramatists. Series 3*. Boston. Houghton. c. 1930

20. Dickinson, T. H., ed. *Contemporary Plays*. Boston. Houghton. c. 1925

21. Dickinson, T. H., ed. *Wisconsin Plays*. New York. Huebsch. 1914

22. Eastman, F., ed. *Modern Religious Dramas*. New York. Holt. 1928

23. *Famous Plays of 1932-33*. London. Gollancz. 1933

24. *Famous Plays of 1933-34*. London. Gollancz. 1934

25. *Famous Plays of To-day*. London. Gollancz. 1930

26. Goldstone, G. A., ed. *One-Act Plays*. Boston. Allyn. 1926
27. Hampden, J., ed. *Nine Modern Plays*. New York. Nelson. 1923
28. Hampden, J., ed. *Ten Modern Plays*. London. Nelson. 1928
29. *Lacy's Acting Edition of Plays*. London. Lacy. Vol. 5
30. Leonard, S. A., ed. *Atlantic Book of Modern Plays*. Boston. Atlantic Monthly Press. c. 1921
31. Lewis, B. R., ed. *Contemporary One-Act Plays*. New York. Scribner. c. 1922
32. Locke, A. Le R., and Gregory, M., eds. *Plays of Negro Life*. New York. Harper. 1927
33. Mantle, B., and Sherman, G. P., eds. *Best Plays of 1909-1910 and the Yearbook of the Drama in America*. New York. Dodd. 1933
34. Mantle, B., ed. *Best Plays of 1920-21*. Boston. Small. 1921 (abridged)
35. Mantle, B., ed. *Best Plays of 1923-24*. Boston. Small. c. 1924 (abridged)
36. Mantle, B., ed. *Best Plays of 1924-25*. Boston. Small. c. 1924 (abridged)
37. Mantle, B., ed. *Best Plays of 1926-27*. New York. Dodd. 1927 (abridged)
38. Mantle, B., ed. *Best Plays of 1928-29*. New York. Dodd. 1929 (abridged)
39. Mantle, B., ed. *Best Plays of 1931-32*. New York. Dodd. 1932 (abridged)
40. Mantle, B., ed. *Best Plays of 1933-34*. New York. Dodd. 1934 (abridged)
41. Marriott, J. W., ed. *Great Modern British Plays*. London. Harrap. 1929
42. Marriott, J. W., ed. *One-Act Plays of To-day*. Series 2. Boston. Small. c. 1924

43. Marriott, J. W., ed. *One-Act Plays of To-day. Series 3.* London. Harrap. 1927

44. Marriott, J. W., ed. *One-Act Plays of To-day. Series 4.* London. Harrap. 1928

45. Mayorga, M., ed. *Representative One-Act Plays by American Authors.* Boston. Little. 1919

46. McDermott, J. F., ed. *Modern Plays.* New York. Harcourt. c. 1932

47. *More Quick Curtains.* Chicago Stage Guild. 1923

48. Moses, M. J., ed. *Dramas of Modernism and Their Forerunners.* Boston. Little. 1931

49. Moses, M. J., ed. *Representative American Dramas, National and Local.* Boston. Little. 1925

50. Moses, M. J., ed. *Representative British Dramas, Victorian and Modern.* Boston. Little. 1918

51. Moses, M. J., ed. *Treasury of Plays for Children.* Boston. Little. 1921

52. Nicholson, K., ed. *Appleton's Book of Short Plays.* New York. Appleton. 1926

53. Nicholson, K., ed. *Hollywood Plays.* New York. French. 1930

54. *One-Act Plays.* New York. Macmillan. 1921

55. *One-Act Plays for Stage and Study.* New York. French. 1924

56. *Same.* Series 2. 1925

57. *Same.* Series 3. 1927

58. *Same.* Series 4. 1928

59. *Same.* Series 5. 1929

60. *Same.* Series 6. 1931

61. *One-Act Plays of To-day. 5th Series.* London. Harrap. c. 1931

62. Pence, R. W., ed. *Dramas by Present-Day Writers.* New York. Scribner. c. 1927

63. Phillips, Le R., and Johnson, T., eds. *Types of Modern Dramatic Composition*. Boston. Ginn. 1927

64. Pierce and Matthews, eds. *Masterpieces of Modern Drama*. Garden City, L. I. Doubleday. 1915. Vol. 1 (abridged)

65. *Same*. Vol. 2

66. *Plays for a Folding Theatre*. Cincinnati. Kidd. 1923

67. *Plays of a Half Decade*. London. Gollancz. c. 1933

68. *Plays of American Life*. New York. French. 1934

69. *Plays of the Harvard Dramatic Club. Series 1*. New York. Brentano's

70. *Portmanteau Plays*. Cincinnati. Kidd. 1917

71. *Provincetown Plays*. Cincinnati. Kidd. 1921

72. *Provincetown Plays*. New York. Harper. 1920

73. *Provincetown Plays. Series 1*. New York. Shay. 1916

74. *Same*. Series 3

75. *Quick Curtains*. Chicago Stage Guild. 1915

76. Quinn, A. H., ed. *Contemporary American Plays*. New York. Scribner. 1923

77. Quinn, A. H., ed. *Representative American Plays, 1767-1923*

78. Sayler, O. M., ed. *Moscow Art Theatre Series of Russian Plays. Series 1*. New York. Brentano's. 1923

79. *Set the Stage for Eight*. Boston. Little. 1923

80. Shay, F., ed. *Appleton Book of Christmas Plays*. New York. Appleton. 1929

81. Shay, F., ed. *Contemporary One-Act Plays (American)*. Cincinnati. Kidd. 1922

82. Shay, F., ed. *Contemporary One-Act Plays of 1921*. Cincinnati. Kidd

83. Shay, F., ed. *Fifty More Contemporary One-Act Plays*

84. Shay, F., ed. *Plays for Strolling Mummers*. New York. Appleton. 1926

85. Shay, F., ed. *Treasury of Plays for Women*. Boston. Shay. 1922

86. Shay, F., ed. *Twenty Contemporary One-Act Plays (American)*. Cincinnati. Kidd. 1922

87. Shay, F., ed. *Washington Square Players*. New York. 1916

88. Shay, F., and Loving, P., eds. *Fifty Contemporary One-Act Plays*. Cincinnati. Kidd. 1922

89. *Short Plays for Modern Players*. New York. Appleton. 1931

90. *Six Plays*. London. Gollancz. 1931

91. *Smart Set Anthology*

92. Smith, A. M., ed. *Short Plays by Representative Authors*. New York. Macmillan. 1920

93. Smith, M. M., ed. *Short Plays of Various Types*. New York. Merrill. c. 1924

94. *Ten One-Act Plays*. New York. Brentano's. c. 1921

95. *Ten Plays*. New York. Huebsch. 1920

96. Tucker, S. M., ed. *Modern Plays*. New York. Macmillan. 1932

97. Tucker, S. M., ed. *Twelve One-Act Plays for Study and Production*. Boston. Ginn. 1929

98. *Twelve One-Act Plays*. New York. Longmans. c. 1926

99. *Washington Square Plays*. Garden City, L. I. Doubleday. 1919

100. Watson, E. B., and Pressey, B., eds. *Contemporary Drama; American Plays*. New York. Scribner. c. 1931

101. Watson, E. B., and Pressey, B., eds. *Contemporary Drama; English and Irish Plays*. New York. Scribner. c. 1931. Vol. I

102. Webber, J. P., and Webster, H. H., eds. *One-Act Plays for Secondary Schools*. Boston. Houghton. c. 1933

103. Whitman, C. H., ed. *Seven Contemporary Plays*. Boston. Houghton. 1931

INDEX

311

INDEX

315

INDEX